As I open this book,
I open myself
to God's presence
in my life.

God's Invitation

God calls me
to be aware of him
in all the people I know,
the places I go,
and the things I do each day.

My Response

When I quiet myself to allow
God's grace to help me,
I see with truth,
hear with forgiveness,
and act with kindness
as God's love works through me.

Thank you God,
for your presence
in my life.

FindingGod

Our response to God's gifts
6

Parish Edition

Barbara F. Campbell, M.Div., D.Min.

James P. Campbell, M.A., D.Min.

LOYOLAPRESS.
A JESUIT MINISTRY
Chicago

Nihil Obstat
Reverend James P. McIlhone
Censor Deputatus
August 20, 2003

Imprimatur
Most Reverend Edwin M. Conway, D.D.
Vicar General
Archdiocese of Chicago
August 22, 2003

The *Nihil Obstat* and *Imprimatur* are official declarations that a book is free of doctrinal and moral error. No implication is contained therein that those who have granted the *Nihil Obstat* and *Imprimatur* agree with the content, opinions, or statements expressed. Nor do they assume any legal responsibility associated with publication.

The Ad Hoc Committee to Oversee the Use of the Catechism, United States Conference of Catholic Bishops, has found this catechetical text, copyright 2005, to be in conformity with the *Catechism of the Catholic Church.*

Finding God: Our Response to God's Gifts is an expression of the work of Loyola Press, an apostolate of the Chicago Province of the Society of Jesus.

Senior Consultants
Jane Regan, Ph.D.
Richard Hauser, S.J., Ph.D., S.T.L.
Robert Fabing, S.J., D.Min.

Advisors
Most Reverend Gordon D. Bennett, S.J., D.D.
George A. Aschenbrenner, S.J., S.T.L.
Paul H. Colloton, O.P., D.Min.
Eugene LaVerdiere, S.S.S., Ph.D., S.T.L.

Peg Bowman, M.A.
Gerald Darring, M.A.
Brian DuSell, D.M.A.
Teresa DuSell, M.M.
Bryan T. Froehle, Ph.D.

Thomas J. McGrath
Joanne Paprocki, M.A.
Daniel L. Snyder, M.Div., Ph.D.
Christopher R. Weickert
Elaine M. Weickert

Catechetical Staff
Daniel W. Gast, M.A.
Jeanette L. Graham, M.A.
Marlene Halpin, O.P., Ph.D.
Thomas McLaughlin, M.A.
Joseph Paprocki, M.A.

Grateful acknowledgment is given to authors, publishers, photographers, museums, and agents for permission to reprint the following copyrighted material; music credits where appropriate can be found at the bottom of each individual song. Every effort has been made to determine copyright owners. In the case of any omissions, the publisher will be pleased to make suitable acknowledgments in future editions. Continued on page 335.

Cover Design: Think Design Group
Cover Illustrator: Christina Balit
Interior Design: Three Communication Design

ISBN-13: 978-0-8294-1826-2; ISBN-10: 0-8294-1826-1

Manufactured in the United States of America.

LOYOLA PRESS.
A JESUIT MINISTRY

3441 N. Ashland Avenue
Chicago, Illinois 60657
(800) 621-1008
www.loyolapress.com

RRD / Menasha, WI USA / 04-11 / 5th printing

Table of Contents

Creator and Father

Saint Jerome

Saint Jerome translated the entire Bible from Hebrew and Greek into Latin. He is the patron saint of librarians.

Saint Jerome

Saint Jerome was born about A.D. 345 in what is now northern Italy. As a young man, he traveled and studied in the great European cities of Rome and Trier. He then went to live in the desert. While there, he said that he had "no other company but scorpions and wild beasts." He began to study Hebrew. He found the language difficult to learn, but his great effort was worth it. His knowledge of Hebrew made it possible for him to become a biblical scholar and translator.

In 382 Jerome began a huge task. He began to translate the entire Bible from the Hebrew and Greek texts into Latin. His endeavor took many decades and eventually produced a version of the Bible in the ordinary language of that time. Jerome's Latin translation of the Bible became the standard for use in the Church.

Saint Jerome in His Study, Domenico Ghirlandaio, 1480

Jerome traveled to many places while working on his translation. He lived in Constantinople, Antioch, Alexandria, and Bethlehem. Yet he knew that translating the Bible was not the only important task; so when war broke out and many refugees came to Bethlehem, Jerome took action. He gave up his work and study for a time to help people in need. He said, "We must translate the words of the Scriptures into deeds; and instead of speaking saintly words, we must act them." His feast day is September 30.

The Bible, God's Story

Think of Bible stories you know. Share your favorite with the group.

PRAYER

Loving God, help me to appreciate your word in the Bible. Keep me faithful in praying from it so that I can come closer to you.

How the Bible Came to Be

The Bible is the Word of God, but it is not just one book; it is a collection of many books. These books were written by different authors using different styles. However, all of these authors were **inspired** by the Holy Spirit. That is, although human beings wrote the Bible, the Holy Spirit guided them.

The Bible is divided into two sections: the Old Testament and the New Testament.

The Old Testament

Jews wrote the Old Testament hundreds of years before Jesus was born. It tells the story of the Hebrew people and their faith in God. For example, the book of Exodus tells the story of how Moses led the Hebrews out of Egypt and across the Red Sea.

The New Testament

Just as the Old Testament is the story of the Jews, the New Testament is the story of the early Christians. It was written because Christians wanted to explain their new faith and teach others how to experience salvation through Jesus. Some of the books are actually letters written by leaders such as Saint Paul. The most important books in the New Testament are the Gospels, which tell us about Jesus' birth, life, death, and resurrection. Although some of the books tell the same stories, each is written from a different point of view.

Did You Know?

The Old Testament is made up of 46 books. The New Testament is made up of 27 books.

Copying the Bible

From the time the Bible was first written until the invention of the printing press in the 15th century, copies of the Bible were written by hand. Saint Jerome worked with handwritten copies of the Bible in Hebrew and Greek and wrote his translation by hand in Latin. This Latin translation is called the **Vulgate** version of the Bible.

Writing out a whole Bible took a long time. Because of this, not many copies were in existence. For about a thousand years, monks and nuns in **scriptoriums,** places where writing took place, made copies of the Bible by hand so that more people could use it for prayer and worship.

Illuminated Bible page

The monks and nuns wanted the Bibles to be easy to read, so they developed a clear kind of handwriting that is the basis of the writing we use today. They also wanted the Bibles to be as beautiful as possible, so they "illuminated" them. This meant that they added large, colorful letters and pictures of plants, animals, and scenes from everyday life.

Be an Illuminator

Choose one of the following verses and illuminate the first letter on a separate sheet of paper.

Noah was six hundred years old when the flood waters came upon the earth.

Genesis 7:6

The LORD is my Shepherd;
   there is nothing I lack.

Psalm 23:1

Let the children come to me and do not prevent them.

Luke 18:16

Saint Ambrose in an illuminated letter

Understanding the Bible

Sometimes the Bible is hard to understand. Some passages are about events and people that we know little about today. Other passages describe things that are difficult to understand because we don't think the same way people did long ago.

God has given the authority to interpret the Scriptures to the Catholic Church and the **Magisterium,** the pope and the bishops teaching together. Their **interpretation** helps us avoid confusion and leads us to a better understanding of God's word. Reading the Bible with the guidance of the pope and the bishops also makes it easier to learn about God's intention for us and for the salvation of the world.

Bishops entering St. Peter's Basilica at the Vatican

When we read the Bible with the help of the Holy Spirit and the Church, we learn the meaning of God's revelation for our lives. This is especially true when we read about the words and actions of Jesus. The Church encourages us to read the Bible in order to learn about God, to grow in our relationship with God and others, to understand God's message of love and forgiveness, and to teach a new generation what the Church believes.

Reading God's Word

Know this first of all, that there is no prophecy of scripture that is a matter of personal interpretation, for no prophecy ever came through human will; but rather human beings moved by the holy Spirit spoke under the influence of God.

2 Peter 1:20-21

The Second Letter to Timothy

Saint Timothy was a pastor in the early Church. The Church was having problems at that time with teachers who were not teaching the truth. Besides that, the Church was just starting out, and Christians often were persecuted, so the future seemed uncertain to Timothy and the people he was trying to lead.

A leader of the Church wrote Timothy some advice:

> All scripture is inspired by God and is useful for teaching, for refutation, for correction, and for training in righteousness, so that one who belongs to God may be competent, equipped for every good work.

2 Timothy 3:16-17

Locating a Scripture Passage

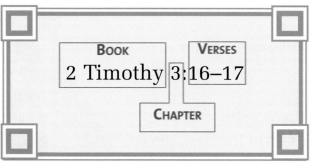

Book		Verses
2 Timothy	3:	16–17
	Chapter	

Solving a Problem

Think of a time when you, like Timothy, were confused or troubled and asked an older, more knowledgeable person for advice. How did that person help you?

_____

_____

_____

_____

PRAYER

Spend some time now praying to the Holy Spirit.
Think about how the Holy Spirit has inspired
and guided those who wrote the Bible and the
popes and bishops who have helped us to
understand it. Begin with this traditional
prayer to the Holy Spirit.

Prayer to the Holy Spirit

Come, Holy Spirit, fill the hearts of your faithful.
And kindle in them the fire of your love.
Send forth your Spirit and they shall be created.
And you will renew the face of the earth.

Lord,
by the light of the Holy Spirit
you have taught the hearts of your faithful.
In the same Spirit
help us to relish what is right
and always rejoice in your consolation.
We ask this through Christ our Lord.
Amen.

You have asked the Holy Spirit to fill your heart.
The Spirit that renews the face of the earth can
renew you as well. Ask the Holy Spirit to help
you grow in understanding the Bible as you
study it this year. Thank God for the gift of the
Spirit and the grace and guidance always
available to you. Rest quietly in God's
presence, aware of his great love for you.

Faith Summary

The Bible is God's revelation. By reading it, especially the stories of Jesus, we learn what God has done for us and how we can help others.

Living My Faith

Words I Learned

inspired   interpretation   Magisterium   scriptorium   Vulgate

Holy spirit

room

St. Jerome

Ways of Being Like Jesus

Jesus was a Jew, and he studied the writings that now make up the Old Testament. To understand what Jesus read and studied, read one or more of the following psalms from the Old Testament: 8, 84, 98, 114, 150.

With My Family

A family Bible often contains a list of family members and information about the birth, Baptism, marriage, and death of each one. It also records other events. You can learn about the history of your family by reading this list. If your Bible does not contain this information, begin collecting it. Start by asking an older relative to tell you about your grandparents, great aunts and great uncles, and relatives who died before you were born. Write or type the information neatly and keep it in your family Bible.

PRAYER

Thank you, God, for the Bible and all the ways it helps me learn about you.

My Response

What will you do this week that reflects what you have learned from the Bible? Write your answer on a sheet of paper.

a parent page

Focus on Faith

God's Story and Ours

We all love stories. Telling stories about our personal and family lives is the foundation for teaching fundamental values to our children. Popular entertainment also tells stories and teaches values. During the hours in which our children play video games, watch television, and listen to popular music, they are being shaped by stories. Our Catholic tradition is filled with stories, beginning with those from the Bible. This year your child will be introduced to a number of these stories from the Old Testament and New Testament. They are stories about shepherds and kings, prophets and sinners, and heroic men and women. These stories shape the larger story of who God is as our Creator and Redeemer. Reading them along with your child gives you the opportunity to expand your imagination and recognize the presence of God in your lives.

Dinnertime Conversation Starters

Dinnertime conversation provides a good opportunity to listen to the stories that your child is hearing in the popular culture. It is important that in listening there be no immediate corrections of what is being said, as this will discourage further sharing. Tell a story that helped to shape your life.

Our Catholic Heritage

Johannes Gutenberg was born into a noble family in Germany about 1400. After early training as a goldsmith, he began experimenting with printing. His Bible, the oldest surviving printed book in the Western world, was published about 1455. Before the invention of the printing press, it took a copyist about 10 months to produce one copy of the Bible, so the price was high. After the invention of the printing press, thousands of copies could be produced swiftly and cheaply, giving many people access to the Word of God. You can view digital versions of the Gutenberg Bible on the World Wide Web.

Hints for at Home

If your family has not displayed your family Bible in a special place in your home, you may want to do so. Choose a small table or shelf that is accessible to everyone. Cover the table or shelf with a cloth and place the Bible on it. Place a votive light beside the book. You may wish to use different colored cloths for different times of the liturgical year—violet for Advent and Lent; white for Christmas, Easter, and feasts of the Blessed Virgin; and green for Ordinary Time.

Focus on Prayer

Your child is reviewing the Prayer to the Holy Spirit. To help with memorization, pray the prayer together as a family. You can find this prayer at www.FindingGod.org.

God Creates the World

Think of something you can do to care for creation and then share your thoughts with the group.

 PRAYER

Creator God, help me learn to value people and all of creation as you do. Guide me to be true to you and myself so that I may be worthy of being made in your image.

The Book of Genesis

In Genesis we have two stories about how the world was created.

The First Story of Creation

In the first creation story, God spoke, and every part of the universe came into being—the sun and moon, the water and land, the plants and animals. God even made man and woman in this story, and he made them in his own image. When he finished, he looked at everything and found that all of it was good.

based on Genesis 1:1—2:4

The writer of this story in Genesis wanted to make clear that God created every part of the world and that God saw everything as very good. Everything good in the creation story includes all physical things, such as plants, animals, oceans, mountains, and rocks, as well as human beings. God was pleased with how everything turned out.

It's All Good

The first creation story tells us that all of God's creation is good. Think of a plant or an animal or some other aspect of creation that you believe also has some negative qualities. Then, in the space provided, write what is good about it, rather than what is bad.

_____

_____

_____

_____

_____

Far From Home

When the first creation story was written, the Jews lived in **exile** in Babylon. They had been forced to leave their homeland to live in a place where the beliefs and customs were strange to them. Beliefs, customs, language, and dress make up a group's **culture**.

The Jews who lived in Babylon were not treated as equals with the Babylonians. Mistreatment of people because of their ethnic origins is called **racism**. The culture of the people in Babylon was very different from the culture of the Jews. Babylonian creation stories were filled with images of death and destruction caused by their gods. The Jews' creation story was peaceful and good. In their story, God created the universe calmly with wisdom and love.

Babylonian monument honoring a priest from the ancient Temple of Marduk (900–800 B.C.)

 ## Meet a Saint

Frances Xavier Cabrini was born in Italy in 1850. Her devotion to missionary work eventually took her to the United States. While there,

she helped to establish schools, hospitals, and orphanages for poor Italian immigrants who were not treated well by society. She insisted that Italians living in the United States be treated the same way as everyone else. Today she is known as the patron saint of immigrants.

Saint Frances Xavier Cabrini tending to poor Italian immigrants

The Second Story of Creation

In this story God created man and woman and put them in a garden to care for it. Together, man and woman—Adam and Eve—were to share equally and care for the earth as God does. They were allowed to eat the fruit from any tree in the garden except for one, from which God had forbidden them to eat. When they were tempted and ate the fruit of the forbidden tree, God made them leave the garden.

based on Genesis 2:4 — 3:24

Although this story appears after the first creation story in Genesis, it was actually written long before the Jews became exiles in Babylon. It was probably written while David and then his son Solomon reigned as kings of Israel. The land surrounding Israel was inhabited by Canaanites and other groups. They had creation stories, too, about all sorts of gods whose acts seem cruel and frightening to people.

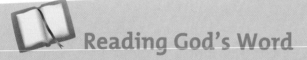

Reading God's Word

What are humans that you are mindful of them,
    mere mortals that you care for them?
Yet you have made them little less than a god,
    crowned them with glory and honor.
You have given them rule over the works of your hands,
    put all things at their feet.

Psalm 8:5-7

God Created Man and Woman as Equals

The story of Adam and Eve shows us a loving God who created man and woman—each a unity of body and soul—to be equal and to help God take care of the earth. When the man and woman disobeyed and rebelled against God, they had to leave God's presence in the Garden of Eden. From then on, life was different from the way that God had intended it to be.

God had created women to be equal to men; but ever since the rebellion of Adam and Eve, women have not been treated equally with men in many cultures. This mistreatment is called **sexism**. Opposing sexism, like opposing racism, is one of the duties of Catholics today.

To Make or to Break?

Humans were made to be good, but we can sometimes be destructive.

List three ways in which humans are creative.	**List three ways in which humans are destructive.**

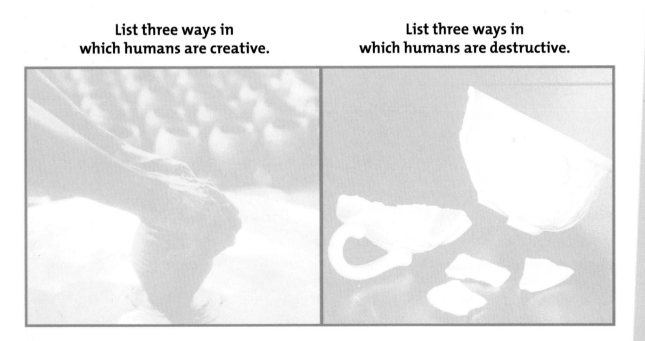

Link to Liturgy

The Liturgy of the Word at Mass includes a Responsorial Psalm, which is divided into verses and responses.

PRAYER

Quiet yourself by taking a few deep breaths. Now imagine that you are in a completely dark place. You look all around, but you can see nothing. You hear the sound of splashing as you feel a gentle wind blowing over water. God is about to create the universe.

Bring into your mind images that you have seen of galaxies, planets, and stars. Enjoy the beauty of the many shapes and colors. Then imagine our solar system with the yellow sun, the giant planet Jupiter, and the delicate blue and green Earth. This is your home in the midst of this beautiful creation.

On the earth you can see mountains, deserts, forests, rivers, and lakes. You see many types of fish in the sea, birds in the air, animals that crawl on land, and animals that walk. God makes each one and then says that each one is very good.

Finally, look at the great expanse of humanity, people young and old, of many shades of skin color, harvesting crops, hunting, fishing, and building machines. God has made each one and called each one good.

Now spend some time giving thanks for the great variety in creation. In your own words thank God for all that he has made. God has given all of this to you to care for. What promise can you make today that you will do your best to take care of his creation? Spend a few moments in God's awesome presence, aware of his care for all that he has created.

Faith Summary

The human family is created in the image and likeness of God. We reflect God's image by helping to care for the earth—its plants, creatures, and resources.

Words I Learned

culture   exile   racism   sexism

Ways of Being Like Jesus

If people want to know what God is like, all they have to do is look at his Son, Jesus. Jesus understood that it was his responsibility to work with God to love people and care for the world. You are like Jesus when you are kind to other people and when you care for God's creation.

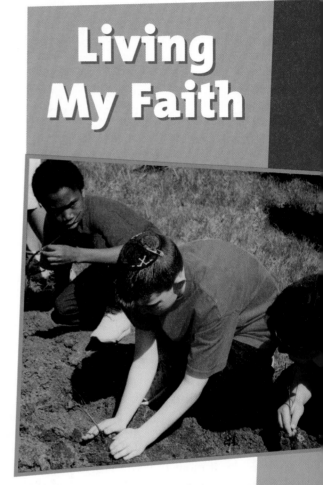

Living My Faith

With My Family

This week, do something as a family to care for God's creation. Maybe you can pick up trash in the neighborhood or plant a tree or flowers.

 PRAYER

God, thank you for making the earth a good place and for creating people to be good. Help me to act in ways that show people that I am made in your image.

My Response

When you get up each morning this week, go to a mirror and say, "God created me, and he's happy with the way I'm turning out." Write what you will do this week to be kind to people and God's other creatures.

Focus on Faith

God Created Everything Good

We are all fascinated by the story of how things began. Our children are fascinated by stories of how they were born, who was present, how exciting it was. We have that same sense of wonder about the beginning of the world. This is the story told in the first chapter of Genesis. This story was written when the Jewish people were in exile in Babylon between 597 and 537 B.C. They wrote the story because their children in Babylonian schools were learning the Babylonian story of creation that was filled with bloody battles. The Babylonians taught that the human family was created from the blood of an evil god. The Jewish writer of Genesis wanted to make it clear that the world was and continues to be created by God and that his creation is good. Celebrate God's good world today.

Dinnertime Conversation Starter

Discuss how you as a family celebrate God's good world.

Hints for at Home

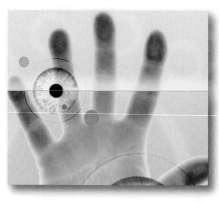

The Catholic Church teaches that human life is sacred and that the dignity of the human person is the foundation for a society's moral strength. To demonstrate to your child that he or she is unique, have your child list facts about himself or herself on a sheet of paper. Included can be likes, dislikes, friends, hobbies, favorite books and classes, and faith experiences. When your child has finished, have him or her sign it and put fingerprints on it (using ink or finger paints). Store the document in a safe place and then show it to your child a few years later. Your child will be interested to see that his or her fingerprints have remained the same despite any changes in personality or growth in faith.

Spirituality in Action

No matter who we are or where we come from, we all have dignity because God created us. Although we can never lose the fundamental human dignity that God gave

us, we can lose some of our dignity as members of a community when we hurt God's creation, especially other people. With your family, look through a newspaper or magazine and discuss some of the ways that people care for or hurt God's creation.

Focus on Prayer

Your child is reviewing the Lord's Prayer. To help with this review, pray this prayer as a family.

Sin and Salvation

What have you done recently that showed your trust in someone who cares for you?

PRAYER

God, my Creator, help me to love and trust you so that doing what is right and avoiding anything that is wrong becomes my way of living.

Trusting God

When we stop trusting God, things start going wrong. In Genesis Chapters 3, 4, and 6, we find three stories that show lack of trust.

Adam and Eve Disobey God

God placed Adam and Eve in the Garden of Eden and gave them everything they needed. Their life was very pleasant there. They tended the Garden and cared for the animals, and they had each other for companionship. God told them that if they ate the fruit from one tree in the middle of the garden, they would die. It was the tree of knowledge of good and evil.

One day a snake convinced Adam and Eve that they were missing out on something. The snake said that they would not die if they ate from the tree but would have wisdom like God's. They forgot that God loved them and would tell them anything they needed to know. They didn't need to disobey him by eating from the tree in order to be wise. They could walk and talk with God every day. Even so, Adam and Eve ate the fruit. That act of disobedience resulted in original sin. It changed everything. God sent Adam and Eve out of the Garden. From that time on, life became difficult for human beings.

based on Genesis 3:1-24

Reading God's Word

I will put enmity between you and the woman,
  and between your offspring and hers;
He will strike at your head,
  while you strike at his heel.

Genesis 3:15

Cain and Abel

After leaving the Garden, Adam and Eve had two sons, Cain and Abel. Cain and Abel had never known what it was like in the Garden. They'd never walked and talked with God as their parents had, so it's no surprise that Cain and Abel didn't get along. Most brothers argue sometimes, but Cain became so angry one day that he killed his brother, Abel. Just a few years out of the Garden and away from God's presence was all it took for people to start hurting each other. When people stop trusting God, they stop trusting each other as well.

The Killing of Abel, Wiligelmo

God had mercy on Cain and allowed him to live, but he sent Cain away from home. Cain had his own family, and his children had families as well. As time passed, there were many people living in the world. By then Adam and Eve were dead, and no one remembered the Garden. No one knew what it was like to walk and talk with God.

based on Genesis 4:1-16

God's Mercy

When do you need God's mercy? Maybe you have failed to do something you should have done. Complete these sentences:

When I disobey you by _____, Lord, have mercy.

When I need to _____, Lord, have mercy.

When I have trouble _____, Lord, have mercy.

When it's hard for me to _____, Lord, have mercy.

When I feel tired, afraid, angry, or _____, Lord, have mercy.

God Chooses Noah

During the many years after Adam and Eve had left the Garden, the world had become full of cruelty, greed, and sadness. It was such an awful situation that God decided to do something extreme.

God chose one family that showed love and trust and obedience. In the middle of a very sinful world, Noah and his wife and his sons and their wives had kept listening for God and looking for him. They wanted to walk with God and talk with him; so when God told them to build a huge boat and put two of every creature on it, they obeyed. They looked completely ridiculous, building a boat where there was no water. People laughed at them and made cruel jokes.

Then the rains came—and kept coming. Noah's family and all of the animals got on the boat (called an ark), and God shut the doors himself. For forty days and forty nights it rained. The entire world was flooded. Weeks later, the water went down, and the ark finally came to rest on land. Noah and his family had survived the worst disaster of all time because they trusted God and obeyed him.

based on Genesis 6:5 — 9:17

Peruvian sculpture of Noah's ark

Link to Liturgy

In the Penitential Act we reflect on and ask for God's mercy. The acclamation *Lord, have mercy* praises God for his great mercy.

God's Promise

God must have understood how frightening the flood had been. To help Noah and his family have hope about the future, God put a rainbow in the sky. God said that this rainbow was a sign of his promise that there would never again be such a flood.

When two people make an agreement today, they sometimes hire a lawyer and sign papers that say exactly what each person will do. In the story of Noah, the rainbow is God's signature. God promised that he would never again flood the whole world. Even after the disobedience of Adam and Eve, after Cain's murder of Abel, and after the world had become evil, God chose to make a commitment to the human beings he had created. That commitment is what we call a covenant.

A covenant is only as good as those who make it. And because God is faithful to his promises, he continues to keep the promise he made to Noah. What was that promise? Never to give up on people, even when they sin.

? Did You Know?

Scientists have discovered that a rainbow appears when water, light, and air come together in a certain way. Rainbows appear all the time in all sorts of places! Maybe God chose the rainbow as his signature because he knew that we would see rainbows so often.

PRAYER

The disobedience of Adam and Eve resulted in original sin, but God did not give up on people. With the words of the angel to Mary, "Hail, full of grace," something new began. Mary gave birth to Jesus, who redeems and saves us. Pray the Hail Mary now, stopping to reflect on each sentence.

Hail Mary, full of grace, the Lord is with you!

God gave Mary the help she needed to accomplish what he called her to do. God also gives us the grace we need to live as Jesus wants us to live.

Blessed are you among women, and blessed is the fruit of your womb, Jesus.

Mary was a person who was special because of her willingness to answer God's call in her life. God calls us each day to be a sign of his love in the world.

Holy Mary, Mother of God, pray for us sinners, now and at the hour of our death.

Mary prays for our needs and the needs of the world. We ask her to support us as we present our own needs to God.

Take a moment to speak with Mary. Ask her to be with you as you present your needs before God.

Amen.

Mother and Child,
Yasuo Ueno, 1997

Faith Summary

The story of Cain and Abel shows how quickly people began to sin after Adam and Eve lost trust in God and disobeyed him. God renewed that trust through Noah and through his promise to help us even though we sin. When we trust God and obey his commands, we can avoid sin and live peacefully together.

Ways of Being Like Jesus

After his baptism, Jesus was tempted. He resisted temptation by remembering God's commands in the Old Testament. You are like Jesus when you rely on verses from the Scriptures to strengthen your faith in God.

With My Family

Noah and his family were given the rainbow as a sign that God loved them and would work with them in starting the world over. God wants to work with your family too. Find an object that will remind your family of God's love. It may be a photograph or a statue or any object that reminds you of a time when God took care of your family. Display this object in a prominent place in your home.

PRAYER

God, thank you for not giving up on people, even though we often forget you. Let me listen to you every day and do what you prompt me to do.

My Response

When are you most tempted to stop listening for God's voice? Make a list of things that you can carry with you this week to help you remember that God is always ready to help you.

Focus on Faith

God's Rainbow

A rainbow is a marvelous sight! It can come at the end of a summer thunderstorm, when the blackness of the day, the fearsome lightning, and the quaking thunder pass. Against the clouds, the sun brightens the sky with an arc of color. The people in biblical times were as affected by the sight of the rainbow as we are. They saw it in the context of the story of Noah and the Great Flood. Through Noah and his family, God had saved the human family. At the end God promised that he would never send another such flood. The rainbow was the sign of his promise, called a covenant. God promises to treat the human family with mercy and love, a promise he will never break.

Noah's Ark, Edward Hicks, 1846

Dinnertime Conversation Starter

We can make covenants within the family, promises to support one another in important ways. Identify with your family a promise that each can make to support the family during the next week. End your family conversation with a prayer and a pledge to ask God for help in keeping the promises made.

Our Catholic Heritage

Throughout the years, Catholic artists have put animals in their artwork to represent different Christian ideas. Lambs, peacocks, lions, owls, and lizards have been painted on the walls of tombs and churches. One animal, the dove, has been used as a symbol for many things: the soul, the Holy Spirit, and peace. It was a dove that gave hope to Noah after he drifted for a long time on the water. He released a dove that returned with an olive branch; thus, Noah knew that land could not be far away.

Hints for at Home

Begin a habit in your family called the *"Lord, have mercy moment."* Whenever someone is having trouble, any person in the family can say, "Lord, have mercy!" When someone is frustrated or sad, it's all right to ask whether this is a *"Lord, have mercy moment."* Sometimes it may even be appropriate to stop and pray the Hail Mary or some other short prayer, asking for God's help. A humorous version of this

is a "Mom, have mercy" or "Dad, have mercy" moment. One of these expressions can be used when a child has made a mistake, forgotten instructions, or spilled the milk. By using a "Mom" or "Dad" version, your child can relate God's love to a parent's love.

Focus on Prayer

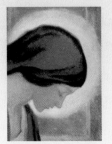

Your child is reviewing the Hail Mary. To help with the review, pray the Hail Mary together as a family. You can find the words to this prayer at www.FindingGod.org.

Abraham Listens to God

What are some of the things that your parents ask you to do that are difficult for you?

PRAYER

God, my Creator, over the years you have strengthened people's faith. Please strengthen mine now. You know what I need.

Sarah and Abraham Have a Child

The story of Sarah and Abraham took place many years after Noah and the flood. The world had many people in it once again.

Abraham and Sarah had been married a long time, but they did not have children. One night God took Abraham outside and said, "Look up at the sky and count the stars, if you can." He told Abraham that he would have as many descendants as there are stars in the night sky.

Years later Sarah had still not become pregnant. Then three visitors, sent from God, came to Abraham and Sarah. They said that in a year Sarah would have a son. Even though Abraham and Sarah thought they were too old to have children, Sarah gave birth to Isaac one year later.

based on Genesis 15:1-5; 18:1-10

？ Did You Know?

Patriarchs, prophets, and other Old Testament characters have been and always will be honored as saints by the Church.

Abraham Is Put to the Test

When Isaac was a young boy, God called out to Abraham and told him to kill Isaac and burn him on an altar. Abraham obeyed God's request and brought Isaac up a mountain, where he built an altar. As Abraham prepared to take his son's life, a messenger of God appeared and stopped Abraham just in time. God allowed Abraham to offer an animal instead of Isaac as a sacrifice.

based on Genesis 22:1-13

Why Did God Test Abraham?

The story of Abraham became a popular tale in Jewish culture at a time when the practice of sacrificing a firstborn child was a common part of life in the

The Sacrifice of Isaac, Rembrandt, 1635

area. In an attempt to criticize this practice, Jewish storytellers and writers offered this story in which God stopped Abraham from killing Isaac.

In the ancient world the story of Abraham set Judaism apart from other religions. The story not only condemned child sacrifice but also provided a human model of the perfect Jew, Abraham, who was completely obedient and faithful to God.

Reading God's Word

Realize then that it is those who have faith who are children of Abraham.

Galatians 3:7

The Chosen People

Because Abraham was willing to obey God, God promised that Abraham would be the father of not only Isaac but an entire nation of people.

When God made a covenant with Abraham, he started a new chapter in the story of our relationship with God. Abraham and Sarah lived many years after the great flood and the saving of Noah's family. In each generation, God calls people to know him in a special way.

God promised that Abraham would be the father of many nations. Ever since God's covenant with Abraham, Abraham's descendants have been known as God's **Chosen People**. God's Chosen People were given a mission to help other people learn to know and trust God.

Jesus was one of Abraham's descendants. Through Jesus, all of us can now be God's people. Just as Abraham and Sarah knew God, trusted him, and carried out his plans for the world, Christians today can do the same.

 Link to Liturgy

Christians have customs that set us apart and say to the world that we are God's people. One of those customs is the sign we make that represents God the Father, God the Son, and God the Holy Spirit. This gesture is called the Sign of the Cross. All Catholic liturgies include this prayer in the opening rites.

The Messengers of God

God performed a miracle for Sarah and Abraham in their old age by giving them a son. God also sent messengers to Abraham and Sarah. Recall the three visitors who came to Abraham and told him that Sarah would have a son. The visitors were angels sent by God. Also, when Abraham was about to kill his son, God sent an angel to stop him.

Angels help people understand God's plan, and they give people the courage to follow God's instructions. Angels are still working as God's messengers.

Angels in Action

Each of the following Bible citations refers to a story in which an angel appears and performs an act for God. Read each passage and write what the angel did in it.

Matthew 1:18–21

_____

_____

_____

Luke 2:8–14

_____

_____

_____

Mark 1:12–13

_____

_____

_____

PRAYER

Abraham and Sarah had reasons not to hope, yet God led them to increased faith and trust. Hope is an important Christian characteristic. We hope because we believe that God has made a commitment to us, to care for us and show us how to live.

Pray the Act of Hope and think about your trust in God.

Act of Hope

O my God, relying on your infinite mercy and promises, I hope to obtain pardon of my sins, the help of your grace, and life everlasting, through the merits of Jesus Christ, my Lord and Redeemer. Amen.

After you pray the Act of Hope, spend a few minutes with God. Thank him in your own words for his grace and for the hope that you will live with him forever. Rest a few moments in his presence.

Faith Summary

God called Abraham and Sarah to believe in him. We also are called to believe what God says and to obey God because we trust in him.

Word I Learned

Chosen People

Ways of Being Like Jesus

When Jesus lived on the earth, he had to learn to trust God. God asked Jesus to do some very difficult things. Jesus often prayed when his trust in God was put to the test. When your trust in God is challenged, you can pray as Jesus did to find strength.

With My Family

Each person needs to learn how to trust God, and each family does too. With your parents' help, write a special prayer asking God to help your family have hope in God's promises. Post the prayer on the refrigerator or someplace else where everyone can see it and be reminded every day to trust God.

 PRAYER

God, thank you for the story of Abraham and Sarah. You keep your promises and do great things for us. Help me always to trust in you.

My Response

When is it hardest for you to trust in God? This week, every time it's hard to trust, say this to yourself: "If Abraham and Sarah could believe, so can I."

Focus on Faith

Abraham's Sacrifice and Ours

The story of Abraham's willingness to sacrifice Isaac is a frightening one. How could God ask this of him? What the story actually is teaching is that God does not want our children in sacrifice. He stopped Abraham's sacrifice to show that the surrounding cultures' practice of sacrificing children was wrong. This Scripture story points to issues we as parents can consider. What expectations do we have of our children? Do we insist on academic or athletic excellence beyond their capacity or interest? Do we insist that our way of doing things is the only way our children should follow? Are we frightened by the prospect of their wanting to follow vocations that we do not approve of? What help do we need from God to not place excessive demands on our children?

Dinnertime Conversation Starters

Have a listening session in which your child can share his or her hopes and dreams of the future. Create an atmosphere in which you listen without judging choices or warning about how much study will be required to accomplish those goals.

Hints for at Home

Throughout our lives the stories of the Bible take on different personal meanings as we go through changes, hardships, and joys. To help you continue to think about Bible stories, work with the family to decorate a small box. On separate small pieces of paper, write the names of different biblical characters that your child has learned about and put the papers into the box. Once every month set aside time for the family to get together and draw a name out of the box. Share the story associated with that character. Talk about the challenges or events in that Bible character's life that brought him or her closer to God. Discuss how those kinds of challenges occur in your own lives.

Spirituality in Action

As Christians, we believe that God does not give up on us but is always working to help us on our journey through life, just as he helped Abraham. Ask each person in the family to think of one thing to do this week to demonstrate a hopeful attitude to others.

For one person this might mean being patient with a person or project. Another person might say positive things when with friends who are often negative toward others. Dad or Mom might make plans for a celebration that the family can enjoy after a major task around the house is finished.

Focus on Prayer

Your child is reviewing the prayer Act of Hope. To help reinforce this prayer, pray it together as a family. You may find the words to this prayer at www.FindingGod.org.

Review

The stories in the Old Testament reveal the human family's relationship with God the Creator. Share an Old Testament story that you especially like. What does that story say about our relationship with God?

PRAYER

God, our Creator, help me to remember always that you created me, that you love me, and that you'll never give up on me.

Faith Summary

God created everything that exists. When he was finished creating, he was very pleased with how his creation, especially human beings, had turned out.

The human family was created in the image and likeness of God. We reflect God's image by helping to care for the earth—its plants, creatures, resources, and people.

In the Garden of Eden, man and woman disobeyed God. The result of this disobedience is called original sin. Ever since, humans have struggled with trusting God, loving God, and obeying God. We also have trouble trusting and loving one another.

God doesn't give up on us, even when we sin and find it hard to trust. He cared enough about the world to give it a fresh start. He sent a flood and started the human family all over again with Noah and his family.

Noah's Ark, Alexis Ngom, 1986

God leads us to greater faith as we go on our life's journey. He led Abraham and Sarah by promising them a son, when they were both too old to have children, and then giving them one. Abraham and Sarah had to learn how to trust and follow God throughout their lives. They are good examples for us. We, too, need to learn how to trust and obey God in our own lives.

We can learn about Noah, Abraham and Sarah, and many other people of God by reading the Bible. God uses the Bible to reveal himself to us, especially in the life, death, and resurrection of Jesus Christ.

Just Imagine!

Now it's time to use your imagination! You're going to explore the Bible characters you've read about in Unit 1. Each person in your group will be either a Bible character or a news reporter who is interviewing a Bible character. The characters are these:

If you're not a Bible character, you will be a reporter who interviews one of the characters. If you are a reporter, make a list of questions to ask the person you're going to interview. Try to develop at least five questions. Here are some suggestions:

"How did God call you to build the ark, Noah?"

"How long were you and your family on the ark before the flood was over?"

What Did You Discover?

After completing the interviews, answer these questions.

1. What did you learn about any of the characters that you had not known before?

   _____

   _____

2. Describe what you have in common with two of the Bible characters who were interviewed.

   _____

   _____

   _____

3. Now describe what two of these characters have in common with Jesus.

   _____

   _____

   _____

4. The characters in the Old Testament are not the only ones who are called by God. What are two things that you are called by God to do?

   _____

   _____

5. Think of all the stories you have learned in this unit. Did God's relationship with human beings change or stay the same from story to story? Explain your answer.

   _____

   _____

   _____

PRAYER SERVICE

Leader: *Let us praise God, who enlightens our hearts, now and forever.*

All: *Amen.*

All: *God, our Creator, we gather to remember how much you love us.*

Leader: *You made the seas and skies, the mountains and valleys, and the trees and flowers.*

All: *And they are good.*

Leader: *You made the creatures of the sea and those on the land and in the air.*

All: *And they are good.*

Leader: *You made people of all kinds—women and men of all races and cultures.*

All: *And they are good.*

Leader: *You have made us families, with parents and children, brothers and sisters, friends and neighbors.*

All: *And they are good.*

Leader: *Thank you for this world, full of wonder and variety.*

All: *Thank you for making us part of this universe. Amen.*

Pray the Lord's Prayer together.

Living My Faith

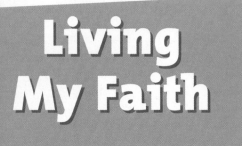

Ways of Being Like Jesus

When Jesus was a boy, he studied the sacred writings that we know as the Old Testament. He also listened to the religious teachers of his time and asked them questions about God. You are like Jesus when you discuss your questions about God or faith with your family or the members of your church.

Torah scroll

With My Family

Ask your parents to help you make a time line that shows how you have grown. Include milestones that you think are important. If you look carefully, you will see that you are always growing and learning. Imagine what kind of time line God could make about you, showing how your faith has grown.

PRAYER

Creator God, you provide so many ways for me to grow in my love and trust for you. Thank you for helping me to know that you will never give up on me. Most of all, thank you for making me and calling me into your love forever.

My Response

What can you do this week to celebrate your faith journey? You might draw a picture of what it's been like so far or write a poem about the things you've learned about God.

Son of God, Son of Mary

Saint John Neumann

John Neumann was one of the first American citizens to be declared a saint. He was also one of the founders of Catholic education in the United States.

41

Saint John Neumann

Saint John Neumann,
Gagliardi

John Neumann was one of the most influential bishops in the United States. He was one of the first American citizens to be declared a saint by the Catholic Church.

John was born in 1811 in Bohemia, which is now part of the Czech Republic. Although he studied for the priesthood in Bohemia, he was ordained in New York City. Soon after his ordination, John was sent to the northern part of New York State, near the city of Buffalo.

The people in that part of the state were immigrants from Germany, Ireland, France, and Scotland. Father John knew eight languages, so he was able to communicate with his new parishioners. Over the years, he served the people of New York, Pennsylvania, and Ohio. In 1852, in recognition of the wonderful work he had done, Father John was appointed bishop of Philadelphia. While bishop, he established schools, wrote books of religious instruction and newspaper articles, and strongly encouraged devotion to Jesus Christ in the Blessed Sacrament.

After being bishop of Philadelphia for only eight years, John Neumann died suddenly while leisurely walking along a city street. The Catholics of Philadelphia mourned the loss of their spiritual leader. The Church honors him on January 5.

God Is Faithful

God works through people to bring about good in the world. Think of a way that God works through someone you know to bring good into the world. Share your thoughts with the group.

🔥 PRAYER

Loving God, help me to see your presence in all of the ordinary events in my life.

Jacob Deceives His Brother

Jacob and Esau were twin brothers, and they competed with each other from the day they were born. Esau was born first, and Jacob was born holding onto Esau's foot! They were completely different in looks and personality, and unfortunately their parents each favored a different son. Their mother, Rebecca, favored Jacob; their father, Isaac, favored Esau. This probaby heightened the brothers' competitiveness.

Esau was to receive the birthright—a special right passed from the father to his firstborn son—but Jacob wanted the birthright for himself. One day Esau came home hungry from hunting. Jacob, who had been cooking, realized that this was his opportunity to take the birthright from Esau, so he convinced Esau to trade it for a bowl of stew!

That wasn't the last time Jacob took advantage of Esau. When their father, Isaac, was near death, he wished to give his final blessing to Esau, his favorite son. Isaac was old and could not see very well, so he asked Esau to go hunting and bring back some food for his favorite meal. While Esau was hunting, Rebecca helped Jacob pretend to be Esau and trick his father into giving the blessing to him instead. When Esau found out, he was so angry at Jacob that he wanted to kill him. Jacob had to leave, never to return to his parents' home.

based on Genesis 25:19-34; 27:1-45

Link to Liturgy

During Mass, before we receive Holy Communion, we pray, "Lord, I am not worthy that you should enter under my roof, but only say the word and my soul shall be healed." With these words, we are asking for God's help and forgiveness.

Jacob Is Tricked

Shortly after leaving home, Jacob met Rachel, and he agreed to work for her father, Laban, for seven years to win permission to marry her. This time Jacob learned what it was like to be on the receiving end of trickery. Laban switched daughters at the last minute, and Jacob married Rachel's older sister, Leah, who was heavily veiled, instead. Jacob still wanted to marry Rachel, and Laban let him, but Jacob had to work an additional seven years as payment. (In that time and culture, a man often had more than one wife.)

God made sure that Jacob found his destiny. He spoke to Jacob and reestablished the promise he had made to Abraham and Isaac. Then he gave Jacob a new name: Israel. After that, Jacob was able to face the brother he had tricked years ago. Esau forgave Jacob, and finally their competition ended.

based on Genesis 29:15-30

Good Results From a Loving God

Jacob certainly had his flaws: he was ambitious and deceitful. God had plans for him, though, and even a misled young man couldn't ruin them.

Jacob's story is a good example of **Divine Providence,** the means by which God's wisdom and love influence all creatures to help in continuing the work of creation. As Jacob's story shows, God was able to bring about good results from bad choices. Both Jacob and his grandfather Abraham fulfilled their destinies, and their faith and character grew in the process.

Remember That God Remembers You

Although God can take our sins and mistakes and bring about good results, some people think that they can count on God to get them out of trouble when they deliberately do something wrong. Such an attitude doesn't come from real faith—it comes from disrespect for God's love and patience. It is never acceptable to do a bad thing in the hope of bringing about something good.

Accepting Consequences

Think back through Jacob's story and list the ways in which he had to suffer the consequences of his actions.

_____

_____

_____

Sometimes, when we have acted in ways that have hurt friends or family members, being sorry and saying so don't seem to be enough. We need to show that we are sorry. Think of a few things you could do other than say, "I'm sorry," and write them below.

_____

_____

_____

Jesus, Descendant of Jacob

Jesus descended from a long line of men and women, including Jacob and King David. Jesus' ancestors were people who made mistakes and learned from them, just as we do.

Through the example of Jesus and his ancestors we can see that our choices and actions are part of God's plan. We all face difficult choices in life, and sometimes the choices we make hurt other people. Although we may not always understand God's plan, Jesus teaches us to trust the goodness and faithfulness of God.

Reading God's Word

And concerning the resurrection of the dead, have you not read what was said to you by God, "I am the God of Abraham, the God of Isaac, and the God of Jacob"? He is not the God of the dead but of the living.

Matthew 22:31-32

PRAYER

God can bring about good results from our sins and mistakes, as he did with Jacob. With this prayer you can offer God every part of your life. Because God is faithful to his people, he will take all of these things and bring something good from them.

Morning Offering

My God, I offer you my prayers, works, joys and sufferings of this day in union with the holy sacrifice of the Mass throughout the world. I offer them for all the intentions of your Son's Sacred Heart, for the salvation of souls, reparation for sin, and the reunion of Christians.
Amen.

Pray this prayer silently to yourself. When you come to the words "my prayers, works, joys, and sufferings," list in your mind some of those things. You may want to write them on paper and offer them to God.

Faith Summary

Jacob trusted in God. Divine Providence can bring about good results from bad choices and situations.

Word I Learned

Divine Providence

Ways of Being Like Jesus

When Jesus needed to reflect on how God was working through him, he would spend time alone praying and listening to God. You are like Jesus when you spend quiet time thinking about how God works through you and the people you know.

With My Family

Your family has its own history of faith. Ask a parent or grandparent to help you record the highlights, in a small book, with pictures and photographs. The highlights may include parishes your family has belonged to, relatives who have done religious work, and stories of answered prayer.

Living My Faith

Anthony is the latest of the Cucco family to wear this baptismal garment.

PRAYER

Loving God, thank you for being faithful to me even when I sin. Help me to trust in you through everything that happens to me.

My Response

You may not always be able to know what the consequences of a choice will be. Think about what steps you can take when you must make a difficult decision; then write them on a piece of paper.

Focus on Faith

Every Child Is Special

Sibling rivalry is common in all families. In the Old Testament, Isaac and Rebecca had the problem with their twin sons, Jacob and Esau. The boys competed for their father's affection and the right for his blessing. Through trickery and with the help of Rebecca, Jacob gained Isaac's blessing but lost his family. He fled for his life when Esau sought revenge. It is easy for parents to make comparisons between their children. The subtle hints convey that one child's behavior and gifts meet with approval while those of the others somehow fall short. Making any comparisons between children in a way that sets them against one another damages family solidarity. Each child is unique and blessed by God. Celebrate that uniqueness in special and noncompetitive ways.

Dinnertime Conversation Starter

One evening, set your child's place at the table with a unique or decorative plate. Tell him or her that your family recognizes how special he or she is to the family. Invite each family member to mention one gift that the child brings to the family. Honor a different family member each night.

Hints for at Home

Help your child to create a faith family tree. On a large sheet of paper, write the names of people who have had a significant impact on the faith life of your family. Include family members, teachers, priests—even writers or artists who are in some way connected to your family's practice of the Catholic faith. Include any ethnic or regional influences as well. Share with one another stories about how these persons affected your family faith life.

Our Catholic Heritage

Saint John Neumann is entombed at St. Peter's Church in Philadelphia, where his body rests within a glass encasement under the main altar of the lower church. To this day, St. Peter's Church is staffed by the same brotherhood of Redemptorists that founded the church. Catholics from around the world still journey to St. Peter's Church to see the National Shrine of Saint John Neumann. In 1979, when Pope John Paul II visited Philadelphia, he too visited the shrine.

Focus on Prayer

Your child is reviewing the Morning Offering. Say this prayer together before he or she leaves for school to help with memorization. You can find the words for the Morning Offering at www.FindingGod.org.

Passover and the Eucharist

How does your family celebrate important events? Share with the group a story about a celebration you have had during the past year.

PRAYER

Faithful God, help me to remember the sacrifice of Jesus when we celebrate the Eucharist. Help me to keep giving as Jesus did, even when it is a sacrifice for me.

God Leads a Nation to Freedom

During a time of famine, Jacob's family—all of his sons and their families—moved to Egypt, hoping that they might find relief there. His son Joseph already lived in Egypt and was an important government official. Jacob's family prospered in Egypt, and after many generations, his descendants filled the country. They were known as the **Israelites** because God had given Jacob the name Israel. They were also known as Hebrews.

Long after Jacob's son Joseph died, the pharaoh—Egypt's ruler—became worried that the numerous Hebrews might have the strength to take over the country. He probably did not know about the service that Joseph had provided for one of the former Egyptian rulers, so the pharaoh made slaves of all the Hebrews.

The Hebrews suffered for nearly four centuries, laboring for the Egyptians. They prayed to the God of Abraham, Isaac, and Jacob to save them, and God heard their prayers. Responding to the cries of the people, God chose a man named Moses to lead them out of slavery. Although Moses was a Hebrew, he had actually been brought up as the son of the pharaoh's daughter.

based on Exodus 1:1 — 2:10

The Finding of Moses (detail), Raphael, 15th century

? Did You Know?

The pharaoh's daughter gave Moses his name, which in Egyptian means "is born." *Moses* is also similar to the Hebrew word meaning "to draw out," which is exactly what the pharaoh's daughter did when she found Moses inside a basket floating on a river; she drew him out of the water. You can read about this in Exodus 2:1–10.

God Appears to Moses

Despite the fact that Moses had been brought up as an Egyptian, he knew that he was a Hebrew, and in his heart he felt great sympathy for the Hebrew slaves. One day Moses saw an Egyptian abusing a Hebrew slave, so he intervened and killed the Egyptian. When the pharaoh learned what he had done, Moses had to leave the country, and he settled in the land of Midian.

While Moses was in Midian, God appeared to him in a strange way. As Moses tended his father-in-law's herd, he heard a voice that came from a bush that was on fire but didn't burn up.

God said that he was the God of Abraham and Jacob and that he had come to set the Hebrew slaves free. Moses asked God's name. God responded in Hebrew, **"Yahweh,"** which means "I am who I am." The name is mysterious, but it helps us trust that God will always be with us as he promised the Hebrew people. We recognize God's presence today as the presence of the Holy Spirit.

based on Exodus 2:11 — 3:16

Moses Accepts His Mission

Although God chose Moses to lead the Hebrew people out of slavery, Moses was hesitant because he thought that he was unable to succeed at such a task. He eventually accepted God's appointment, but he knew that, to do so, he would have to trust God and follow God's instructions.

When Moses went back to Egypt to convince the pharaoh to free the slaves, the pharaoh was stubborn and didn't believe that their God would help the Hebrews. God had to perform many mighty wonders before the pharaoh would change his mind. The last of these wonders was called Passover.

Passover and the Sabbath

God told Moses that on a certain night the angel of death would travel over Egypt and kill the firstborn child in every family but that, if the Hebrew people followed God's instructions, their firstborn children would be spared. So Moses told each Hebrew family to kill a lamb and to sprinkle its blood on the door of the house. If they did so, the angel would see the blood and pass over the house without causing harm.

The Israelites were also instructed to eat a special meal. This meal and the prayers offered on that night became a memorial for the Hebrew people, known as the Passover. A memorial is a celebration that helps people remember an important event. Even today Jewish people (another name for Hebrews) celebrate Passover every year. It helps them remember the night that the angel of death passed over the Hebrew houses.

based on Exodus 12:1-30

The **Sabbath** is another celebration that continues to be observed today. When God created the world, he rested on the seventh day, and he commanded people to rest on that day every week. This day of rest was called the Sabbath. Christians now celebrate the Sabbath on Sunday and on this day recall the new creation, which began with the resurrection of Christ.

What Has God Done for You?

Write about some of the things God has done for you. How do you celebrate them?

Celebrating Eucharist

The Hebrews celebrated Passover as a memorial to God for saving them from slavery. The last meal Jesus shared with his disciples before he was crucified added new meaning to this celebration. From that time on, this meal would be a memorial to the sacrifice Jesus made in order to save humanity from sin. Jesus' Death and Resurrection began a new covenant between God and people, and this covenant is what we remember and celebrate in the **Eucharistic liturgy.** We believe that Jesus' sacrifice becomes present to us as we say the prayers of the Mass and share in the Body and Blood of Jesus Christ.

Catholics all over the world, including the **Eastern Catholic Churches,** celebrate the Eucharist. All of us share the same apostolic tradition, honoring the same Jesus and the same covenant between God and his people. Although we are obligated to receive the Eucharist once every year, we are encouraged to receive it as often as we can. The Eucharist forgives venial sin and unites us with Christ. Those who are in a state of mortal sin may receive the Eucharist only after receiving absolution in the Sacrament of Penance.

Reading God's Word

Jesus said to them, "Amen, amen, I say to you, unless you eat the flesh of the Son of Man and drink his blood, you do not have life within you. Whoever eats my flesh and drinks my blood has eternal life, and I will raise him on the last day."

John 6:53-54

PRAYER

When we gather for the Eucharist, we remember how God leads and cares for his people. We give thanks. We commit ourselves to making the world a place where every person comes to the table to be restored in body and spirit.

Pray together this psalm for your prayer today.

The LORD is my shepherd;
    there is nothing I lack.
In green pastures you let me graze;
        to safe waters you lead me;
        you restore my strength.
You guide me along the right path
    for the sake of your name.
Even when I walk through a dark valley,
        I fear no harm for you are at my side;
        your rod and staff give me courage.

You set a table before me
    as my enemies watch;
You anoint my head with oil;
    my cup overflows.
Only goodness and love will pursue me
    all the days of my life;
I will dwell in the house of the LORD
    for years to come.

Psalm 23

Now spend a few minutes reflecting on God's goodness and love that you find in your life. Thank God in your own words for his guidance along the right path and the courage he gives you in difficult times. Rest in God's presence.

Faith Summary

During Passover, Jews recall the night that God spared their children as he punished the Egyptians for enslaving the Hebrew people. Jesus' last meal may have been a Passover meal, but he added a new meaning to this meal, one that we celebrate in the Eucharistic liturgy.

Words I Learned

Eastern Catholic Churches   Eucharistic liturgy
Israelite   Sabbath   Yahweh

Ways of Being Like Jesus

Jesus performed many miracles during his life. On one occasion he turned a few loaves of bread into enough food to feed thousands of hungry people. When you and your family contribute to food drives, you are continuing the work of Jesus.

With My Family

When you participate in Mass with your family, pay special attention to the eucharistic prayer and talk later about phrases and actions that stood out for you.

 **PRAYER**

Thank you, Jesus, for helping us to understand God's covenant with us in a new way. You allowed your own blood to be shed so that we would be saved from sin.

My Response

God gave people the Sabbath as a day to rest and worship him. What do you do on Sunday to celebrate this gift from God? Write your answer on a piece of paper.

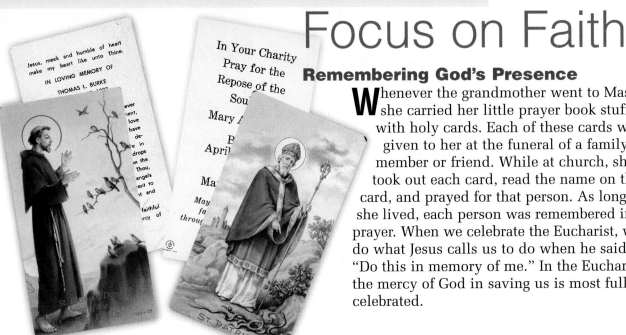

Focus on Faith

Remembering God's Presence

Whenever the grandmother went to Mass, she carried her little prayer book stuffed with holy cards. Each of these cards was given to her at the funeral of a family member or friend. While at church, she took out each card, read the name on the card, and prayed for that person. As long as she lived, each person was remembered in prayer. When we celebrate the Eucharist, we do what Jesus calls us to do when he said, "Do this in memory of me." In the Eucharist the mercy of God in saving us is most fully celebrated.

Spirituality in Action

Become involved with a ministry that helps to feed the hungry. Your family can contribute to a food pantry or participate in Operation Rice Bowl. Perhaps there are people in your neighborhood who can afford food but need your assistance to go shopping. Explore these Web sites with your children: **www.catholicrelief.org** and **www.oxfamamerica.org**.

Dinnertime
Conversation Starter

As you say grace before your meal, add a prayer for deceased family members and friends. After dinner, write the names of those remembered and bring the list to a Sunday Eucharist as a reminder to pray for them at Mass as well.

Focus on Prayer

Pray through Psalm 23 with your child and talk about what the different phrases mean.

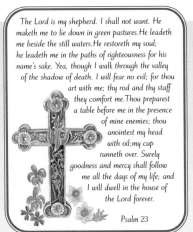

The Lord is my shepherd. I shall not want. He maketh me to lie down in green pastures. He leadeth me beside the still waters. He restoreth my soul; he leadeth me in the paths of righteousness for his name's sake. Yea, though I walk through the valley of the shadow of death, I will fear no evil; for thou art with me; thy rod and thy staff they comfort me. Thou preparest a table before me in the presence of mine enemies; thou anointest my head with oil; my cup runneth over. Surely goodness and mercy shall follow me all the days of my life; and I will dwell in the house of the Lord forever.

Psalm 23

Hints for at Home

Set aside an evening for your family to get together and then bake a loaf of bread. Place the bread on the dinner table. Before beginning the meal, each person in your family should hand a piece of bread to the person next to him or her and say the following prayer: "Let this bread remind us of Jesus Christ, the Bread of Life."

God Leads His People

Think about some of the trips you've taken—vacations, visits to friends and relatives, or trips to important places. Share something about a trip with the group.

PRAYER

Faithful God, lead me and guide me to be more committed to the journey of faith.

The Great Exodus

After the Passover the pharaoh could no longer refuse Moses' request that the Hebrews be released from slavery. He had seen the incredible power of God and insisted that the Hebrew people leave immediately. After living in slavery in Egypt for hundreds of years, the Hebrews, led by Moses, began their long journey to freedom. This journey is known as the **Exodus.**

For 40 years the Israelites wandered in the desert before they settled in the land of Canaan. Their journey was filled with anxiety and hardship. There were many times when people lost their trust in God and complained to Moses about his having brought them out of Egypt to die in the desert. They were frightened, but throughout their journey God provided everything they needed.

God gave them food, manna, which fell from the sky, and water, where there was none to be found. He even sent a cloud by day and a pillar of fire by night to show them which direction to go.

The Gathering of the Manna (detail), Master of the Manna, 1470

God Saves the Israelites

The most miraculous events in the Hebrews' flight from Egypt occurred when they crossed the Red Sea. After Moses and the Hebrews left Egypt, the pharaoh decided to pursue the Hebrews and destroy them. He sent a grand army of chariot riders and soldiers.

The Egyptian army closed in on the Israelites, trapping them against the sea. At that moment God told Moses to stand before the Red Sea and raise his staff. As he did, the water in the sea split apart, and a path of dry ground stretched clear across to the other side.

Moses and his people crossed the sea on the dry path, and the Egyptian army followed close behind. After pursuing the Israelites onto the path, the Egyptians realized that the Hebrews had God on their side, so the Egyptians began to retreat. Before they could return to the shore, God told Moses to raise his staff again; as he did, the walls of water came crashing down, destroying the Egyptian army.

based on Exodus 14:10-30

Moses releasing the waters of the Red Sea, Bible illumination, 10th century

Trusting God Through It All

Are you ready to trust God in difficult situations? Complete the sentences below.

When I don't succeed at _____, I trust that God

_____

When I feel _____, I trust that God

_____

When I need _____, I trust that God

_____

God Gives Moses the Ten Commandments

Moses went to Egypt to challenge the pharaoh for the sake of the Hebrew people. The pharaoh would not cooperate and began a battle with God that he could not win. After finally releasing the Hebrew people, the pharaoh tried once again to stop them, but God crushed his army, while Moses led his people across the sea.

When the Hebrews reached Mount Sinai God gave Moses the Ten Commandments. God asked the Hebrews if they wanted to be his people. In response the people said yes and agreed to follow these commandments.

Jesus lived by the Ten Commandments and told others to do so. With God's help, these basic instructions guide us to the right relationship with God and each other.

Reading God's Word

Hear, O Israel! The LORD is our God, the LORD alone! Therefore, you shall love the LORD, your God, with all your heart, and with all your soul, and with all your strength.

Deuteronomy 6:4-5

Exploring the Ten Commandments

A short version of the Ten Commandments is written below. On the line below each commandment, rewrite it in your own words. You might try rewriting negative statements to make them positive ones and vice versa. For example, after "You shall not steal," you could write, "Be generous to others." You will not be rewriting the Bible; you will be exploring the meaning of these verses.

I am the Lord your God: you shall not have strange gods before me.

_____

You shall not take the name of the Lord your God in vain.

_____

Remember to keep holy the Lord's day.

_____

Honor your father and your mother.

_____

You shall not kill.

_____

You shall not commit adultery.

_____

You shall not steal.

_____

You shall not bear false witness against your neighbor.

_____

You shall not covet your neighbor's wife.

_____

You shall not covet your neighbor's possessions.

_____

PRAYER

Choose several of your answers from Exploring the Ten Commandments and use them as the words of a prayer. If one of the rewritten Ten Commandments was "Be generous to others," for example, the words of your prayer might include "God, help me to be generous to others."

This is your personal prayer, based on God's Word. Be creative!

_____

_____

_____

_____

_____

_____

_____

Silently pray it to yourself, knowing that you are in the presence of God.

Faith Summary

The Exodus event renewed the covenant between God and the Israelites that began with God and Abraham.

Word I Learned

Exodus

Ways of Being Like Jesus

The Ten Commandments were important to Jesus, as were the other teachings of the Old Testament. Jesus added new meaning to our faith, but he didn't set aside the faith of Abraham, Isaac, Jacob, and Moses. When you follow the Ten Commandments, you are being like Jesus.

With My Family

Sometime this week ask everyone in your family to help write ten family commandments to follow. When you have decided on these commandments, display them in a place where everyone can see them.

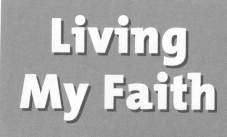

Pillar of fire,
stained-glass window,
Temple Menorah

PRAYER

Dear God, thank you for helping me to find my way each day.

My Response

Explain in your own words why the Ten Commandments are important to you.

_____

_____

_____

a parent page

Focus on Faith

The Ten Commandments

When Jewish people worship, they bring out the scroll containing the Torah, or the Law, with great reverence. They remember that God had saved the Israelites from slavery in Egypt. When God asked the people whether they wanted him to continue to be their God, they said yes. The Law, centered on the Ten Commandments, was given to them as a gift. The first three commandments taught them that only by loving God alone could they remain free. The last seven commandments gave them the basic principles they needed to live in peace with one another. The Ten Commandments remain for us, as Catholics, the fundamental teaching that God gives us in order to live in relationship with himself and others.

Dinnertime Conversation Starter

Choose a commandment that affects family life, such as the fourth, seventh, or eighth. Help the family determine positive ways to live that commandment.

Hints for at Home

With your family, develop a checklist of weekly deeds that cultivate peace and justice according to God's commandments. The list should include actions that are relevant to each member of your family. For example, say a prayer for someone you know who is going through a difficult time. Make a list for each family member and display the lists in a place where everyone can see them. Each time a family member has accomplished one of the deeds listed, that person should put a check mark next to that point. At the end of the week, gather the family and talk about what has been accomplished.

Focus on Prayer

Your child was encouraged to create a prayer of his or her own. Ask your child to help you write a prayer of your own. Don't ask to see your child's prayer but be willing to discuss it if your child wants to show it to you and talk about it.

Our Catholic Heritage

For many centuries Christians have recited certain prayers at particular times throughout the day. These sets of prayers are called the Liturgy of the Hours. Miriam's Song of Deliverance, found in Exodus 15:1–18, is one of the prayers found in the Liturgy of the Hours.

Being Faithful to God

How many choices do you make in a day? How many *important* choices do you make in a day? Describe one choice you have made this week that definitely involved right and wrong.

PRAYER

Generous God, show me how I can make choices that will honor you.

Two Stories, Two Choices

Many stories in the Old Testament are told on a grand scale: the entire world is flooded, nations are freed from slavery, and armies are destroyed. However there are also personal stories in the Old Testament, stories about people who had to make difficult decisions that eventually changed their lives. These personal stories help us to understand the importance of making good decisions in our lives, and they also show us the consequences of making bad decisions.

Since we all have times when we must make difficult decisions that can have serious consequences, we can read these stories and learn from them. The stories of David and Ruth in particular show us how important moral choices can affect our relationships with God and people.

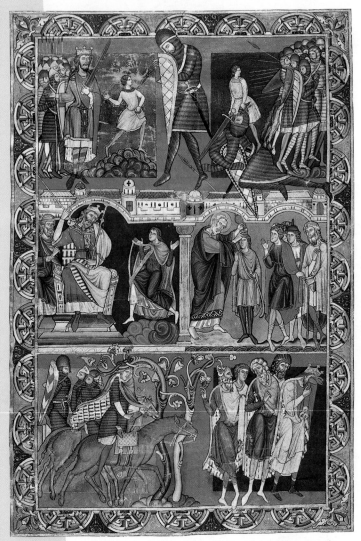

Scenes from the Life of David (single page),
Master of the Morgan Leaf, Winchester Bible,
12th century

David's Choice

After the Exodus the Hebrews settled in the land of Canaan and established a kingdom. David, their second king, united the various tribes of the land under one rule and established Jerusalem as the capital of Israel.

David's reign started successfully; the kingdom was prosperous, and the people approved of him. As David's power grew, however, his wisdom and ability to make good decisions did not grow. He became arrogant and used his power to get whatever he wanted.

David's arrogance eventually led him to make some bad decisions. He thought that he could do anything without having to face the consequences.

One day, while his army was at war, David saw Bathsheba, the wife of one of his army captains, Uriah. David was instantly attracted to her, and he wanted to be with her even though she was already married.

David knew that it would be wrong to be with her. Nevertheless, he became envious and resentful of her husband for having what he wanted. David ultimately let envy and lust, rather than the knowledge of right and wrong, guide his decision. He chose to be with Bathsheba while Uriah was away. By committing adultery, David had broken one of God's commandments.

When David learned that Bathsheba was pregnant with his child, he tried to cover up his sin by arranging for Uriah to be in the front lines of battle so that he would be killed. Uriah died in battle, and David quickly married Bathsheba. With that, David had made things even worse. He had become more than an adulterer; he had become a murderer as well.

based on 2 Samuel 11:1-17

Reading God's Word

Two blind men were sitting by the roadside, and when they heard that Jesus was passing by, they cried out, "[Lord,] Son of David, have pity on us!"

Matthew 20:30 **R**

Ruth's Choice

King David would not have even been born had it not been for a young woman named Ruth. Ruth was a converted Moabite who married a Jewish man. Unfortunately, her husband died, and she was left with a difficult decision. Ruth's mother-in-law Naomi, also a widow, had decided to return to her own people in Israel after her husband and her sons died. Ruth could remain in Moab and live with her own family, or she could accompany Naomi back to Israel.

In those days an unmarried woman had to live with her parents, and a widow had to rely on relatives for help. Naomi had relatives in Israel, but Ruth would be a foreigner there. Nonetheless, Ruth felt an obligation to her mother-in-law. She wanted to take care of Naomi, who was old and about to go on a long, difficult journey.

Ruth set aside her own needs and decided to comfort and care for her grieving mother-in-law. She continued to care for Naomi while they lived in Israel, and good things happened to Ruth. Naomi introduced her to a distant relative, Boaz, whom she later married. Ruth eventually became the great-grandmother of King David.

based on Ruth 1-4

Moral Decisions, Moral Consequences

David and Ruth both made important, life-changing decisions, but the choices they made had very different consequences. David may have truly loved God, but his arrogance and his envy of Uriah impaired his ability to make the right decisions. He wanted to satisfy himself at the cost of Uriah's life. Although God forgave him, David had to live with the consequences of his decisions for the rest of his life. He and Bathsheba started a family, but it was beset with division and conflict.

Ruth, however, placed the needs of her mother-in-law over her own needs. Although life was difficult for her at first, her decision to care for Naomi had good, although unexpected, results for both of them. Naomi had someone who cared for her in her old age, and Ruth married a person with whom she started a new family.

Making Choices

Having freedom of choice does not mean doing anything we please. God reminds us that choice is not just a gift granted to human beings; it is a responsibility as well. Knowing whether a choice is right or wrong may not always be easy, because we can't predict the consequences of every decision. Frequently, even if the right moral choice is obvious, emotions such as envy, fear, and lust make choosing to do the right thing difficult.

Therefore, when we face moral decisions, it is important to remember the instructions of God and the Church and to consider the consequences of our actions. Although we may not always make the right decisions, God offers forgiveness to those who seek it. Even so, like David, we will live with the consequences of our decisions for a long time.

PRAYER

We all need God's forgiveness for the bad choices we make. King David made some bad decisions, but deep in his heart he wanted to do what was right. He wanted to love God and be the person God wanted him to be.

Psalm 51 is a prayer for forgiveness that traditionally represents David's sorrow. Parts of this psalm have been rewritten in the prayer below. Group A and Group B should read alternate verses.

A: God, you have so much goodness and compassion. Please help me to put my sins and mistakes behind me. Wash away my guilt.

B: I know what I've done wrong and that I've sinned against you. I deserve the consequences of my actions.

A: Please give me a clean heart, one that wants to trust you and listen to you.

B: Give me greater strength to follow the right way, no matter what.

A: Please don't turn away from me because I've done wrong.

B: Help me to be happy again. Help me to enjoy being your child.

A: When you forgive me and help me, other people will see what it means to be a child of God.

B: Help me to say and do the things that will help other people have faith and avoid mistakes.

All: Thank you for your forgiveness, for giving me a fresh start. Amen.

Faith Summary

The moral choices of David and Ruth teach us how our decisions regarding serious issues affect our relationships with God and other people.

Living My Faith

Ways of Being Like Jesus

Sometimes making the right moral choice is difficult. You are like Jesus when you think about the consequences of important decisions and then act according to God's instructions.

With My Family

At dinner sometime this week, lead your family in an activity in which each of you compliments a good decision made by the person sitting to the left.

PRAYER

Thank you, God, for giving us examples in the Scriptures of both good and bad choices. Help me learn from those stories to avoid making bad choices myself.

My Response

How do you know whether you are making a good choice or a bad choice? Are you facing a choice now that is confusing to you? If you are, talk about this choice with an adult you trust, someone who cares about you and lives a life of faith.

a parent page

Focus on Faith

Acting in Freedom

Sometimes we do not know what to make of the Old Testament. There are so many violent stories of war and betrayal. The story of David and Bathsheba could appear in today's scandal sheets. David had a moral choice to make, and he made the wrong one. He abused the freedom he had as king when he took Uriah's wife and had Uriah killed. The prophet Nathan called David back to his senses and to repentance. Unfortunately, like David, we can be tempted to interpret freedom as a right to do what we want. Our children are especially susceptible to this temptation. Christians can find true freedom only in Christ. Christian freedom is not acted out in selfish ways but in service to God and others.

Our Catholic Heritage

For hundreds of years, people have made pilgrimages. For example, during the Middle Ages pilgrimage to holy sites was a popular activity. At that time there were three primary pilgrimage destinations: Jerusalem, Rome, and Santiago de Compostella in Spain. In Jerusalem Catholics walked in the footsteps of Jesus where he had carried his cross. In Rome they visited the center of the Catholic Church, where Saints Peter and Paul had died. At Santiago de Compostella pilgrims went to the tomb of the apostle James, who was the first apostle to be martyred.

Dinnertime Conversation Starter

Have a discussion about what "freedom" means in your family. Have members share how they would like to be free. Lead the conversation to the relationship between freedom and the necessity on the part of everyone to act in a responsible way.

Spirituality in Action

Examine what your family does to serve others. What can you do in the parish or neighborhood? Talk about things you can do for others nearby or far away.

Focus on Prayer

Psalm 51 is a prayer seeking God's forgiveness and asking for his everlasting closeness. Read Psalm 51 with your family. After reading the psalm, ask family members to share some of the ways they need God's understanding and nearness. Formulate some of these thoughts into a prayer that your family can pray together.

Review

Jesus' ancestors were ordinary people who grew in their faith. Each person had a destiny, and over the course of their lives each learned to be faithful.

PRAYER

God of Abraham and Jesus, help me to remember the many people who have walked with you and learned, day by day, how to be faithful.

Faith Summary

Even though Jacob was a flawed human being who made bad choices, he trusted God.

God delivered the Hebrew people from slavery, and this event is remembered through a celebration called Passover. Centuries later, Jesus added new meaning to Passover during the Last Supper with his disciples, when he began a new covenant with God's people, one that we celebrate in the Eucharistic liturgy.

God chose Moses to lead the Hebrew slaves out of Egypt. This journey, known as the Exodus, along with God's giving the Ten Commandments at Mount Sinai, renewed the Israelite people's trust in God's covenant, which began with their ancestor Abraham.

King David made both good and bad choices, but he continued to turn to God. God forgave David, and David with Divine Providence continued to do God's work for his people. Jesus was born from David's family line many generations later.

Our Ancestors in Faith

Write as many short phrases or statements as you can about these ancestors of our faith. An example is provided for each.

Jacob

was a twin. _____

_____

_____

Moses

killed an Egyptian. _____

_____

_____

David

was an ancestor of Jesus. _____

_____

_____

Ruth

was a widow. _____

_____

_____

Learning From Our Ancestors in Faith

After you have finished writing statements about Jacob, Moses, Ruth, and David, you will be assigned to one of four groups. Each group will be assigned a different person—Jacob, Moses, Ruth, or David—and given poster board and markers or colored pencils.

On the poster write your character's name in big letters and then divide the poster board into three sections with two vertical lines. In the section on the left, rewrite the story of your character, using the statements each person wrote in the previous activity. In the middle section draw scenes, based on the story, with the markers or colored pencils. Then, in the section on the right, make a list of the important lessons learned from that story.

PRAYER SERVICE

Leader: *Let us praise God, who guides us through life.*

All: *Amen.*

Leader: *We are all on a journey together. It is a journey of faith, and while we travel God watches over us and helps us to grow into the people we were meant to be.*

Reader: *A reading from the Book of Psalms.*
[Psalm 107:1–9]

The Word of the Lord.

All: *Thanks be to God.*

Leader: *We let go of all things that hinder our faith journey.*

All: *We want to be free of the sins that hurt us and other people.*

Leader: *We journey to the new country that God has waiting for us.*

All: *We know that God has good plans for our lives.*

Leader: *God's Providence will make a way for us.*

All: *We will trust God's love and guidance, no matter what. Amen.*

Living My Faith

Ways of Being Like Jesus

Throughout his life Jesus learned the stories of Jacob, Moses, Ruth, and David. When you read these stories, think about their meanings and let the stories help you to make important decisions as you grow in faith.

With My Family

During the week remember your faith ancestors. Use photographs, drawings, letters, poems, gifts, or other reminders of them. Include Bible characters as well as people in your family's history. Each night during the week, light a candle among all of these remembrances and thank God for the journey your family has taken.

✦ PRAYER

Thank you, God of Jacob, Joseph, David, Ruth, and Moses. We're all part of the same family. Best of all, we have you, our loving God, watching over us.

My Response

Write a prayer for the people who will come after you— your other relatives who will be born, perhaps even your future husband or wife, children, or grandchildren. Ask God's blessing on the lives of people who have not even been born yet. They, too, will be part of this great family of faith.

_____

_____

_____

Community of Jesus

Saint Helena

Helena lived during the third century A.D. in the Roman Empire. As the mother of the Roman emperor, she used her influence to build churches in holy cities such as Jerusalem.

Saint Helena

Saint Helena, Cima da Conegliano, 1495

Helena was born into a poor family during the third century A.D. She lived in a part of the Roman Empire north of Italy and worked at her father's inn, where she met travelers from all over the world. One of the many travelers she encountered, a general in the Roman Empire, became her husband.

Marrying a Roman general was an event that transformed Helena's life. Her husband soon became more than a general in the Roman army—he became the emperor of Rome. Helena, meanwhile, became a mother, and she named her son Constantine. After the death of Helena's husband, Constantine became the emperor, and he named his mother empress of Rome.

For two hundred years the rulers of Rome had persecuted Christians. Constantine, however, ended the persecution and allowed Christians to worship without fear. Helena herself became a devout follower of Jesus Christ. She was baptized and used her power as empress to help as many people as she could.

After visiting Bethlehem and Jerusalem, Helena ordered that churches be built in these cities so that people could come to pray in those holy places.

Helena could have done many things in her privileged position, but she chose to use her power to help those who wished to follow Jesus Christ. The Church honors Saint Helena on August 18.

God's Presence in the Temple

What makes a place holy? Describe a place you've been to that has made you feel as if God was right there beside you.

PRAYER

Loving God, give me the grace to know your presence and to help other people to welcome you into their lives.

Solomon's Temple

King David dreamed of building a great temple to God, whom he loved, but his son Solomon was the one God chose to fulfill that dream. After David died, Solomon, now king, enlisted the service of thousands of men to begin construction of a temple on Mount Zion, a tall hill in Jerusalem.

Since the Exodus from Egypt, the Hebrews had worshiped God in a tent that they set up wherever they were. Within the tent rested the **Ark of the Covenant**, a large gold box that is said to have held the actual stone tablets on which were written the Ten Commandments that Moses received on Mount Sinai.

Now the people would have a temple at the heart of their kingdom. It was made of the finest materials and designed by the most talented builders and artists. On the day the Temple was dedicated, representatives of the entire kingdom attended. There was a grand procession as the Ark of the Covenant was brought into the **Holy of Holies,** the most sacred room inside the Temple.

At the ceremony Solomon called on God to remember his promise to Moses—that God would be present among his people. Solomon also reminded the people that God had been faithful to them and that they must respond to God in their hearts and obey his commandments.

based on 1 Kings 6:1-18 and 8:1-26

The Ark of the Covenant

God's Presence in the Temple

In ancient Judaism the Temple was an important part of life. Worship, feasts, and festivals recalled God's faithfulness and praised his holiness. Animal **sacrifices** were a common part of these ceremonies. Worshippers offered animals, and priests sacrificed the animals on an altar outside the central Temple building. This practice was a concrete way for worshippers to offer thanks for all that God had provided.

Throughout the centuries people have understood God's presence in many ways. After they left Egypt, when the Hebrews saw the pillars of fire and clouds they believed that God was traveling along with them. Eventually they made a special tent, called a tabernacle, in which to worship God. Then Solomon built a temple, a permanent structure. Although the people knew that God did not actually live in the Temple, the Temple was a place where the people could worship God.

God also made his presence known through the priests, prophets, and kings. He called priests to offer sacrifices in the Temple. He called prophets to help people understand how God wanted them to care for one another. He called kings to care for the people and rule in a just way.

Sacred Site

Construction of Solomon's Temple on Mount Zion was completed in 953 B.C. Although there are no archaeological remains, the Bible describes the Temple in detail (1 Kings 7:12–51). Two large bronze pillars rested on each side of the entrance, and the interior of the temple was decorated with gold-plated wooden sculptures.

God's Presence in Jesus Christ

During his life Jesus had a special respect for the Temple at Jerusalem. For Jesus the Temple was not just a monument to God; it was his Father's house.

After the Resurrection God's presence took on new meaning. Christ himself became the ultimate priest, prophet, and king, and his Death on the cross became the final sacrifice for sin. Jesus is the one mediator between God and the human family. Jesus Christ is now at the right hand of God the Father, where he permanently intercedes for us. Jesus Christ sends the Holy Spirit to gather the new people of God, the Church, which is the new Temple of the Holy Spirit. God no longer dwells in a stone house; he dwells within us, his people.

God's Presence Within Us

Describe what would make your life a holy place. Make a list of character qualities, words, habits, and goals that will provide a place for God to dwell in you.

_____

_____

_____

_____

Reading God's Word

Jesus answered and said to them, "Destroy this temple and in three days I will raise it up." . . . Therefore, when he was raised from the dead, his disciples remembered that he had said this, and they came to believe the scripture and the word Jesus had spoken.

John 2:19,22

Keep the Church Holy

The people of God express God's presence in the world by loving others with God's love. This means that we cannot discriminate against others on the basis of their background, race, sex, or beliefs. **Discrimination** is a way of saying "You are not good enough for God" or "God loves me more than he loves you."

The Sacrament of Holy Orders

Through Baptism Christians become members of the Church and share in the ministry of Jesus as priest, prophet, and king. The priesthood of Jesus Christ is especially visible in the men called to receive the Sacrament of Holy Orders. Priests and bishops are called by the Holy Spirit to offer the Sacrifice of the Mass and to serve as leaders in the Church. Deacons are called as visible reminders for Christians to serve each other as a king serves his people.

Meet a Saint

Roque Gonzalez was a Jesuit priest who worked with native tribes in Paraguay for 20 years. He proclaimed God's presence to them and helped them to build settlements to protect them from the slave trade. Father Gonzalez served as doctor, engineer, architect, farmer, and pastor. In 1628, amid violence between European settlers and natives, Father Roque was killed along with two other Jesuit priests. They were all named saints in 1988, and their feast day is November 17.

PRAYER

Just as the Hebrew people saw the Temple as the dwelling place of God, we believe that the Holy Spirit makes the Church "the temple of the living God." After Baptism we, too, become temples—sanctuaries in which the Holy Spirit may dwell.

Imagine yourself in the presence of the risen Jesus. Silently pray these petitions. After each one pause, look to Jesus within you, and ask him to make you a worthy temple of the Holy Spirit.

Make me beautiful with love and compassion that will bring healing to others.

Lord Jesus, make me a worthy temple of the Holy Spirit.

Make me open, peaceful, and welcoming to all people.

Lord Jesus, make me a worthy temple of the Holy Spirit.

Make me joyful, full of happiness that will give joy to others.

Lord Jesus, make me a worthy temple of the Holy Spirit.

Make me truthful and just so that others know they can come to me for help and hope.

Lord Jesus, make me a worthy temple of the Holy Spirit.

Now spend more quiet time with Jesus. Pray that he may always find a home in your heart. Ask him for what you need at this time. Rest in his presence, aware of his great love for you.

Faith Summary

The Temple in Jerusalem was a place where people could experience God's presence. After his resurrection, Jesus Christ sent the Holy Spirit to gather a new people of God, the Church, where God is present today.

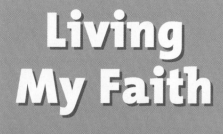

Words I Learned

Ark of the Covenant   **discrimination**
Holy of Holies   **sacrifice**

Ways of Being Like Jesus

Jesus loved the Temple, and he treated it as his Father's house. You are like Jesus when you respect your church, other people, and yourself as a temple of the Holy Spirit.

With My Family

What can your family display in your home that will tell others that God dwells there? Ask your parents, grandparents, or brothers and sisters to help you to find a place to display a piece of art or a picture that signifies that your home is a holy place.

 **PRAYER**

Jesus, my guide, thank you for helping me to open myself to the Holy Spirit dwelling in my life.

My Response

Concentrate on one characteristic that makes your life an expression of God's presence. How will you enhance that characteristic this week?

RAISING FAITH-FILLED KIDS
a parent page

A Quiet Area for Meditation and Worship

Focus on Faith

God Resides in Each of Us

The children came home from the hill where they were playing. They were excited to have that space to play on but could not put into words why it was so special. On reflection one of the children realized that the place was so special because it excited his imagination; he could see possibilities for a dozen kinds of games to play. We all have places where we go that have special meaning in our lives, sacred spaces where we feel inspired and especially close to God. For ancient Jewish society that place was the Temple in Jerusalem. For us it can be our parish church where we have space to quiet ourselves in God's presence and a community of people with whom we are a sign of God's presence in the world.

Hints for at Home

As a family, talk about the discrimination you see at school, at work, at church, and in your neighborhood. Decide on a plan that your family members can follow when they witness or are victims of discrimination.

Dinnertime Conversation Starter

Share with your children what your special places were as a child and why you liked them. Ask your children to share their feelings about places that are special to them.

Focus on Prayer

In this session your child prayed a prayer to the Holy Spirit. Write a prayer with your family that helps you remember that your home and your family are places in which the Holy Spirit dwells.

In Our Parish

Ask one of your church leaders to talk with your family about the history of your church and its present-day goals. Then agree on a day on which your family can create a poster illustrating the history. Let your child choose how to design the poster. Use photographs, magazine clippings, watercolors, markers, colored pencils, or any other medium.

Psalms, the Prayers of Jesus

What is your favorite way to pray? What thoughts do you have? What words do you use when you pray alone?

PRAYER

Lord Jesus, help me learn to express to God my thanks, my needs, my sadness, and my joys, by praying the psalms as you did.

A Prayer Collection

The Book of Psalms is a collection of 150 sacred songs and poems that are examples of how to pray. They are prayed every day in the **Liturgy of the Hours,** which is the official prayer of the Church. The psalms help us to unite our own feelings and situations with the prayers of the Church as a whole.

The most common types of psalms are those of praise, lament (sadness), thanksgiving, intercession (need), and wisdom. They are so simple and direct that they can be prayed by anyone at any time. The psalms call us to prayer, and they give us words for our hearts' response to God.

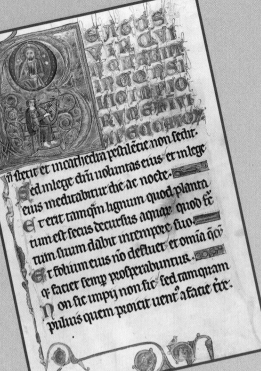

Prayer Together and Alone

When we participate in Mass or other liturgies, we participate in **communal prayer.** On these occasions we pray the same prayer or psalm together with the other members of the Church. Communal prayer allows us to share in the experience of speaking with and listening to God. The Hebrew people practiced communal prayer as well, and many of the psalms were used in this way.

Personal prayer is also important. Personal prayers are conversations between God and ourselves alone. Being still with God and speaking honestly with him help our faith to grow and our spiritual life to develop.

Daily Experiences Make the Word Come Alive

Recall the story of Jacob, who worked for Laban for many years for permission to marry Laban's daughter. Jacob was a diligent shepherd, and he protected his sheep 24 hours a day. He cared so much for his sheep that he would occasionally go hungry rather than eat one of them. In Genesis, Jacob says, "How often the scorching heat ravaged me by day, and the frost by night, while sleep fled from my eyes!"

Genesis 31:40

Jacob's description of his life as a shepherd helps us to understand God's relationship with us. Just as Jacob made sacrifices for the protection of his sheep, in a similar way God cares for and protects us.

Psalm 23 is one of the best known psalms. This psalm presents an image of God as a shepherd providing green pastures, quietly flowing rivers, and a banquet, giving the impression of a peaceful day. Psalm 23 also describes the believer as walking through the darkest valleys and surrounded by pitfalls, disappointment, and failure. The wolves are always near, but the psalm reminds us that God is there for us through the heat of the day and the cold of the night, ever watchful while we sleep.

based on Psalm 23:1-4

Reading God's Word

Man may be merciful to his fellow man,
    but the LORD's mercy reaches all flesh,
Reproving, admonishing, teaching,
    as a shepherd guides his flock.

Sirach 18:11-12

Statue of the Good Shepherd, 4th century

Wisdom Literature

Several books of the Old Testament are known as **Wisdom Literature**. This is literature that helps us to explore life's meaning and gives us practical advice for everyday life.

The Wisdom books are

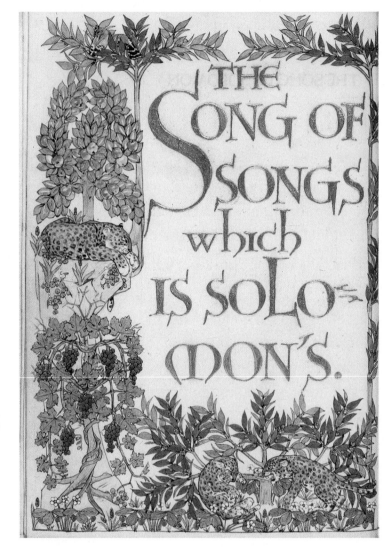

Job: one man's story that explores the meaning of suffering

Proverbs: short, poetic advice for everyday life

Ecclesiastes: a book that explores the meaning of human existence

Song of Songs: a love poem with many meanings

Wisdom of Solomon: poetic verses about justice and wisdom

Sirach: poetic verses about duty, humility, and the law

Why Wisdom?

Wisdom is one of the gifts of the Holy Spirit. It gives us understanding and helps us to follow Jesus Christ. Through wisdom the Holy Spirit prepares us to recognize Christ and receive him as the Son of God and Savior of the world.

Mary, who trusted God with perfect obedience, is called the Seat of Wisdom. She is the most important person in the Holy Spirit's work of preparing the world for Jesus, because she had the understanding and the faith to cooperate with God and give birth to Jesus.

Psalms and Seasons

Below are verses from four psalms. After reading each verse, write which church season—Christmas, Lent, Easter, or Pentecost—you think the psalm would be appropriate for. Then write your reason for choosing that season.

When you send forth your breath, they are created,
    and you renew the face of the earth.

Psalm 104:30

Season: _____ Why: _____

_____

Wash away all my guilt;
    from my sin cleanse me.

Psalm 51:4

Season: _____ Why: _____

_____

I shall not die but live
    and declare the deeds of the LORD.

Psalm 118:17

Season: _____ Why: _____

_____

Then let all the trees of the forest rejoice
    before the LORD who comes,
    who comes to govern the earth,
To govern the world with justice
    and the peoples with faithfulness.

Psalm 96:12-13

Season: _____ Why: _____

_____

PRAYER

The psalms give us a way to express every aspect of life. When we are happy and full of hope, we can pray psalms of praise and thanksgiving. When we feel lost and abandoned, there are psalms that put those feelings right into God's hands. When we have lost our way, we can find psalms that lead us toward the light of God's promise.

Pray this psalm together. Group A and Group B may read alternate verses.

A: The LORD answer you in time of distress;
  the name of the God of Jacob defend you!

B: May God send you help from the temple,
  from Zion be your support.

A: May God remember your every offering,
  graciously accept your holocaust.

B: Grant what is in your heart,
  fulfill your every plan.

All: May we shout for joy at your victory,
  raise the banners in the name of our God.
  The LORD grant your every prayer.

A: Now I know victory is given
  to the anointed of the LORD.

B: God will answer him from the holy heavens
  with a strong arm that brings victory.

A: Some rely on chariots, others on horses,
  but we [rely] on the name of the LORD our God.

B: They collapse and fall,
  but we stand strong and firm.

All: LORD, grant victory to the king;
  answer when we call upon you.

Psalm 20

Faith Summary

The Book of Psalms and the Wisdom Literature give us words to express the real problems and joys in life. Sometimes we express these things alone, through personal prayer, and sometimes with others, through communal prayer.

Words I Learned

communal prayer   Liturgy of the Hours

personal prayer   Wisdom Literature

Ways of Being Like Jesus

When we pray the psalms, we pray the same words that Jesus prayed. As a Jewish boy, he learned to read the books of the Old Testament and probably memorized many of the psalms. Choose a psalm that you enjoy and pray it often. You might even memorize it.

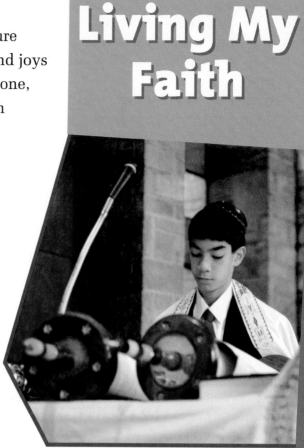

Living My Faith

With My Family

Choose a psalm to be your family's for the week. At the last meal of the week, include the psalm in your family's prayer.

 PRAYER

Father God, thank you for giving us the psalms as prayers that help us to communicate with you about the pains and pleasures of life.

My Response

Choose one or two lines from one of the psalms mentioned in this session. One line could be a prayer for bad times and the other a prayer for good times. When events come up this week and you need a prayer, remember one of these lines and pray it.

a parent page

Focus on Faith

Wisdom for Everyday Life

We all use sayings that help us to get through everyday life. In this computer age "Garbage in, garbage out" is popular. We may remember our parents saying "A watched pot never boils." The Wisdom Literature in the Bible also has sayings to help us understand our relationship with God and others. Sirach 19:11 warns about spreading gossip to untrustworthy people, saying that it is like an arrow stuck in a man's thigh. On the positive side, Sirach reminds us that showing reverence for God and following God's law are the ways to perfect wisdom (Sirach 19:17). We can discover many other wise sayings like these in the other books of Wisdom, and we can have fruitful discussion about their meaning and application to daily life.

Dinnertime Conversation Starter

Brainstorm with your children about some of the sayings prevalent in society today. Discuss the values these expressions are actually teaching.

Hints for at Home

This week use situations in your family life to show something about God's love—anything from caring for an infant to teaching an older child a new skill or comforting one another.

Our Catholic Heritage

Saint Jerome in His Study, Messina

A number of books in the Catholic Bible are found in neither the Jewish Bible nor the Protestant Bible. These books are Baruch, Judith, Sirach (Ecclesiasticus), Wisdom, and 1 and 2 Maccabees. These books are called the deuterocanonical books. They were a part of the Bible used by Greek-speaking Jews in Jesus' time, and they have been a part of the Catholic Bible since Jerome created his Vulgate version. These books were formally canonized, along with all other books of the Bible, in 1563 at the Council of Trent.

Focus on Prayer

Read the following proverbs and talk with your family about what they mean: Proverbs 10:12, 16:3, and 17:1.

The Mission of the Church

Think of an activity in your church that proclaims Jesus' presence; share it with the group.

PRAYER

Call me, Jesus, to act as a member of your Church. Help me to make you present to everyone I meet.

The Beginning of the Church

After Jesus was crucified, he was raised from the dead and appeared to his followers; he told them that he would be leaving. He instructed his followers to wait for the Holy Spirit, who would come to them and help them continue to live as followers of Jesus Christ.

The Holy Spirit soon came to the disciples in a miraculous way, and Peter, one of Jesus' closest followers, explained the meaning of the event. Speaking to Jews and converts to Judaism, Peter proclaimed that Jesus was the Messiah, the one prophesied in the Old Testament who would reunite the people with God. Peter explained how the Scriptures had told of Jesus' coming and even of the events of that day.

Peter talked about Jesus' many signs and wonders and how he had fulfilled the prophecies of the Messiah. After the crucifixion, Peter said, God raised Jesus from the dead, as the Scriptures had foretold, and he now sits at the right hand of God.

When the crowd heard Peter's explanation, many were deeply moved and asked what they could do. Peter said that they could repent, be baptized in the name of Jesus Christ, and receive forgiveness of their sins. The Scriptures tell us that about 3,000 people were baptized, all of them Jews who believed that Jesus was the promised Messiah. Together they formed the early Church.

based on Acts of the Apostles 2:1-41

The Church Leads in Faith

The Church continues to be the sign and instrument of God's communion with all humanity, gathering people together from every land and language. Our journey to God need not be traveled alone. The Church as the people of God goes ahead of us, teaching the truth and communicating the faith.

God calls us to be members of the Church, because it is the means of salvation that God has established for all. Through Jesus Christ in the Church, we are saved from our sins and become part of God's family. As members of the Church, we are enabled by the Holy Spirit to believe in Christ and live as signs of God's presence in the world. By celebrating the sacraments, practicing our faith, and doing good works, we act as members of God's family.

On Your Faith Journey

Why is it important not to be alone on the faith journey?

_____

_____

How do you show that you are a sign of God's presence in the world?

_____

_____

A Brief History of Relationship

In the Garden of Eden, God was present with Adam and Eve, and they could walk and talk with him. Ever since their disobedience and exile from the Garden, God has been bringing us back to a relationship in which we can know him personally.

- Noah's family stayed faithful to God even when no one else did.

- Abraham and his tribe became God's people, the Hebrews, who were God's presence among all other peoples of the world.

- David established rule over the people as king and God's representative.

- Solomon built the Temple, in which God could be present and worshiped.

- Jesus came as God's presence among us. He demonstrated through his life, miracles, and teachings what God is like.

- Jesus Christ returned to the Father and established the Church to be God's presence on earth.

The People of God are all temples of the Holy Spirit. We carry God's presence in our hearts. In addition, we are God's own family, able to talk with God and listen to him in prayer and the sacraments.

Reading God's Word

Your light must shine before others, that they may see your good deeds and glorify your heavenly Father.

Matthew 5:16

Images of the Church

Many images are used to describe the Church. Among them are the images of the Church as the Bride of Christ, the Temple of the Holy Spirit, and the Body of Christ.

Think of another image you could use to describe the Church. Complete the sentence below.

The Church is like _____

because _____.

The Church Respects Other Religions

Those who are not members of the Church are still saved by the grace of Jesus Christ. Jews have already responded to God's revelation in the Old Testament, and Muslims—followers of Islam—believe in the one God of Abraham and his descendants. As Catholics we recognize the value of other religions and respect the elements of truth found in them.

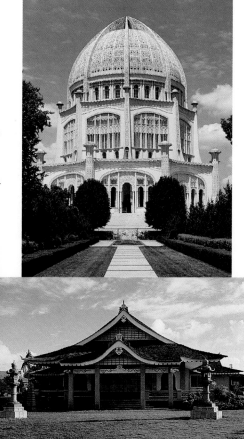

Link to Liturgy

The Dismissal in the Concluding Rites of the Mass is the point at which we commit ourselves to proclaim and be a sign of the Kingdom for the world today. When we say our *Thanks be to God,* we are saying, "I will go forth to proclaim the presence of Jesus Christ that I have heard in the readings and received in the Eucharist."

PRAYER

The Lord's Prayer, which Jesus taught us, is one of our most important prayers. As you pray it, think about the deeper meaning of the words.

Our Father, who art in heaven,

How wonderful that I can call you Father, because you have created me. I am your child, but you are "our" Father. You are in heaven, but you are still with me. You share your life with me and are close to my heart.

hallowed be thy name;
thy kingdom come,
thy will be done
on earth as it is in heaven.

Your name is holy, and you make all creation holy, including me. Keep me on the path to holiness. I pray for your kingdom to come. Thank you for bringing it near in your Son, Jesus Christ. Help me to serve your kingdom in the way I care for others.

Give us this day our daily bread,

You have given me life. How could you not give me the bread that I need? Help me to remember that it is "our" bread, one loaf that I must share with many.

and forgive us our trespasses,
as we forgive those who trespass against us;

How can I ask for forgiveness if I am not willing to forgive? There is no limit to your forgiveness. May there be no limit to mine.

and lead us not into temptation,
but deliver us from evil.

Give me the strength to face the daily struggles to make good choices. May the Holy Spirit help me to grow and give me peace.

Amen.

Faith Summary

Jesus Christ calls us to be members of the Church, which is the sign of God's communion with humanity. The mission of the Church is to proclaim Christ's presence today.

Ways of Being Like Jesus

Jesus taught us to forgive people as God forgives. You are like Jesus when you forgive others for any harm they may have caused you.

With My Family

Assign each member of your family to act as a different part of the family "body" for a week. One suggestion might be to have the "mouth" of the family lead prayers, have the "hands" help out with projects or chores, and have the "eyes" read passages from the Bible.

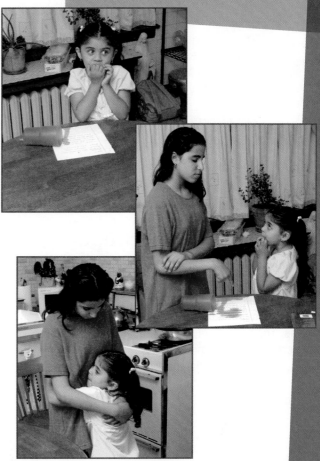

Living My Faith

 PRAYER

Jesus, my brother, thank you for including me in your family, the Church, and for helping me to be a sign of your presence in the world.

My Response

How will you show people that we are all signs of God's presence this week?

RAISING FAITH-FILLED KIDS

a parent page

Our Catholic Heritage

By the end of the fourth century, the Christian Church had spread across the known world and had centers in five major cities of the Roman Empire. The cities were Constantinople, Alexandria, Antioch, Jerusalem, and Rome. The bishops of the first four cities, all in the Eastern half of the Empire where most of the people lived, were called patriarchs. The bishop of Rome, the largest city in the Western Empire, came to be called the pope.

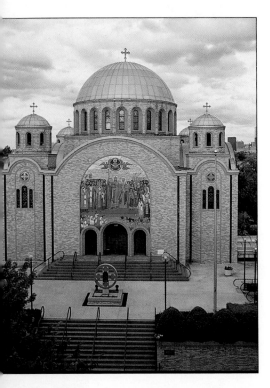

Focus on Faith

Jesus Calls the Church to Mission

The vocation of the Church is to pass on the faith it has received. This is also our vocation as parents. We can do this daily by praying before meals and by praying with and blessing our children in the evening. We can nurture a forgiving family. When there is a beautiful sunset or a rainbow, we can remind our children that it is a gift from God. When we worship at church, we can do so with reverence. We can create that same sense of reverence at home when relating to our children. We give our children their first impressions of what it means to live in relationship with God.

Dinnertime Conversation Starter

What wonder of God's creation have you noticed for the first time today or appreciated in a new way? Share your stories.

Hints for at Home

Check out from the library a book or a video on Judaism or Islam. Read or watch it together and discuss the similarities and differences between those religions and the Catholic faith.

Focus on Prayer

Your child has reflected on a deeper meaning of the verses in the Lord's Prayer. Pray the Lord's Prayer with your child and then ask your child to comment on some of the verses.

The Marks of the Church

If someone asked you what the Church is for, what would you say?
Share with the group what the Church has meant for you and
your family.

PRAYER

*Jesus, lead me to love your Church so that I can be an important part of
bringing your message to the world.*

Paul Speaks of Love and Unity

The apostle Paul wrote many letters while he was in prison for his faith. He may have written to friends and relatives, but the letters we know about were written to other Christians.

Paul was an educated Jew who knew his Jewish faith intimately. He recognized Jesus as the Messiah and set out to tell the world. He probably knew that he could be put in prison, just as some of the Old Testament prophets had been, because it was dangerous to confront people with the truth about their lives.

Paul maintained hope that the Church would continue to cooperate with the Holy Spirit in shaping God's family.

Paul knew that Christians would stand apart and make a difference in the world through humility, gentleness, patience, and love. He believed that members of God's family must have unity if they are to follow the same Christ.

Paul's letters encouraged believers to treat one another with the kind of love that they had learned from Jesus and the apostles. He reminded them that they were all part of one body, with Jesus Christ as the head.

based on Ephesians 4:1-6, 15-16

Saint Paul Preaching in Athens, Raffaello Sanzio, 1515

Peace and Unity

Peace among God's people comes from our confidence in Jesus Christ and in the Church that he established. We can be at peace because our teachers and leaders have a clear understanding of what Jesus and the apostles taught. Therefore, we can learn from our teachers and continue to grow closer to Christ.

The unity of the Church is not disturbed by diversity. The Church is made up of many peoples and cultures, and God gives us many kinds of gifts so that we can do good in the world. We can be assured of unity because we worship the same God and receive help and grace from the same Savior, Jesus Christ.

Exploring Virtues

Explain how each of the following virtues helps us to celebrate the unity and diversity of the Church.

Humility

_____

_____

Gentleness

_____

_____

Patience

_____

_____

Love

_____

_____

Marks of the Church

The **Nicene Creed** was written centuries ago to help Christians remember the important beliefs of the faith. In the Nicene Creed we identify the four marks of the Church. The four marks of the Church are not characteristics that the Church creates or develops or learns. They are qualities that Jesus Christ shares with his Church through the Holy Spirit. The four marks of the Church are that it is one, holy, catholic, and apostolic.

The Church Is One

Just as God is one in the Father, Son, and Holy Spirit, so also is the Church one. The founder of the Church is Jesus Christ, who brought us back to God and made us into the family of God. The Church is one in the Holy Spirit, who dwells in those who believe.

The Church Is Holy

The Church is holy because the Church lives in union with Jesus Christ, the source of holiness. Through the Holy Spirit the Church leads others to holiness. The holiness of the Church is seen in the love that the members of the Church have toward one another and the many sacrifices they make for the sake of the world.

The Church Is Catholic

Catholic means "universal." The Church is universal in two ways. First, the Church is catholic because all baptized people are part of the Church and the Church possesses the means of salvation. Second, the mission of the Church is universal because the Church has been sent to proclaim Christ to the entire human race.

The Church Is Apostolic

The Church traces its tradition directly from the apostles; therefore, the Church is considered apostolic. With the Holy Spirit the Church preserves and continues the teaching of the apostles. The pope and bishops are the successors of the apostles.

Mary, the Example of Perfect Holiness

The holiness of God is reflected in the holiness of faithful Christians, the greatest of whom is Mary. Mary goes before us in the holiness that is the mystery of the Church. Her song of response to God, the Magnificat, is found in Luke 1:46–55. In that song Mary praises God for the gift of grace.

Reading God's Word

The Mighty One has done great things for me, and holy is his name.

Luke 1:49

PRAYER

Below are verses from the Nicene Creed followed by passages of reflective text. These will help you to take the time to talk with God the Father, Jesus the Son, and the Holy Spirit and to think about what they tell you about God's care for you.

I believe in one God,
the Father almighty,
maker of heaven and earth,
of all things visible and invisible.

Creator God, you are maker of heaven and earth. Your care continues for all of creation, even the things that can't be seen. You care for me; you are the Almighty, but you are also my loving Father.

I believe in one Lord Jesus Christ,
the Only Begotten Son of God,
born of the Father before all ages.
God from God, Light from Light,
true God from true God.

Lord Jesus, how wonderful you are. You are God, but you are human, just like me. You are light, yet you know what it is like to be me. God and human together, you saved me.

I believe in the Holy Spirit, the Lord, the
giver of life,
who proceeds from the Father and
the Son.

Holy Spirit, you give us life through the sacraments. You show me Christ, the visible image of God, and bring me into the love of the Trinity.

I believe in one, holy, catholic and
apostolic Church.

May our Church always be one. Help me work to heal its divisions. Keep the Church holy and lead me on the path to holiness.

I look forward to the resurrection of
the dead
and the life of the world to come.

May I be united some day with all who have died to live in your presence forever.

Amen.

Faith Summary

Paul's letters to Christians express his desire for the Christian Church to continue to cooperate with God's grace. The four marks of the Church—that it is one, holy, catholic, apostolic—are symbols of the Church's authority and mission.

Word I Learned

Nicene Creed

Ways of Being Like Jesus

Jesus talked about the one characteristic that would set God's people apart and show the world God's presence. That characteristic is love. Think of a person you haven't treated well recently and do something nice for that person.

With My Family

After Sunday Mass look through your parish bulletin with your family and make a list of all the things your parish is doing that show that the Church is one, holy, catholic, or apostolic.

PRAYER

Jesus, my friend, thank you for creating a Church that shares in your holiness and love. Help me to love the Church and her leaders.

My Response

What can you do this week to celebrate that you are part of God's family? Write a special prayer, help someone, or research part of the Church's history, such as the life of a saint.

Our Catholic Heritage

The Nicene Creed is a proclamation of our beliefs that was first written by the Catholic Church during the fourth century. Its original formulation was developed at the Council of Nicaea in 325. The creed was a response to fourth-century Christians who did not believe that Jesus Christ was God. It was rewritten and formalized at the Council of Constantinople in 381. Today, Roman Catholics, Eastern Catholics, and most Protestants accept the Nicene Creed as a summary of Christian beliefs.

In Our Parish

The Church is one because the people of the Church, regardless of ethnic or national identity, are one human family. Invite a member of your parish who has been a refugee or is an immigrant to speak to your child and his or her peers. Encourage the group to ask questions about how the Catholic faith has helped the speaker to deal with the hardships of immigration.

Focus on Faith

The Marks of Jesus' Church

Many families have particular ways to identify themselves. In Europe there is a rich tradition of crests, shields, and flags carrying a family's identifying symbols. In the Celtic world colorful tartans identify traditional family names. The Catholic Church identifies itself as one, holy, catholic, and apostolic. Jesus Christ is the source of unity and holiness. The Church is catholic in its mission to the world and apostolic in remaining faithful to the faith it has received from the apostles. Were people to look to your family as representative of the Catholic faith, what would they see? What characteristics of the Church would they recognize in the way you speak, act, or relate to others?

Dinnertime Conversation Starter

Talk about any crest, traditional celebration, sign, or fabric pattern that identifies your family as coming from a particular tradition. Share its history and why it is meaningful to you. Then brainstorm with your children about what your family would put on a crest that would show the world what you value.

Focus on Prayer

Your child has been introduced to the Nicene Creed. Pray this together as a family. You can find the words to the Nicene Creed at www.FindingGod.org.

Review

Jesus Christ established the Church to be God's presence on the earth.
What are the many ways that people have experienced God since the
time of Old Testament figures such as Moses and David?

PRAYER

*Lord Jesus, show me how to live as an active and faithful member of your
Church so that I and others can know God's presence here and now.*

Faith Summary

For many years Solomon's Temple in Jerusalem stood as a symbol of God's presence on the earth. After Jesus Christ's resurrection and ascension to heaven, the Holy Spirit established a new temple, the Church. With the help of the Holy Spirit, the Church lives on as a sign of God's presence on the earth.

There are two types of prayer: communal and personal. When we pray together in church, we are participating in communal prayer; most often that communal prayer is during Mass. When we speak with God alone, we are engaging in personal prayer.

During communal prayer we often pray from the Book of Psalms. There are many different types of psalms in this book; psalms of praise, of wisdom, of lament, and of need are some of the most common. Also found in the Old Testament is a collection of books called Wisdom Literature. These books contain poetry and stories that help us to understand the joys and sorrows of life.

As members of the family of God, we have certain responsibilities. Our mission is to help others recognize Jesus Christ as Savior and to enter the life of faith through the Holy Spirit.

The Church has four marks: it is one, holy, catholic, and apostolic. These are characteristics that Christ shares with the Church through the Holy Spirit.

A Proverbs Tree

The Book of Proverbs is an example of Wisdom Literature that has provided truths about human nature for thousands of years.

With a partner select two proverbs, from your assigned chapter, that you think are helpful pieces of wisdom. Write each one on the back of a separate index card, leaving space around the proverb. Now illustrate the proverb using the remaining space around it. You may want to illuminate the first letter the same way monks illuminated Bible verses in scriptoriums.

After you have finished, punch a hole in each index card and put yarn or string through it. Make sure that the yarn is the right length so that when you tie the ends together it forms a loop to use for hanging.

Hang each proverb on the tree.

Each of you may then pick a proverb to think about during this week. You may pick the proverbs you illustrated, but it will be even better if each of you chooses a proverb prepared by someone else.

Turn Your Prayers Into Bookmarks

Write a short, four-line psalm that you can carry with you on a bookmark. Follow the suggestions below to help you write each line of your psalm. When you have finished, write the psalm on one side of your bookmark and then decorate the remaining space.

Line 1: This line sets the tone for the psalm. It can be a description of how you love God or a request for God's help. You don't need to be very specific; just speak to God as you would in one of your personal prayers.

_____

Line 2: This line should reinforce the main idea of the first line. Here you may want to be more specific and explain why you are asking God for his help. You can even repeat what you wrote on the first line but choose a different way of saying it.

_____

_____

Line 3: This line should describe something good that God does for you.

_____

_____

_____

Line 4: The final line should be a way of giving thanks to God. You may simply thank him, or you may describe a way that you will thank him every day.

_____

_____

_____

PRAYER SERVICE

Leader: Praise be to God, who fills our lives with love and joy.

All: Amen.

Leader: We are part of God's family, the Church: one, holy, catholic, and apostolic.

Reader: A reading from the first letter of Paul to the Corinthians.
[1 Corinthians 12:12–20]
The Word of the Lord.

All: Thanks be to God.

Leader: Lord Jesus, help us to be one.

All: Bring us peace and unity through your Holy Spirit.

Leader: Lord Jesus, help us to be holy.

All: Hold us close to your heart and transform us until we are just like you.

Leader: Lord Jesus, help us to be catholic.

All: Teach us to welcome all of God's children and to respect the faith journey of others, while sharing the good news of salvation.

Leader: Lord Jesus, help us to be apostolic.

All: May we learn well from our teachers and pastors, remember the lives of the apostles, and join our prayers with those of all your saints. Amen.

Living My Faith

Ways of Being Like Jesus

Jesus always treated his followers with respect. When you are the leader of a group or the captain of a team, respect your group and work for the members as they work for you.

With My Family

Go around the dinner table one night and have each person talk about special moments in church that they remember. A parent or a grandparent could talk about his or her first Communion, or a child could talk about a favorite song. Share reasons that the Church is so important to your life together.

PRAYER

Thank you, Jesus, for allowing us to be temples for your Holy Spirit. Thank you for sharing God's gifts with us and including us in your family.

My Response

Write one statement that helps you remember how to act as a sign of God's presence. Write it on something that you can keep in your pocket or wallet so that you can look at it anytime.

Saint Ignatius of Loyola

As the leader of the Society of Jesus, Ignatius found strength in his deep prayer life and his love for the Mass.

Saint Ignatius of Loyola

In 1540, a few years after being ordained a priest, Ignatius and six of his companions formed a religious community known as the Society of Jesus, or the Jesuits. Thus began a period of very hard work for Ignatius, who was elected leader of the new community. The Society of Jesus expanded very quickly, and Ignatius had to respond to issues from Europe, where he worked, to as far away as Japan, where his dear friend Francis Xavier proclaimed the gospel as a missionary.

Ignatius could not have kept up the great work that he did without a deep prayer life. As every priest is called to do, Ignatius prayed the Divine Office. The Divine Office is the official public prayer of the Church that is prayed at specific times throughout the day. It is centered on the Psalms and other scripture readings and may be prayed together with others or privately. When Ignatius entered a church where the Divine Office was being sung publicly, he felt that his heart was being transformed by God.

The Miracle of Saint Ignatius of Loyola, Peter Paul Rubens, 1618

The center of Ignatius's prayer life was the celebration of Mass. When he celebrated Mass, Ignatius took two hours to prepare and reflect on the experience of encountering Jesus in the Mass. Ignatius gave orders to his followers that he was not to be disturbed during this time. He loved to celebrate Masses that honored the Blessed Trinity, the Holy Name of Jesus, and Mary, the Mother of God. During Mass, Ignatius would pray for himself, the Jesuit community, and all of the people whom they served. It was during these times of prayer that Ignatius had his deepest experiences of God. These experiences of prayer and devotion gave him the grace to face the issues of his life and of the Jesuit ministry. His feast day is July 31.

Prophets Challenge the People

Some friends will tell us what we want to hear, but our best friends will tell the truth and help us grow. Who are the people in your life whom you can count on to help you live according to your faith?

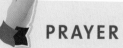 **PRAYER**

Dear God, open my mind and heart to hear the truth of your message.

The Prophets

After the reign of King Solomon, his kingdom was divided into two smaller kingdoms, Israel to the north and Judah to the south. During this time God called on certain people to be **prophets,** and each prophet had a message that suited that particular time and situation.

Prophets held a unique role in ancient Jewish society because they spoke for God. For the most part, the prophets advised people, especially kings, about how to make society exist in harmony with God's commandments. Both kingdoms, Judah and Israel, had their own problems and, therefore, their own prophets to help people overcome the problems.

Amos and Jeremiah

Between 760 and 750 B.C., in the northern kingdom, the prophet Amos spoke against the way the poor were being treated by the wealthy. In fact, Amos's concern for justice is part of the basis for the Church's teachings about justice today.

In the southern kingdom the prophet Jeremiah spent a lifetime sharing God's message with the people of Judah. He harshly criticized the rulers, the priests, and the people for not obeying the terms of the covenant established with Abraham and Moses. When the Babylonian empire conquered Judah in 587 B.C., Jeremiah witnessed the destruction of Solomon's Temple in Jerusalem. This was one of the saddest events in Jewish history. It was the beginning of the Babylonian exile, when thousands of Jews were forced to leave Judah to settle in Babylon. Jeremiah, nonetheless, gave encouraging advice to the exiles; he urged them to remember that God's love would be with them regardless of where they were.

God Calls Isaiah

When God calls on someone to be a prophet, he usually does it in a rather dramatic way. One such calling came to a man named Isaiah, who prophesied in Jerusalem before the time of Jeremiah.

Isaiah was in the Temple of Jerusalem when he had a sudden, powerful vision of God sitting on an enormous throne, wearing clothes that flowed across the room. Six-winged angel guardians, called **seraphim,** hovered above, crying, "Holy, holy, holy is the Lord of hosts!" The entire Temple shook and filled with smoke.

This certainly got the attention of Isaiah, who responded—in effect—"I am so not ready for this! Here is God, so awesome that the whole place is smoking. I'm not good enough to stay in the same room—in fact, nobody I know is good enough. I'd better get out of here!"

Isaiah's actual words were "I am a man of unclean lips," so one of the angels took an ember from the live coals on the altar and touched Isaiah's mouth with it. The angel said, "See, now that this has touched your lips, your wickedness is removed, your sin is purged." In other words, "You may not be holy, but at least we have taken care of *that* problem."

Image of a Seraph, late 16th century

Then Isaiah heard God's voice saying, "Whom shall I send? Who will go for us?" Isaiah, now free from feeling unworthy to be in God's company, said, "Here I am; send me!" Thus, the man who a few moments before had been terrified was now ready to do God's work.

based on Isaiah 6:1-8

Reading God's Word

All this took place to fulfill what the Lord had said through the prophet:
"Behold, the virgin shall be with child and bear a son,
and they shall name him Emmanuel,"
which means "God is with us."

Matthew 1:22-23

Being a Prophet Is Not Easy

God's prophets had a holy job to do—a ministry to perform. They were called by God to intervene in societies that were no longer following God's commandments.

Prophets often called on citizens and rulers to share wealth, food, and other necessities with everyone in a society. This tradition of calling people to share is an important part of the Church's mission today. It follows from the understanding that the goods of God's creation are meant for everyone.

In ancient Jewish society—as well as today—such messages were not always well received. People often ignored prophets who called on them to share, even though the people knew that the goods created by God were not meant for only a few of them. Every now and then, a ruler would go so far as to throw a prophet in prison or out of the country in hopes of silencing him. Through it all, though, the prophets kept talking. They kept delivering God's words to ordinary people, priests, and kings. God had called them, and God gave them the strength and wisdom to act.

A Prophecy for Today

If God were to send your country a prophet, what do you think the message would be?

_____

_____

If God were to send your neighborhood a prophet, what do you think the message would be?

_____

_____

If God were to send you personally a prophet, what do you think the message would be?

_____

_____

What It Means to Reform

Some of the kings in the history of Israel and Judah did their best to bring **reform** to their societies. With the help of the prophets, they would call the people to turn from their evil ways, honor God, and treat each other—especially the poor and the weak—with respect.

Reform continues to be an important part of society today. People are still trying to make positive changes in their governments, schools, and communities. One of the reasons that people work for reform is that the laws of society are not always the same as the moral laws required by faith. As Catholics, we follow the moral laws of our faith even when they are contradictory to the laws of society.

Pope Paul VI speaking to the United Nations

Dorothy Day standing between two peace activists

Meet a Modern Prophet

Dorothy Day (1897–1980) was a Catholic who cared deeply about poverty and issues of social justice. With her friend Peter Maurin she founded the Catholic Worker Movement, a community of laypeople dedicated to serving the poor, the hungry, and the homeless. She was a passionate advocate for peace, and her actions led to her being arrested a number of times for protesting her country's involvement in war. She might be considered a modern-day prophet, whose work is an example of every Catholic's duty to fight injustice. In the year 2000 the archbishop of New York formally asked the pope and bishops to consider declaring Dorothy Day a saint.

PRAYER

Prophets have always helped us to relate the issues of the present to God's everlasting message. With this prayer you can ask God to help you to hear people who are like prophets and to be more like a prophet for others.

Holy God,
help me to listen with my heart
when you tell me the truth about my life.
Help me to agree when you show me my sin
and help me to hope when you show me how to change.
Help me to live out your truth in my own life
and to encourage others to do the same.
Thank you for speaking to my heart,
helping me to feel your love and concern.
Thank you for using my mind, voice, and body
to carry out your ministry in the world.
In the name of Jesus,
my prophet, priest, and king.
Amen.

Now take time to thank God for sending prophets to help us to live out God's truth in our lives. Think about one thing God might be asking you to change in your life. Ask God to help you to make that change and to live as he calls you to. Thank him for the grace and guidance of the Holy Spirit in your life.

Faith Summary

God's prophets were called to remind people of God's message. Sometimes they pointed out the consequences of people's sinful lives, and sometimes they brought encouragement during hard times.

Words I Learned

prophet   reform   seraphim

Ways of Being Like Jesus

Jesus was also a prophet, and he knew what it felt like to be treated like one. He was aware of the injustices in the society that he was a part of, and he called on people to reform. You are like Jesus when you speak out against the injustices in your society.

With My Family

Find an article about a social injustice in a magazine. With the help of your family, write a letter to the editor of that magazine, expressing your response to the article.

Living My Faith

PRAYER

Holy God, thank you for sending your prophets to tell us what we need to hear. Help me to be more open to listen to the people in my life who are honest with me and encourage me.

My Response

How is God calling you to tell the truth or encourage people? Whom do you know who might need your encouragement? What will you say to help that person?

Focus on Faith

God Calls Us

Near the end of the Confirmation ceremony, the young priest led the congregation in singing "Here I Am," a song based on Isaiah 6:1–8. In the reading God asks for someone to bring his word to the people. Isaiah finally stands up and says, "Here I am; send me!" These words are also the chorus of the song. At the last chorus the priest invited everyone to stand and sing. The atmosphere changed. This was not just a call to those confirmed that day. In the act of standing, everyone realized that each person was being asked to respond to God's call in his or her own way.

Dinnertime Conversation Starter

God never stops calling us to serve him. What is your family being called to do for others?

Hints for at Home

As a family, keep track of how you share your time with volunteer social services. At the end of every month, evaluate what you have done and discuss what that says about your family. Decide how your family can balance the time spent addressing issues at home and in the community.

Our Catholic Heritage

In 1975 Jesuits from all over the world met and discussed their goals. They decided then that any ministry with the name Jesuit attached to it should serve others and promote justice. Jesuits in the United States directly engage the social problems of today as prison chaplains, community organizers, and lawyers, working for the rights of the poor and marginalized.

Portrait of Saint Ignatius, Jacopino del Conte

Focus on Prayer

Talk to your child about God's calling for his or her life. Emphasize that we are not always called to do big or dangerous things and that we have different callings at different times. We are called simply to go about daily life as obedient children of God. Afterwards, pray with your child, asking God's guidance and help for whatever ministry you're given, now or in the future.

Prophets Give Hope

Have you ever been forced to go somewhere you did not want to go?
Maybe you had to move to a new town or start at a new school. Think
about how you made the best of your situation.

PRAYER

*Lord Jesus, help me to hear the message of the prophets so that I can better
know the story of my Christian faith.*

The Jews in Exile

The Jewish people of Judah had been taken away by their enemies to Babylon, and not only did they not know when they would return home, but they were not at all sure they would ever get home. Their great city of Jerusalem and the Temple had been destroyed, and they were captives living in the land of their enemies. They were severely mistreated, and they mourned for the people who had been killed during the war. They saw no end to their misery.

During this time a new prophet began ministering to the exiled Jews in Babylon. He admired Isaiah and even took the same name, although today we call him Second Isaiah. Second Isaiah proclaimed to the people that God still loved them and would care for them, even during this time in this unfriendly place. The prophet emphasized that God would continue to act for his people, as he had done in the past. He urged them to feel secure, knowing that God, who had led their ancestors out of Egypt, would lead them on another Exodus back to the **Promised Land**—the land God had given to his people.

Second Isaiah was called by the Holy Spirit to comfort the exiles. There was good reason for the prophet to speak encouraging words. The period of exile (587–537 B.C.) had been bitter. The people dreamed of returning to Jerusalem. As time went on, the Jews' memory of their homeland became more and more distant.

Early Christians Turn to the Prophecies

The Gospel writers used the Old Testament to help them understand Jesus. In doing so, they found the teachings of Second Isaiah to be the most supportive. They interpreted Second Isaiah's message of renewal and hope as being ultimately fulfilled in the life, death, and resurrection of Jesus Christ. For example, Luke refers to Isaiah 40:3–5 to describe the ministry of John the Baptist in announcing Jesus' arrival (Luke 3:4–6).

Of course, the Jewish exiles understood Isaiah's message as meaning that they would be saved by God and taken back home to Jerusalem. Early Christians, however, believed that the messages of Second Isaiah and other prophets actually referred to Jesus Christ, who would save all people, not just the Jewish exiles.

John the Baptist in the Wilderness, Geertgen tot Sint Jans, late 15th century

Reading God's Word

Do not think that I have come to abolish the law or the prophets.
I have come not to abolish but to fulfill.

Matthew 5:17

Jesus and the Prophecies of Old

The New Testament book of Matthew contains many references to the prophetic books of the Old Testament, especially Isaiah. This makes sense, because Matthew was a Jew and was quite familiar with the Old Testament prophecies. He was talking primarily to Jews, and he wanted to use their own Scriptures to prove how Jesus had fulfilled prophecies concerning the Messiah.

1st ISAIAH

The people who walked in darkness have seen a great light; Upon those who dwelt in the land of gloom a light has shone. (IS 9:1)

? Did You Know?

The Book of Isaiah was written by different writers in three times and places. Chapters 1–39 were written between 738 and 700 B.C. This was the time when Judah was a kingdom and had been invaded by the Assyrians. Chapters 40–55 were written while the Jewish people were in exile. Chapters 56–66 were written after the people returned to Jerusalem from exile. The returning people felt disappointed and hopeless because the kingdom that had once supported them was gone. The prophet called them to continue to believe in God, who had rescued them from Babylon.

Making Connections: Matthew and Isaiah

Complete the activity below by determining the passage from the Book of Isaiah that Matthew referred to in connecting the story of Jesus with the prophets of the past. In the middle column write the verse from Isaiah that Matthew referred to. In the column on the right, describe the event that the passages refer to. Choose from the following passages from Isaiah: 7:14, 40:3, 50:6, 53:4, 53:7.

New Testament	Old Testament	The Event
Matthew 1:23	Isaiah ___:___	_____
Matthew 3:3	Isaiah ___:___	_____
Matthew 8:17	Isaiah ___:___	_____
Matthew 26:63	Isaiah ___:___	_____
Matthew 27:30	Isaiah ___:___	_____

2ND ISAIAH

Comfort, give comfort to my people,
    says your GOD.
Speak tenderly to Jerusalem, and proclaim to her
    that her service is at an end,
    her guilt is expiated. (Is 40:1-2)

3RD ISAIAH

The spirit of the Lord God is upon me,
    because the Lord has anointed me;
He has sent me to bring glad tidings to the lowly,
    to heal the brokenhearted,
To proclaim liberty to the captives
    and release to the prisoners, (Is 61:1)

PRAYER

The following prayer is the first part of Psalm 143. It is a call to God for strength during difficult times.

A: LORD, *hear my prayer;*
  in your faithfulness listen to my pleading;
  answer me in your justice.

B: *Do not enter into judgment with your servant;*
  before you no living being can be just.

All: *I stretch out my hands to you;*
  I thirst for you like a parched land.

A: *The enemy has pursued me;*
  they have crushed my life to the ground.

B: *They have left me in darkness*
  like those long dead.

All: *I stretch out my hands to you;*
  I thirst for you like a parched land.

A: *My spirit is faint within me;*
  my heart is dismayed.

B: *I remember the days of old;*
  I ponder all your deeds;
  the works of your hands I recall.

All: *I stretch out my hands to you;*
  I thirst for you like a parched land.

Be aware of God's love and strength surrounding you. Ask God for what you most need right now. Thank him for his love and presence. Rest peacefully in God for a few moments.

Faith Summary

The book of Isaiah consists of the prophecies of three prophets. Second Isaiah, who prophesied during the Babylonian exile, was seen by early Christians as one who had foretold the coming of Jesus Christ. His message to the exiled Jews, however, was to remain hopeful by remembering what God had promised.

Word I Learned

Promised Land

Living My Faith

Ways of Being Like Jesus

Isaiah and the prophets offered hope during difficult times. All of our hope is fulfilled in Jesus Christ. We are like Jesus when we ourselves offer hope to those who need it.

With My Family

Think of a friend or relative whom your family has not been in touch with recently. Write that person a card or send flowers or a gift to remind that person that your family is thinking about him or her.

PRAYER

Thank you, Jesus, for fulfilling what all of the other prophets and priests and kings began. I no longer have to hope for some distant savior—you're with me now.

My Response

Keep a "hope diary" this week. Every day, rather than recording your worries and fears, write down something you can be hopeful about.

RAISING FAITH-FILLED KIDS

a parent page

In Our Parish

Organize a newcomer's festival at your church. Plan

a day or evening for welcoming newcomers into the community with enjoyable activities, music, and food (of course!). Encourage all of those present to give personal introductions, sharing something about their lives or faith journeys. Include games to help break the ice, a prayer service, or a guest speaker to discuss the history of the parish.

Focus on Prayer

Your child has prayed part of Psalm 143. Pray through this psalm with your child and discuss its meaning.

Focus on Faith

God in the Midst of Exile

Every person experiences what it is like to live in exile. Exile can be exclusion from the "in" crowd at school, lack of appreciation at work, or a sense of disconnection from your family. The Jewish people in the Old Testament knew what it was like to be in exile. Their Temple was destroyed. They were brought from Judah to Babylon. They had to make new lives in a strange land. It was a very difficult time, but it was also a time for understanding the mercy of God. God sent a prophet whose words "Give comfort to my people" are written in Isaiah 40:1. These words speak to us today as full of hope as they did when the prophet proclaimed them to the people.

Dinnertime Conversation Starter

Recall with your child some times in the life of your family when you turned to God for hope and comfort. Discuss any special prayer or ceremony that helped in time of need.

Our Catholic Heritage

Four passages in the book of Isaiah are known as the Suffering Servant oracles. Although they refer to events of that particular time, they also convey the message of Jesus' ministry and the meaning of his life, death, and resurrection. Those passages are Isaiah 42:1–4, 49:1–7, 50:4–11, and 52:13–53:12.

Baptism and Confirmation

What has been the most important event in your life? How has that event changed you?

PRAYER

Lord Jesus, call me to live as a member of your family so that I can enjoy the strength that comes from you and your people.

The Piece That Holds Everything Together

Helicopter pilots rely on a small metal nut that secures the main rotor system to the mast of a helicopter. If that small piece of metal ever comes off, the helicopter will crash. That nut has come to be called the Jesus Nut because, as the saying goes, "If it fails, whether you know Jesus or not, you are on your way to meet him!"

In a passage in the Letter to the Ephesians, Jesus is compared to a keystone. Just as a tiny piece of metal keeps an entire helicopter flying properly, a keystone is the stone in the very center of an arch that holds the entire arch together. The writer of Ephesians called the apostles and prophets the foundation of the household of God and Jesus the keystone. "Through him the whole structure is held together and grows into a temple sacred in the Lord; in him you also are being built together into a dwelling place of God in the Spirit."

Ephesians 2:21-22

The household of God—the Church— is built on the teachings of Jesus, the prophets, and the apostles; and each of us is like a stone that is added to the building. The stone that holds it all together is Jesus. This household of God, made of living stones—the people of God—becomes God's presence in the world.

The Gallarus Oratory, 7th-century chapel, Ireland

Reading God's Word

Come to him, a living stone, rejected by human beings but chosen and precious in the sight of God, and, like living stones, let yourselves be built into a spiritual house to be a holy priesthood to offer spiritual sacrifices acceptable to God through Jesus Christ.

1 Peter 2:4-5

Entering a New Life With God's Family

We become members of Christ and the Church through the Sacraments of Initiation: Baptism, Confirmation, and Eucharist.

The Old Testament has many images of water that help us to understand Baptism. Each year during the **Easter Vigil,** the baptismal waters are blessed, and prayers call these images to mind. At the time of Creation, the Spirit breathed upon the waters. During the great Exodus, the waters of the Red Sea parted, allowing the people of Israel to cross from slavery into freedom. Later, in the New Testament, John the Baptist baptized Jesus in the waters of the Jordan River.

A water blessing during the Easter Vigil at St. Stephen's

Knowing that Baptism is necessary for salvation, parents have their babies baptized not long after they are born. Baptism marks the baby as a member of the Church. The community of believers and the parents make a commitment to care for and teach this child as he or she grows up in the faith.

Infant Baptism, however, was not the usual way that people became members of God's family in the early Church. Traditionally, people who wanted to become members of the Church were adults, and they had to go through a long period of conversion. This type of preparation for Baptism still exists today, and the people who are going through this process are called **catechumens.** During this time the person learns about what God has done through Jesus, what the Church teaches, and how the catechumen can respond in faith to God's call.

Changed for Life

Have you ever been through an event that changed you? Some life experiences change forever the way you look at life. For most parents the birth of a child is that kind of event.

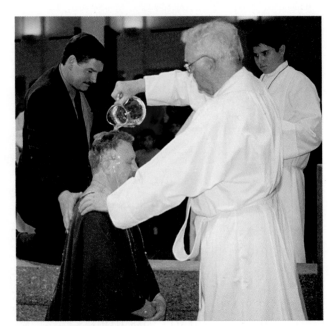

Baptism by immersion

Through Baptism we are saved, and we receive a permanent mark, or character. We are baptized only once, but we belong to Christ forever. We receive the gift of sanctifying grace.

Confirmation deepens our life of faith. The Holy Spirit gives us a deeper awareness of Christ in our lives and the wisdom to live as God wants us to. Confirmation deepens our bond to the Church. We are sealed by the Holy Spirit, who gives us strength to know Christ and to live like Christ. We receive the grace to become more active Christians in the world.

When we are confirmed, we are anointed on the forehead with chrism—a special oil blessed for this purpose. The bishop lays hands on us and says, "Be sealed with the Gift of the Holy Spirit." Like Baptism, Confirmation leaves a permanent spiritual mark and therefore cannot be repeated.

Turning Points

Baptism and Confirmation are important events in people's lives. What do these ceremonies mean to you?

_____

_____

What other ceremonies mark turning points in people's lives?

_____

_____

Changed Lives Are Meant to Change Lives

We are not baptized and confirmed simply so that we can be happy and safe in God's family. Just as Jesus' baptism marked the beginning of his ministry, our Baptism obligates us to do God's work, now that we have been brought into Jesus' family. As we live out the faith and love that grow in us, day by day, we show others what a fulfilling life really is. We demonstrate a life of love, forgiveness, and hope because we personally know these things from our relationship with God through Jesus Christ and the Holy Spirit.

Did You Know?

There are seven sacraments of the Church, and they're divided into three groups:

Sacraments of Initiation
Baptism
Confirmation
Eucharist

Sacraments at the Service of Communion
Matrimony
Holy Orders

Sacraments of Healing
Penance
Anointing of the Sick

PRAYER

When you face a new situation, you have much learning ahead of you. Even though you have been growing in faith since you were a baby, there will always be more to learn about life in God's family.

This prayer reminds us of the day-by-day growth we experience as Christians. It is based on a prayer by Saint Richard of Chichester, who lived during the 13th century.

Thanks be to you, our Lord Jesus Christ,
For all the benefits that you have given us,
For all the pains and insults that you have borne for us.
Most merciful Redeemer, Friend, and Brother,
May we know you more clearly,
Love you more dearly,
And follow you more nearly,
Day by day.
Amen.

You have been marked for life. Spend some quiet time now with Jesus. Thank him for the day-to-day growth you have experienced since your Baptism. Ask him for the help you need to follow his ways and grow in your love for him.

Faith Summary

The house of God—the Church and all of its people—is a community of living stones with Jesus Christ as the keystone. That house continues to grow and increase in strength as people are initiated into the Church through Baptism and become more fully involved with the Church's mission through Confirmation.

Words I Learned

catechumen   Easter Vigil

Ways of Being Like Jesus

Jesus' public ministry began after John baptized him. You are like Jesus when you think about the meaning of your Baptism and act as a person who has been brought into a forgiving and caring community.

Living My Faith

With My Family

Sometime this week, talk about how your family can be a domestic church. Discuss ways that your family members can bring love, forgiveness, and hope to one another.

 PRAYER

Jesus, thank you for accepting me into your family. Because I belong to your family, there will always be someone to love me, and there will always be other people for me to love.

My Response

Your faith has probably undergone many changes since you were baptized. Write one way that you hope your faith will develop as you continue to grow.

a parent page

Focus on Faith

Jesus Holds Us Together

Families that live in places where earthquakes are an ongoing threat know that when they feel a severe tremor one of the safer places to go to in a building is a doorway. The extra bracing surrounding a doorway offers protection against the collapse of the building. Ephesians 2:19–22 describes Jesus Christ as the keystone, the most important stone in a building, the stone that holds the building together. As Christians, we are the household of God made of living stones. The stone that holds us all together is Jesus. Families who center their lives on Jesus have chosen a firm foundation for their faith.

Dinnertime Conversation Starter

What steps can you as a family take to make the presence of Jesus more central to your life?

Our Catholic Heritage

The season we now know as Lent began as a period during which new believers prepared to be received into the Church. In the early Church new believers first received the Eucharist on Easter. Eventually, this time of preparation for new believers—repentance, study, and prayer— became a season of repentance and renewal for people who were already baptized into the Church as well.

In Our Parish

Find out whether your parish has people involved in the Rite of Christian Initiation of Adults (RCIA). If so, talk with the RCIA leaders in your parish about the process these adults go through to become members of the Church. Encourage all the members of your family to participate in the next Easter Vigil, which is when these catechumens will be baptized, be confirmed, and receive the Eucharist.

Focus on Prayer

Your child was introduced to a prayer written by Saint Richard of Chichester. Refer to www.FindingGod.org for the words to this prayer and pray it with your child.

Sacraments of Healing

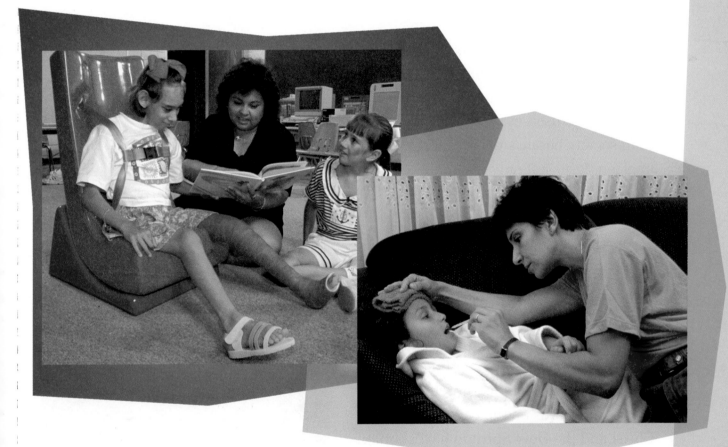

Recall a time when you were very sick. How did the sickness change your daily life? Who helped you to recover? How did you thank that person?

PRAYER

Jesus, my guide, help me always to know that you are ready to offer me healing in body and spirit.

Jesus Sends Forth Healers

Before Jesus went to Jerusalem, where he was crucified, he summoned the twelve apostles to give them the mission of spreading the good news about God's kingdom. He also granted them the authority to heal the sick, as he had done. The disciples who had been following Jesus, amazed at his miracles, were now able to perform those miracles through his power.

based on Luke 9:1-6

Healing, however, is not meant only to help people with their physical ailments; healing is needed for spiritual and social ills as well. Sickness and disease are a sad but common part of life. During the time of Jesus, people with diseases were often kept apart from society because they were considered unclean. Jesus not only restored the physical health of people with diseases or disabilities but also restored their status as persons with the same dignity that everyone is granted by God.

The Church Continues to Heal

Just as Jesus shared with his disciples the authority to heal, he continues to heal people through the Church today. The Church calls on the power of Jesus Christ and the Holy Spirit to heal people. The Holy Spirit gives the Church gifts for healing both body and spirit. We find these gifts especially in the two Sacraments of Healing, the Anointing of the Sick and Penance.

Jesus healing a woman, catacomb fresco, Rome, 4th century

Reading God's Word

This is my commandment: love one another as I love you.

John 15:12

Healing for the Body

An important way that the Church continues Jesus' healing ministry is in the Anointing of the Sick.

When a person is seriously ill, preparing for surgery, of advanced age, or in danger of death, he or she may celebrate the Anointing of the Sick with a priest.

The priest anoints the person with the oil of the sick, which is olive oil that has been blessed by a bishop. This sacrament

Parish celebration of the Anointing of the Sick

- helps a sick person to identify his or her physical suffering more closely with Christ's

- gives strength, peace, and courage to a person who is dealing with serious illness or difficulties of aging

- forgives the sins of a person who is unable to participate in the Sacrament of Penance

- may even bring physical healing, if that is God's will

- helps to prepare a believer for eternal life

The Dignity of Human Life

The Church teaches that human life is sacred because it comes from God. When people are seriously ill, they still have dignity simply because they are created by God. Christ's healing power is with us at all times, no matter how bad a situation may look. Because life is sacred, the Church condemns the practice of euthanasia. It is not acceptable to end a person's life just because that person is old or seriously ill.

Healing for the Soul

In the Sacrament of Penance, the Holy Spirit gives us the grace of healing from serious sin and the effects of sin. All sin separates us from God and others. Mortal sin especially separates us from God, and mortal sin that is not repented of can leave a person in danger of hell, the eternal punishment of separation from God. All mortal sins must be confessed in the Sacrament of Penance.

The Sacrament of Penance is celebrated after a careful examination of conscience. In the sacrament a person makes a confession to a priest, who offers absolution, conveying God's forgiveness of the sins confessed.

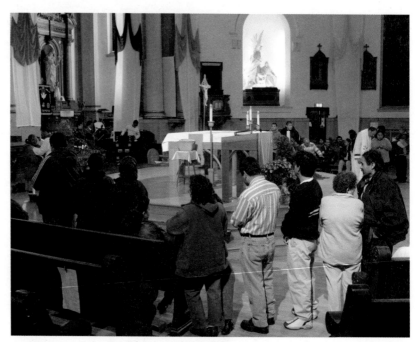

Parishioners waiting to make confession to a priest

The Catholic tradition offers us some general steps for making a good confession:

1. Make a thoughtful and honest examination of conscience.

2. Express true sorrow for the sins committed.

3. Make a firm purpose of amendment.

4. Confess those sins to the priest.

5. Receive absolution.

6. Perform the penance assigned by the priest.

The Sacrament of Penance brings reunion with God and the Church. It gives our consciences peace and comforts us spiritually.

Purgatory is the state of final preparation and purification for those who are saved but, at the time of death, are not yet ready to be in God's presence. It is a temporary state. The prayers of other Christians help those in purgatory to attain full union with God.

Removing the Effects of Sin

If a person has been forgiven for stealing something, that person still must give back or pay for whatever was stolen. Even after sins are forgiven, their effects can remain in a person's life; so, after a person has received absolution, he or she must also make restitution to the victim. That is, he or she must make up for the offense.

After being forgiven, a person may still feel inclined to commit a particular sin; something in that person's life remains that may tempt him or her to sin again. A penance of prayers and good deeds may help a person to overcome these temptations.

Through prayers and good deeds we receive indulgences, which compensate for some of the wrong we have done and help us prepare to live in God's presence after death.

Do Over!

Imagine that you have stolen something without getting caught. You continue to feel guilty about what you have done. What do you do to make restitution for what you have done?

_____

_____

_____

_____

Imagine that you have insulted somebody and afterward feel guilty about what you have said. How will you make up for what you have done?

_____

_____

_____

_____

PRAYER

We all know what it is like to feel sad or guilty after doing something we know is wrong. With this prayer we call on God's mercy and forgiveness.

Act of Contrition

My God,
I am sorry for my sins with all my heart.
In choosing to do wrong
and failing to do good,
I have sinned against you
whom I should love above all things.
I firmly intend, with your help,
to do penance,
to sin no more,
and to avoid whatever leads me to sin.
Our Savior Jesus Christ
suffered and died for us.
In his name, my God, have mercy.
Amen.

Now spend some time with God. Ask him for the help you need to avoid what leads to sin and for the strength to ask forgiveness when you've done something wrong. Thank him in your own words for the forgiveness he offers.

Faith Summary

In celebrating the Sacrament of Penance and the Anointing of the Sick, we find the healing presence of God in our everyday lives. Through restitution, penance, and indulgences, we continue to remove the effects of sin even after confession and forgiveness.

Ways of Being Like Jesus

Jesus included every person in his mission to heal the physical and spiritual ailments of society. As part of your dedication to Jesus, make sure that you include everybody in group activities, at school or elsewhere.

With My Family

Concentrate on areas in which the whole world needs healing. Each day this week, write one "sickness" on a piece of paper and attach it to your refrigerator. With your family, pray for the healing of that sickness before each meal.

 PRAYER

Jesus, thank you for healing me in every way. Help me turn to you when I need my body or my spirit to be healed.

My Response

Jesus sent the disciples to teach and heal anyone who was in need. Do you know anyone who is sick and in need of encouragement or assistance? How can you offer your help to that person this week?

Focus on Faith

God Forgives Us

On May 13, 1981, an attempt was made to assassinate Pope John Paul II. The pope was rushed to the hospital and underwent surgery for six hours. In his first public statement after the incident, he asked all to "pray for the brother who shot me, whom I have sincerely forgiven." On a visit to the prison cell of the person who shot him, the pope repeated his words of forgiveness. The pope through his words and actions is an example of the healing grace of forgiveness we receive when we celebrate the Sacrament of Penance. Recognizing that God forgives us opens us to the grace to forgive others.

Our Catholic Heritage

When people celebrate the Sacrament of Penance, they take time to do an examination of conscience. In his *Spiritual Exercises,* Saint Ignatius of Loyola gave people instructions on how to stop to look at their lives every day. This part of the exercises is called the examen. It is not the same thing as the examination of conscience that is part of penance. Instead, it is designed to help people be more aware, from day to day, of both their blessings and their sins. Ask yourself these two questions: What have I done today to be closer to Jesus? What have I done today to separate myself from Jesus? This daily examen can help prepare us for penance by encouraging us to pay attention to our spiritual life on a daily basis.

Dinnertime Conversation Starter

In what way can we become a forgiving family?

Hints for at Home

The next time your family knows of someone in the hospital, write that person a get-well card and include a passage or two from the Bible. One person may decide how to design the card, and another person may look for appropriate messages of encouragement. The Book of Psalms is a great place to start your search for get-well messages.

Focus on Prayer

Review with your child the Act of Contrition, the focus of prayer in this session. This prayer can be found at www.FindingGod.org.

Review

Jesus and the prophets healed people with messages of encouragement and reform. The Church continues to share in the healing powers of Jesus Christ. What have you discovered recently that has strengthened your faith in the healing powers of God, Jesus Christ, and the Church?

PRAYER

Jesus, help me to carry on your work of healing and teaching just as you and the prophets did.

Faith Summary

During a time in Jewish history when the people were divided and forgetting who they were as God's people, God sent prophets to warn them about their sins and remind them of God's continuing commitment to them.

God sent prophets with messages for specific times and situations. However, the prophets' words often pointed to a time far beyond their own, to a Messiah who would bring ultimate peace, justice, and communion with God. The promise of the prophets has been fulfilled in Jesus Christ, who is our prophet, priest, and king.

In Baptism we are born into the family of Jesus Christ, a bond that is strengthened in Confirmation. We, too, are God's Chosen People, through our faith in Christ and the grace of the Holy Spirit.

Long ago, through the preaching of the prophets, God warned people that they must turn from their sin. God offered healing, which they needed badly because sin had damaged and wounded them. Now, in the life of God's family, we celebrate the healing Sacraments of Penance and the Anointing of the Sick.

Break time at Casa Maria, a Catholic Worker house

Celebrating the Sacrament of Confirmation

A neighborhood march against violence, sponsored by St. Rita's parish

The Prophets' Messages Today

You will be placed into one of three groups. Each group will be assigned one of the Old Testament prophets listed below. After your group has been assigned a prophet, follow the instructions.

Amos: 5:11–15, 8:4–7
Isaiah: 2:4–5, 10:1–3
Jeremiah: 7:1–7, 22:13–17

1. At the top of a piece of poster-sized paper, write the name of the prophet in large letters.

2. Read the scripture passages that have been selected for the prophet. After your group has finished reading, write the important points of the prophet's message at the top of the poster, under the prophet's name.

3. Draw a vertical line through the middle of the remaining space on the paper. At the top of the left section, write the word *Problems.* At the top of the right section, write the word *Solutions.*

4. Think about the problems in society that the prophet would speak out against if he were alive today. Look through newspapers and magazines and cut out headlines, short articles, and pictures that reflect these problems. Attach them to the left section of your poster. To the right section of your poster, attach stories about people or groups that are providing solutions to these problems.

5. In any available space, write a list of people who are spreading the same message of hope that your prophet proclaimed.

Teen Dies of Drug Overdose

New York City–A memorial service was held this morning for the 18-year-old honor student who died Friday night of a drug overdose. Hundreds of people turned out for the service, ...ludi... rel-...ts

Unemployment on the Rise

For the second month in a row the unemploymen... rate has risen, bol... fears that the rece... likely to continue i... year. Corporate d... ing and a decrease... ...r demand ha... ...to the...

Prosecutor Seeks Death Penalty

For the th... ro...

City Razes Low Income Housing to Make Room for New Mall

School Districts in Financial Trouble

Across the nation school ...istricts are facing the ...rst financial crisis in ...re than two decades. ...ing technology costs ... poor fiscal manage-... ...t are largely t... ...ame ... the crisis ...

On the Road of Faith

Follow the path below. On the lines next to each illustrated scene, write what you think is going on and explain its importance. In the final scene draw a picture that depicts how you see yourself living faithfully 20 years from now. Explain your drawing on the lines provided.

_____

_____

_____

_____

_____

_____

_____

_____

_____

_____

_____

_____

_____

_____

_____

_____

PRAYER SERVICE

Leader: *The grace of our Lord Jesus Christ be with us.*

Students: *Amen.*

All: *In the name of the Father and of the Son and of the Holy Spirit. Amen.*

Reader: *A reading from the Book of Isaiah.*
[Isaiah 43:1–3]

The Word of the Lord.

All: *Thanks be to God.*

Leader: *God our Creator, help us to be patient when times are hard, when we feel far from home, or when we are far from the kind of people we want to be.*

All: *Help us to put our hope in you.*

Leader: *Help us to remember how you led your people wherever they needed to go.*

All: *Help us to trust that you are always with us. Help us to listen for your encouragement.*

Leader: *Help us to believe all of the good news you have for us—especially the good news of Jesus Christ, who has given us life with you and a future that no bad times can take away.*

All: *In Jesus' name we pray.*
Amen.

Living My Faith

Ways of Being Like Jesus

Jesus and the prophets were aware of the problems in their societies, and they never hesitated to speak out against them. Despite harsh resistance from the people they criticized, Jesus and the prophets persevered. You are like Jesus when you follow the path that is good and persist despite the resistance of others.

Nobel Peace Prize winners Betty Williams (left) and Mairead Corrigan (right)

With My Family

Cut out several small pieces of paper large enough for a person's name. Every time a member of your family does something to restore peace in the home, write that person's name on one of the pieces of paper and put it in a container. Do this for a month and then have someone in your family randomly draw out a person's name from the container. The rest of the members of your family can do something special for the peacemaker whose name has been chosen.

PRAYER

Thank you, God, for sending your Son, Jesus, so that I can be close to you.

My Response

Think about something important that you want to accomplish this year. The next time you are with one of your best friends, share your goal with that person and ask him or her to share an important personal goal with you. Decide how each of you can help the other person to accomplish that specific goal.

Living Like Jesus

Saint Benedict of Palermo

Benedict was a former slave who became the leader of a community of monks in 1578. He was known for his humble manner and for the ability to give insightful advice.

Saint Benedict of Palermo

Benedict was born in Messina, Sicily, in 1526. Although his parents were slaves who had been taken from Africa, Benedict was given his freedom at the age of 18.

After gaining his freedom, Benedict worked for his former master for a few years. One day while working, he was approached by a neighbor, Father Jerome Lanza. Father Lanza convinced him to follow Jesus. Benedict sold his few possessions, gave the money to the poor, and joined the monastery.

At the monastery Benedict and others lived as hermits, enduring harsh conditions. They ate very little, did difficult manual labor, and knelt in prayer for hours on stone floors. Benedict felt that even this lifestyle was too comfortable. After making a pilgrimage to the deserts of Syria and Egypt, Benedict decided to leave Father Lanza's monastery.

Eventually Benedict retreated to a cave in the mountains overlooking Palermo, Sicily. It was there that Benedict became known as an especially holy man. People from a wide area came to see him and ask for his blessings. His reputation grew even greater after he joined the Convent of St. Mary, where he was appointed the superior. Humble Benedict, however, did not want to be in a position of authority. After serving as superior for a short time, he resigned, preferring to work in the kitchen as a cook.

Benedict died in 1589 and was declared a saint in 1807. He is a patron saint of African Americans, and his feast day is April 4.

Jesus' Way of Love

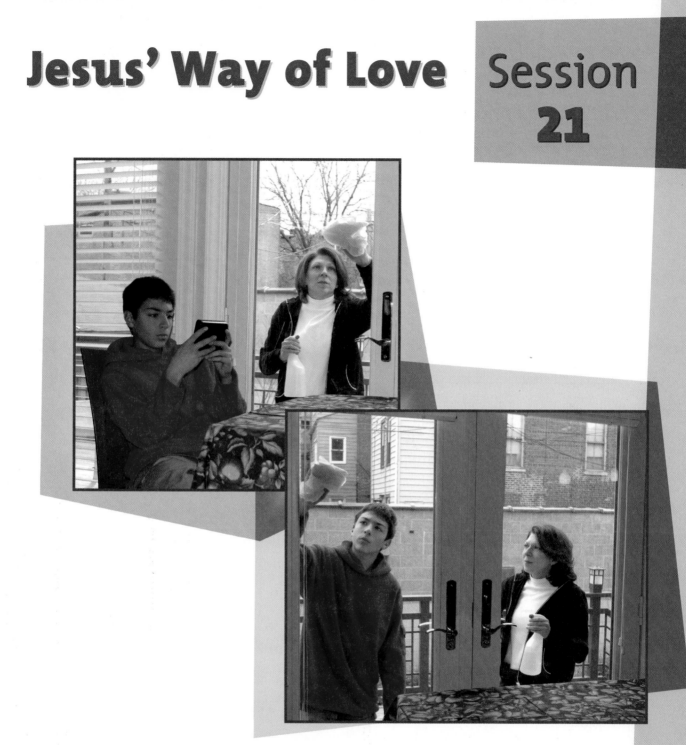

When was the last time you chose to help someone rather than do something for yourself? What did you do?

PRAYER

Jesus, help me to choose to love even when it is difficult and help me to live out my love in my relationships with you and others.

A Young Woman Who Listened to God

Thérèse of Lisieux was born in 1873 in France, the youngest of nine children. As a young girl, she wanted to join the Carmelite convent as her older sisters had, but the head of the convent didn't think young Thérèse was ready; convent life was strict and rigorous. Nonetheless, Thérèse persisted. Nothing would stop this young woman from fulfilling her dreams. She wanted to do great things for God.

At the age of 14, she went on a pilgrimage to Rome with her father. As far as she was concerned, this was her best chance to get into the convent. Although she and the other pilgrims were forbidden to speak with the pope, as soon as she saw him, she ran up to him and begged him to let her enter the Carmelite Order.

Saint Thérèse as a novice at the convent of Lisieux

The pope didn't grant her permission to enter the convent. A Church official noticed her courage, however, and urged the head of the Carmelite convent to admit her. At the age of 15, Thérèse entered the convent, joining two of her older sisters.

Thérèse loved God. She discovered that she could show her love for God and others by making small sacrifices every day. Thérèse knew that God wanted her to live in constant awareness of his presence in her life.

Reading God's Word

Hear, O Israel! The LORD is our God, the LORD alone! Therefore, you shall love the LORD, your God, with all your heart, and with all your soul, and with all your strength.

Deuteronomy 6:4-5

Kingdom Qualities Are Possible in Our Lives

Have you ever tried to pay attention to God for an entire day? It's not easy. This kind of close attention to God is really a gift of the Holy Spirit. Thérèse gave such close attention to God all day that she was told by others to write about how she did it. Thérèse wrote this story and called it *The Story of a Soul,* which still helps people all over the world.

Thérèse died at the young age of 24. She practiced faith, hope, and charity so well that she was **canonized,** declared a saint of the Church, in 1925. Pope John Paul II declared her a **Doctor of the Church** in 1997. Her feast day is October 1.

Although Thérèse's life was short, her story is an inspiring reminder that we can all live as members of God's kingdom. Our identity as members of the Kingdom of God is based on how we act—just as our identity as members of a society is defined by the way we speak, the clothes we wear, and the way we interact with people.

As citizens in God's kingdom, we share three important qualities: faith, hope, and charity. These are called theological virtues because they are all gifts from God and they express the nature of God. They are also the source of our prayer life. When we demonstrate these qualities in our speech and actions, we show others what God is like and are truly acting like Kingdom people!

Saint Thérèse
of Lisieux

Did You Know?

There are three female Doctors of the Church: Saint Catherine of Siena, Saint Teresa of Ávila, and Saint Thérèse of Lisieux. A Doctor of the Church is one who gives special guidance to Christians seeking a deeper spiritual life.

Saint Catherine
of Siena

Saint Teresa
of Ávila

The Three Theological Virtues

The three theological virtues are given to us by God. We do not acquire them through human effort. The three virtues are also deeply connected to one another. We can hope because we have faith; and as Saint Paul writes in the First Letter to the Corinthians, both come to completion in charity.

Faith

Faith is the ability to believe in God and give our lives to him. Through the Church the Holy Spirit shares with us the ability to believe. Faith calls us not only to believe in God but to decide to give ourselves totally to him. When you give your life to God, you are truly acting for the good of others.

Hope

Christian hope is our desire for all of the good things God has planned for us. Hope helps us to trust that if we live according to Jesus' teachings, we will see God's kingdom. Hope also helps us to do what pleases God even when that is difficult or when we get tired and discouraged. Through Christian hope we know that we have **eternal life**—our existence with God forever in heaven.

We often say offhandedly that we "hope" something will happen. This expression is more like a wish than Christian hope, which is based on the Bible and the teachings of the Church. With Christian hope we are confident that God's plan will unfold as it should, even if it doesn't happen right now or in the way we expect. The Holy Spirit gives us this kind of hope.

Charity

Charity is the virtue we express in our love for God. This love is more than just feelings for God; it is the way we think about God and act toward God. When we love God, we allow God to be at the center of life, to help us in everything we do and say.

Charity is also expressed in our love for other people. We often use the word *charity* to mean the giving away of money or possessions to the poor. Jesus taught us that sometimes we are also called to make sacrifices as an expression of our love for all.

The practice of charity brings all of the virtues together in perfect harmony. Saint Paul wrote in his letter to the Corinthians, "If I have faith to move mountains but do not have love, I am nothing. . . . Love is patient and kind, love is not jealous or boastful. Love believes all things, hopes all things, endures all things. . . . So faith, hope and love remain, these three. But the greatest of these is love."

adapted from 1 Corinthians 13:1-13

Living the Virtues

Imagine what the world would be like if we all lived with faith, hope, and charity. How do you think the world would be different?

_____

_____

_____

_____

_____

_____

PRAYER

Through prayer, we strengthen our relationship with God and accept the gifts that the Holy Spirit grants us: faith, hope, and charity.

Act of Faith

O my God, I firmly believe that you are one God in three divine Persons, Father, Son, and Holy Spirit. I believe that your divine Son became man and died for our sins and that he will come to judge the living and the dead. I believe these and all the truths which the holy Catholic Church teaches, because you have revealed them, who can neither deceive nor be deceived.
Amen.

After you pray the Act of Faith, think about how God, Jesus, and the Holy Spirit influence your life. Ask God to strengthen your faith, give you hope, and encourage you to be charitable.

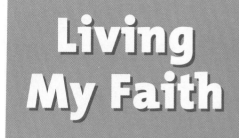

Faith Summary

The three theological virtues—faith, hope, and charity—are gifts from God. Faith calls us to make a personal decision to give our lives fully to God. Hope gives us the strength to live for the Kingdom of God and accept the Holy Spirit in our lives. Charity is the virtue that guides our actions to love God and others.

Words I Learned

canonize   Doctor of the Church   eternal life

Ways of Being Like Jesus

Jesus taught that the loving thing to do is sometimes the very opposite of what we might want to do. In particular, he taught us to love our enemies. Think of a person you haven't been very friendly with and do something nice for that person. That might be all it takes for the two of you to get along.

With My Family

Develop a family motto based on the three theological virtues. Keep it short—one or two sentences—design it, and hang it up on a wall or on the refrigerator.

PRAYER

God, thank you for the gifts of faith, hope, and love, which make me secure in you.

My Response

What will you do this week to demonstrate love to people in your family? to people in your neighborhood? to people in your class at school?

RAISING FAITH-FILLED KIDS

a parent page

Focus on Faith

A Saint for Our Time

Thérèse of Lisieux (1873–1897) was the youngest of nine children in a devout Catholic family. She received permission to enter the Carmelite community in 1888. Thérèse wanted to die as a missionary. She discovered instead that God had called her to make small sacrifices each day and to live in constant awareness of his presence. Her older sister Pauline, her superior in the community, recognized that Thérèse had special gifts from God and directed her to write her autobiography, *The Story of a Soul.* After years of physical and spiritual suffering, Thérèse died from tuberculosis in 1897. She was canonized in 1925 and declared a Doctor of the Church by Pope John Paul II in 1997.

Dinnertime Conversation Starter

Imagine that your child was writing an autobiography. What special gifts from God would he or she include? Help your child discern those qualities and talents that make him or her unique.

Hints for at Home

Help your family remember the importance of faith, hope, and charity by displaying these virtues in a family art project. One night this week, have each person in your family write a sentence that states how he or she will live out each virtue. Group the statements by virtue and then copy them on one side of three pieces of sturdy paper so that the statements about faith are on one piece, hope on another piece, and charity on the final piece. On the other side of each piece of paper, make a collage of magazine clippings that represent the virtue. Display the finished artwork in your home.

In Our Parish

Find out what your parish is doing this month to show God's love to others. Your parish may be in charge of a food pantry, collecting toys and clothing, taking up special collections, or visiting elderly members or those who are sick. Often these activities are listed in your church bulletin. You can also ask your pastor or other staff member what charitable activities are currently going on. Participate as a family.

Focus on Prayer

Your child has been learning about the virtues of faith, hope, and charity. Write a prayer with your child that helps both of you to remember to live according to these virtues.

Sacraments of Service

What do you think your life will be like in 20 years? What kind of job will you have? Will you be married?

 PRAYER

Jesus, help me to trust that the decisions I make will lead me to a life filled with love and holiness. Make me holy as you are holy.

Two Pictures of Holiness

Imagine two churches. Both are filled with people, dressed in their best clothes and beaming with happiness and anticipation. In both churches a grand ceremony is about to begin, and the air is filled with a sense of expectation.

In the first church a woman and a man, dressed very elegantly, kneel before a priest. Friends and family surround them. Here and there, people are dabbing at their eyes with handkerchiefs. You guessed it; it's a wedding!

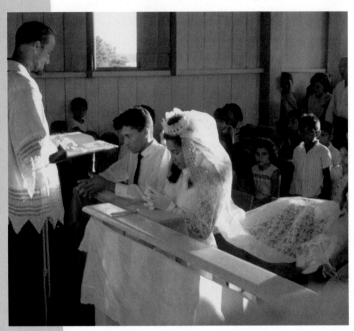

A wedding ceremony in Brazil

In the second church men wearing special garments lie prostrate on the floor. Everyone is singing, asking all the saints to pray for them. The bishop says, "Hear us, Lord our God, and pour out upon these servants of yours the blessing of the Holy Spirit and the grace and power of the priesthood." In this ceremony the Church is ordaining new priests.

Ordination of new priests

Reading God's Word

As he who called you is holy, be holy yourselves in every aspect of your conduct, for it is written, "Be holy because I [am] holy."

1 Peter 1:15-16

Serving God, the Church, and the World

Both of these ceremonies are joyous and important. The people involved have had to think carefully about their decisions. They also have had to prepare for this step in their lives. In both ceremonies the people are about to make promises to God and the community. In each church the community is present to witness and celebrate.

The Sacrament of Holy Orders

What are being celebrated in these churches are the Sacraments of Matrimony and of Holy Orders. Both priesthood and marriage are vocations. A vocation is a way of life that God calls us to so that we can live out the mission of the Church in our individual lives. Through our vocations we use the gifts God has given us to love others and to serve the Kingdom of God.

The Sacraments of Holy Orders and Matrimony are two means through which people are called to holiness. Together they are called the Sacraments at the Service of Communion because they are ways of life that help us to lead others to salvation. The Holy Spirit calls everyone to holiness. We read in the Book of Leviticus, "I, the Lord, am your God; and you shall make and keep yourselves holy, because I am holy."

Leviticus 11:44

Meet a Saint

Paul of the Cross lived in Italy during the 18th century. As a young man he was inspired to start a congregation of preachers who were dedicated especially to the passion of Christ. His congregation became known as the Passionists. Today, the Passionists still preach about the crucified Christ to a suffering world.

Holy Orders

In the Sacrament of Holy Orders, the Holy Spirit calls men to a life of holiness and service as leaders of the Church. The ordained ministry has three levels: deacon, **presbyter** (priest), and bishop.

Bishops are part of the Episcopal college, and they are responsible for the part of the church community that is entrusted to them. Usually a bishop is the visible head of a number of parishes in a region (called a diocese). Bishops serve God's family by being leaders to the people and priests of their parishes.

The bishops are the successors of the apostles. The pope is the successor of Saint Peter, who was the leader of the apostles. Together, the bishops and the pope share in the apostolic responsibility and mission of the whole Church.

Special Duties

Deacons, priests, and bishops each have specific ways they can serve communities. What do you know about their special duties? In the columns below, write all the different ways deacons, priests, and bishops serve.

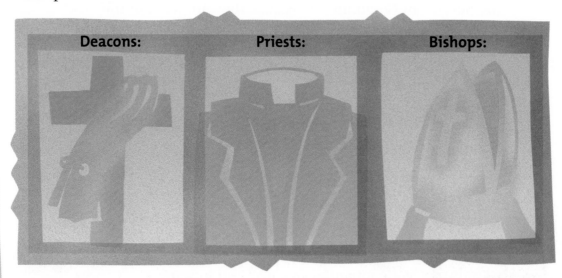

Deacons: Priests: Bishops:

Did You Know?

Charisms are gifts of the Holy Spirit that help members of the Church serve the common good. Among these are the gifts of teaching, proclaiming the gospel, giving to the poor, and showing hospitality.

Marriage: A Holy Calling

In the Sacrament of Matrimony, a woman and a man are called by the Holy Spirit to enter into a marriage covenant with God and each other. They make this commitment before the community in a public celebration before a priest, a deacon, or another authorized witness of the Church.

Husband and wife, called to holiness through their Baptism, receive the grace to help each other grow in holiness. They live out their vocation by loving each other and their children, whom they care for and educate in the faith. Their relationship reflects the union between Christ and the Church. They give themselves completely to each other, physically and emotionally, loving each other and giving their bodies to no one else.

Chastity, which unites us sexually and spiritually as persons, helps a husband and wife to give themselves completely to each other. They say to each other in the marriage ceremony: "I promise to be true to you in good times and in bad, in sickness and in health. I will love you and honor you all the days of my life." They are two individuals promising to live as one couple. This promise cannot be ended simply by a human decision.

It may seem difficult to be united for life with another human being, yet the two are committing themselves to just that. Through faithfulness and the grace of the sacrament, a married couple can be witnesses to God's faithfulness and infinite love. Such love is always open to the gift of children. A child, created in the image and likeness of God from the moment of conception, must be treated as a human being even while that child is still in the mother's womb.

 **PRAYER**

Holiness is our everyday attitude. Whether we serve as priests or laypersons, as teachers or students, we are all called to lives of holiness.

This prayer may help to remind you that God will always be with you to guide you along your unique path in life. Pray it silently to yourself.

God, my creator, my provider,
As I struggle to seek the right way in life,
Help my heart find guidance in your love.
Help my mind reflect the depth of your wisdom.
Help my hands create peace.
Help my feet support hope.
And strengthen my love for you,
As I grow strong in your love for me.
Amen.

Pray the prayer again. What words or phrases stand out? Spend time discussing them with God. Listen to God with your heart.

Faith Summary

Although every person is called to the vocation of a holy life, some people are called to holiness through Holy Orders or through Matrimony. These sacraments are celebrations of people who have chosen to make a public commitment to service and holiness.

Word I Learned

presbyter

Ways of Being Like Jesus

You are like Jesus when you follow your calling in life—whatever it may be—with holiness and service to others.

With My Family

Ask the older members of your family whether they remember what they thought about when they were your age. What did they want to be when they grew up? How did they want to serve people and live holy lives?

PRAYER

Thank you, God, for making it possible for me to live a holy life by serving others with love.

My Response

Every day this week, pray for the person you will be in 10 years. Ask God to show you the vocation that is best for you. Ask God to help you make choices now that will lead you to an adulthood of holiness and faithfulness.

RAISING FAITH-FILLED KIDS

a parent page

Focus on Faith

Jesus Calls Us

He was a personable young man with an excellent singing voice. In preparation for a career in show business, he was taking a fine arts degree in college. One day he was present when a priest gave a presentation to his class. He noticed that, unlike most of the people he dealt with in show business, the priest was very happy with himself and with his vocation. The young man asked himself what he really wanted out of life. In response, he left college, entered the seminary, and has faithfully served as a diocesan priest for many years. Our children are presently in the process of preparing for their future. What values are they learning from us, their parents, that will help them discern where God is calling them?

Dinnertime Conversation Starter

Challenge your son or daughter to consider a life dedicated to God as a priest or a member of a religious order. Discuss what such a vocation would involve. With your family consider adding a prayer for vocations to your mealtime prayer.

Our Catholic Heritage

Francis Borgia (1510–1572) was born into a noble Spanish family. He became one of the wealthiest and most powerful men in Spain. Francis's life changed drastically when a good friend died in 1546. He underwent an emotional and spiritual transformation; he gave up all of his possessions and joined the Society of Jesus (Jesuits). After being ordained a priest in 1551, Francis Borgia began a busy life establishing

The Conversion of the Duke of Gandia, Francis Borgia, Carbonero

schools and novitiates across Europe. Francis Borgia died in 1572 and was canonized in 1671.

Hints for at Home

Encourage your child to begin exploring career ideas. Show that no matter what he or she chooses to do, your child can live a life of holiness. Begin by having your child make a simple list of his or her favorite hobbies and activities. Talk about how these ideas could become careers later in life. Ask how he or she might be able to serve people through a chosen career.

Focus on Prayer

Pray with your child this week, asking God to help you live out your holy calling as a parent. Allow your child to hear you ask for God's help to be the mother or father you are called to be.

Caring for the Earth

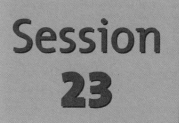

Think about a place outdoors that has a special meaning to you.
Describe that place and explain how it makes you feel.

PRAYER

*God, my Creator, help me to see you in all of creation so that I will praise you
and remember to care for the earth.*

Gospel of Life: A Letter to the Church

Human beings have always had a special relationship with the natural world. We find joy in its beauty and diversity, and we have the ability to harness its natural resources for social benefits. We also depend on nature for our own survival. All of the people in the world must share the goods of the earth and should have enough to meet their basic needs. That is why it is important for us to understand how to have a healthy relationship with the environment that we live in.

In 1995 Pope John Paul II wrote an **encyclical,** which is a letter of instruction to the Church, called "The Gospel of Life." The pope's main message was that all life is a sacred gift from God and that, as God's people, we have a special responsibility to care for the environment.

Pope John Paul II wrote, "To defend and promote life, to show reverence and love for it, is a task which God entrusts to every man, calling him as his living image to share in his own lordship over the world. . . . As one called to till and look after the garden of the world, man has a specific responsibility towards the environment in which he lives, towards the creation which God has put at the service of his personal dignity, of his life, not only for the present but also for future generations."

Link to Liturgy

The Prayer of the Faithful occurs at the end of the Liturgy of the Word. We pray for the needs of the world, the Church, and the parish community through a series of intercessions. The prayer may be introduced by the priest and then announced by a reader or a cantor. After each intercession, the people respond with, "Lord, hear our prayer" or similar words. The priest then offers a concluding prayer.

Ruling With Love and Wisdom

In the first creation story God created man and woman and gave them dominion over the fish of the sea, the birds of the air, and all living things that move on the earth. That sounds like an amazing birthday present, but God gave human beings more than everything on the earth; he gave them something else—responsibility. He entrusted human beings with the responsibility of caring for his magnificent creation.

based on Genesis 1:28-31

What exactly does *dominion* mean? It is control or rule. Pope John Paul II wrote in his encyclical that "the dominion granted to man by the Creator is not an absolute power." Just as we uphold the moral law in our relationships with one another, so too must we uphold the moral law with regard to our relationship with the natural world. We are not to abuse and misuse natural resources; that is not at all what God intended.

Another way to understand how to have dominion over everything on the earth is to think about how God has dominion over us. God cares for us with love and wisdom. In the same way, our dominion over the planet should include great love for nature and wisdom about how to protect all of its creatures, resources, and habitats.

Top: Energy conservation workshop
Middle: Rescuing a bird from an
     oil spill
Bottom: An eco-village in Ithaca, N.Y.

Environmental Abuse

Give examples of how people have misused parts of the environment, whether those parts be animals, plants, or natural resources.

_____

_____

_____

Solidarity

The responsibility we have to care for the earth requires that we consume its goods with moderation, taking only what we need. Just

think of all the food and water we waste in a single day, while there are people all over the world who don't have enough food to eat or any clean water at all.

Visitors at a display of the AIDS quilt in Washington, D.C.

This is why we must strive to live in **solidarity,** unity, with groups of people in all parts of the world, by recognizing their needs and rights. We are called to do what we can to help them protect their environments so that all people can be provided with the food and other materials that they need.

In the Bible there is no division between justice toward people and justice toward the environment. Throughout the Scriptures, the natural world is even spoken of as though it were a person—it can rejoice or mourn.

Reading God's Word

Let the heavens be glad and the earth rejoice;
    let the sea and what fills it resound;
    let the plains be joyful and all that is in them.
Then let all the trees of the forest rejoice
    before the LORD who comes,
    who comes to govern the earth,
To govern the world with justice
    and the peoples with faithfulness.

Psalm 96:11-13

Exercise Your Dominion!

Imagine that your home is in the center of a circle with a radius of one mile. Now imagine that you're in an airplane looking out over that area. Draw a sketch or a diagram of everything that lies within a mile of your home. Include everything you can think of—animals, plants, buildings, streets, any natural areas such as forest preserves, fields, or bodies of water.

After you have finished your drawing, think about some of the places in your neighborhood where you could improve the environment. Are there any parks or alleys in your neighborhood that need to be cleaned? Is there an unused piece of land where you could start a community garden? Mark these places on your drawing.

PRAYER

Quietly pray this prayer and then read the reflection that follows.

Act of Love

O my God, I love you above all things with my whole heart and soul, because you are all good and worthy of all my love. I love my neighbor as myself for the love of you. I forgive all who have injured me and I ask pardon of those whom I have injured. Amen.

Now reflect on the love that God has asked us to have for all of life. God has given care of the earth to us. Think about the small things you can do to make sure that the gift of creation can continue to be shared by people all over the world.

Reflect on how you show your love of God by caring for creation and your neighbors who share it with you.

Faith Summary

Pope John Paul II wrote an encyclical that calls us to remember that all of creation is a gift from God and that we have a responsibility to use the gifts of the earth in ways that honor God. By increasing our solidarity with people all over the world, we can work to bring about environmental and social justice.

Words I Learned

encyclical   solidarity

Ways of Being Like Jesus

Like Jesus, we can see the goodness that God has revealed to us by respecting the natural world around us and by recognizing the presence of God in every living thing.

With My Family

Go on a short field trip with your family—to a park, a national forest, a river, or a lake. Find a private area where you can stand together and pray that people will care for the plants and animals that live there.

 PRAYER

Creator God, thank you for this marvelous world you've made. Show me how to care for it with love and wisdom, now and for the future.

My Response

What will you do this week to show respect and care for the environment? Invite your friends to help you!

a parent page

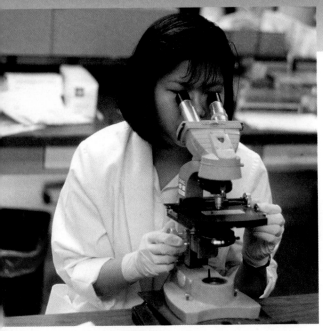

Focus on Faith

Gospel of Life

In 1995 Pope John Paul II issued the encyclical "The Gospel of Life." This document seeks to address the positive contribution of Catholic teaching regarding life in all of its forms. John Paul II notes that we have a specific responsibility toward the environment in which we live and toward the whole of creation that God has put at our service. Our dominion of the earth must be based on God's dominion. This requires discerning ways to serve the needs of the world rather than seek ways to exploit it. Decisions that we make today not only will influence us but also will affect our children in all the years to come.

Spirituality in Action

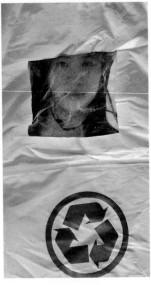

Make a list of five environmental issues that are most meaningful to your family. Search for information about the environmental groups that are working to make a difference in some of the issues that your family listed. Decide as a family how you can contribute most effectively to one or two of those groups. Try to find a group that is doing work locally. Your family may be able to volunteer to help for a few days every month.

Dinnertime Conversation Starters

What steps can you take as individuals and as a family to assume responsibility for the environment?

Our Catholic Heritage

Some of the first people to study the environment were Jesuit priests. Jesuit botanists stationed all over the world discovered and named hundreds of plants and herbs, and Jesuit astronomers helped to invent more-accurate calendars. They understood that it is a joy and a responsibility to honor and understand our planet and to use its resources for the benefit of everyone.

Focus on Prayer

Your child has reflected on the Act of Love and how that relates to our care for God's creation. This prayer can be found at www.FindingGod.org. Sometime this week, with your child write or look for another prayer that expresses your love for God and all of his creation.

Jesus' Call for Justice

What does justice mean to you? Think of a time when you witnessed a simple act of justice; share this experience with the group.

PRAYER

Jesus, lead me to a greater faith so that my actions always reflect God's love and justice.

The Slave Becomes the Servant

Saint Patrick knew what it was like to lose his fundamental rights as a person. He was born and raised the son of a Roman military officer in Britain but was captured by pirates and enslaved in Ireland. For six years he worked as a shepherd, suffering from hunger, cold, and loneliness. Still, he never lost his faith in God, and he prayed to him every day and every night.

Eventually, Patrick's dream of returning home came true. Late one night he escaped. In his renewed freedom, he understood what his mission was; he would work to help others achieve the same rights he had once lost. Patrick became a priest.

After a number of years in parish ministry, Patrick was ordained a bishop. He now felt that God was calling him to return to Ireland, where he had been a slave for so many years. Patrick went back to Ireland and preached to the Celtic tribes, introducing them to Christianity. He worked to change the social life of Ireland by establishing monasteries, convents, and parishes; and by adapting pagan celebrations to Christian feasts.

Patrick forgave those who had enslaved him. He worked for their benefit, and he helped to establish systems and practices that supported people's dignity and freedom. His feast day is March 17.

Faith That Works

In slavery Patrick's faith led him to freedom; in freedom his faith led him to service. His understanding that a life of faith is a life of good works is an idea expressed many times in the Scriptures.

The Letter of James explores the theme of faith and good deeds by explaining that faith without action is empty. At the very beginning James says, "What good is it, my brothers, if someone says he has faith but does not have works?" He goes on to explain that our faith must lead to good works that help other people. If we are not treating people with dignity and respect, what is the point of having faith at all?

adapted from James 2:14-26

What Do the Scriptures Say?

Read James 2:14–26 and answer these questions:

What example does James give of faith that is not followed by good works?

_____

_____

What does he call faith without works?

_____

What work justified Abraham?

_____

What did Abraham need to have before he could ever give up his son?

_____

Living in Community

Each of us is a part of many communities, large and small. We are members of families, and we are members of parishes. We are residents of a neighborhood community, and we are residents of a global community as well. In communities we share common goals and find support in our solidarity.

When God created human beings, he intended them to live in communities. In order to make our communities function well, the Holy Spirit calls us to care for each other with respect and tolerance.

Jesus Christ also has brought us together in a community—the Church. As members of this community, we live with others as Jesus lived, in justice and with compassion. We reach out particularly to those in need, such as persons with disabilities, the poor, the homeless, and the lonely.

Think about how life in your community would be different if people treated everyone the same way they treated their closest friends.

Reading God's Word

This is the commandment we have from him: whoever loves God must also love his brother.

1 John 4:21

Community Justice

Because God created us to live in communities, it is very important that the institutions in any community follow God's **natural law** of justice. That is why governments must support the fundamental rights of the individual and why laws must direct and encourage people to treat each other fairly, as equals. All civil authority must be exercised responsibly and with morally acceptable means.

Even though people are of equal value in God's eyes, their life circumstances are certainly not equal. We are called to work especially for those who are poor or who need special help, such as refugees and homeless people.

A teacher watches as a teenager works in a wheelchair-accessible garden bed.

Society itself should be organized so that people can help one another, encourage one another to be virtuous, and live with one another in peace. Society should do everything possible to avoid war. The basic rights that a government should protect are the right to religious liberty, the right to personal freedom, the right to receive necessary information from the media, the right to life, and the right to be protected from terror and torture.

In the News

Think about world events that you're hearing about in the news.

What problems have to do with people's rights to be treated as equals?

_____

What problems seem to be connected to poverty?

_____

What problems seem to be connected to a loss of freedom?

_____

PRAYER

The Church prays the Magnificat at every evening prayer. In this song and prayer Mary expressed her own sense of justice after learning that she would give birth to a special child.

The Magnificat

All: *My soul proclaims the greatness of the Lord,*
my spirit rejoices in God my Savior;
for he has looked with favor on his lowly servant.

A: *From this day all generations will call me blessed:*
the Almighty has done great things for me,
and holy is his Name.

B: *He has mercy on those who fear him*
in every generation.
He has shown the strength of his arm,
he has scattered the proud in their conceit.

A: *He has cast down the mighty from their thrones,*
and has lifted up the lowly.

B: *He has filled the hungry with good things,*
and the rich he has sent away empty.

All: *He has come to the help of his servant Israel*
for he has remembered his promise of mercy,
the promise he made to our fathers,
to Abraham and his children forever.

Talk to God quietly and thank him for the gifts that he has given Mary and you.

detail from *Madonna Clothed in a Robe of Wheat,* 15th century

Faith Summary

We are reminded by Saint Patrick's life and the Letter of James that faith is meaningless unless it is accompanied by good deeds. Our faith leads us to help every person to have fundamental rights, such as freedom and religious liberty. Sometimes this means that we must work to change unjust institutions and laws. By following the example of Jesus, we make our global community work by having compassion for others and working for justice.

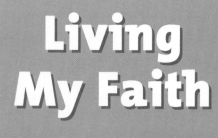

Living My Faith

Word I Learned

natural law

Ways of Being Like Jesus

In Luke's Gospel the story of the Good Samaritan reminds us that all people are capable of good and are deserving of our respect. You are like Jesus when you treat all people with the same love and respect.

With My Family

Visit your local community organization and learn how your family can become involved in the important issues in your neighborhood.

 **PRAYER**

Jesus, thank you for showing me that I have the ability to make my community a place of peace and justice.

My Response

Think about injustices in your community. List ways you can work to correct one of them.

Focus on Faith

Faith and Works

James 2:14–26 is a powerful teaching about the relationship between faith and action. James says that if a person has nothing to wear or nothing to eat and all we do is tell that person to go in peace without materially helping him or her, our good wishes are worthless. So is our faith if it does not lead to good works on behalf of others. James continues by saying that, just as the body without the spirit is dead, faith without good works is dead. An active faith is one that impels us to address the needs of the poor and vulnerable. In today's society this means not only making personal contributions to help others but also working against the social structures that keep people imprisoned in poverty.

Dinnertime Conversation Starter

With your family identify the social structures that keep people in your community trapped in poverty. What step can your family take to change the structure while also assisting the poor?

Spirituality in Action

You have probably been the new person at work at some point in your life, so you know how difficult it can be. The next time a new person starts at your workplace, go out of your way to welcome that person with acts of kindness for the first few weeks that he or she is there. In fact, if you happen to notice anyone who is feeling isolated or frustrated at work, do something for that person as well.

Our Catholic Heritage

On a small island in Lough Derg, Ireland, is a place of legend and pilgrimage called St. Patrick's Purgatory. According to folklore, at this island God gave Patrick the ability to see

and show others the suffering that sinners endured in purgatory. It was a kind of warning. To this day, pilgrims come to this place for a three-day retreat of fasting and prayer. Pilgrims arrive at the island in the afternoon, having eaten nothing since midnight, and they participate in an all-night vigil.

Focus on Prayer

Your child reflected on the Magnificat. Recite this prayer as a family. You may find the exact words to this prayer at www.FindingGod.org.

Review

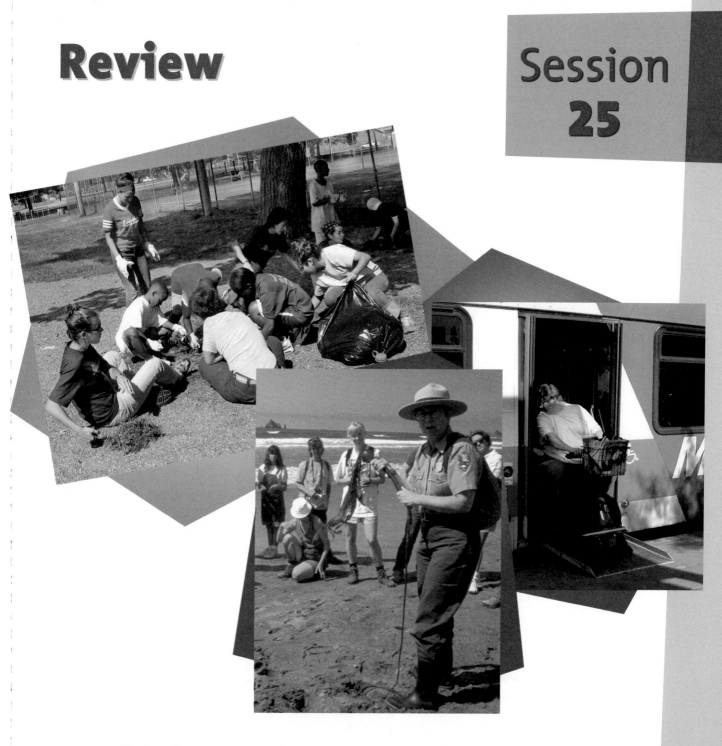

We are called to live as Jesus lived, using the goods of the world responsibly and working for justice with compassion.

PRAYER

Lord Jesus, help me to live out your love in specific ways so that I can, day by day, live as you lived and love the world as you did.

Faith Summary

Jesus calls us to practice the three theological virtues of faith, hope, and charity. In faith we dedicate our lives to God, with hope we trust that God's plan will be accomplished, and through charity we act with love for God and all people.

Although every person is called to the vocation of a holy life, some people are called to holiness through two special sacraments: Holy Orders and Matrimony. In these sacraments people receive the grace to serve the world and the Kingdom of God. Married couples dedicate their lives to each other and to bringing up their families in the faith. Ordained men serve the Church community as leaders and teachers.

All of creation is a gift from God, and the goods of the earth are to be used in ways that honor God, so we are called to care for the earth responsibly. We do this by protecting the environment, respecting plants and animals, and helping people all over the world to find the resources they need.

As people of a just God, we are called to support the common good and the fundamental rights of each person. We strive to live in a way that is good for everyone. This means that we work to help those who are the victims of injustice.

Fundamental human rights include health care, freedom of religion, freedom of speech, and fair housing opportunities.

Building Bridges Between Cultures

You will be placed into one of two groups. The goal of each group is to create its own unique culture. Think about all of the different things that make up your group's unique identity. Start by answering simple questions, such as "What is the climate of the environment we live in?" and "What kind of clothing do we wear?" Then determine some of the more complicated aspects of your culture, such as "What are the major problems facing our people?" and "What kind of government do we have?"

One person in the group will be responsible for listing all of the aspects of your culture on a sheet of paper. When your group is finished, decide on five questions to ask the other group. One member of your group will present these questions to the other group. Through these five questions alone, your group will learn about the other group. Word your questions specifically in order to get specific answers.

Now each group is to send an ambassador to the other group to ask the questions. The ambassador will be allowed to take notes. After five or ten minutes, the ambassadors are to return and give their reports to their own groups.

Now each group will write a letter of support and encouragement to the other group. In this letter suggest one way in which your group might help the other to deal with its major problems.

Bringing Charity to Communities

The circles on this page represent different communities. In each one, draw pictures and write ideas about how you can bring the virtue of charity to that community. In the last circle, do the same thing for a community of your own choosing, such as a team or group in which you participate.

~Family~

~Parish~

~School~

~World~

PRAYER SERVICE

Leader: *Each of us is called to live a holy life. God has given us gifts, and through these gifts we can serve the Kingdom of God. We are offering God the gifts we have for the sake of his Kingdom in the best way we know how.*

Reader 1: *A reading from the Letter to the Ephesians.*

[Ephesians 4:1–7, 11–13]

The Word of the Lord.

All: *Thanks be to God.*

Leader: *Let us offer our petitions to God.*

Reader 2: *For Christians everywhere, that they may practice the virtues of faith, hope, and charity, we pray to the Lord.*

All: *Lord, hear our prayer.*

Reader 3: *For those called to the vocations of Holy Orders and Matrimony, that they may receive the grace they need truly to love and serve others, we pray to the Lord.*

Reader 4: *For the earth and all of its creatures, that they may be treated with care by men, women, and children, we pray to the Lord.*

Reader 5: *For those who suffer injustice, that they may find justice and peace, we pray to the Lord.*

Leader: *Let us pray the Lord's Prayer, the words Jesus taught us.*

Leader: *As we go forth to live and share God's Word, let us offer each other a sign of peace.*

Living My Faith

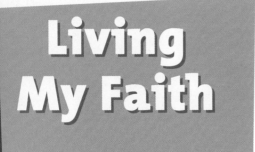

Ways of Being Like Jesus

God's creation exists for our good and the good of everyone on our planet. It exists so that, in our caring for it, we can find inspiration and enjoyment in all of its beauty and wonder. Don't forget to take the time to enjoy the beauty of life, in all of its forms, just for enjoyment's sake!

With My Family

Attach a piece of paper to your refrigerator and write across the top *In a Perfect World.* . . . On this paper your family can keep an ongoing list of social issues that they are concerned about. Whenever a member of your family feels that an institution at work, at school, or anywhere else needs to be changed, he or she may add that idea to the list. At the end of the week, discuss all of the issues. Then, on the opposite side of the paper, list all of the things your family can do to help improve those institutions.

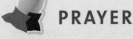

PRAYER

Thank you, Lord Jesus, for giving us the gifts we need in order to live as holy people.

My Response

This week go to a favorite place in nature that is nearby and spend half an hour with God. During this time, reflect on the gifts you have been given and think about what your vocation might be. Talk to God about your hopes and fears about whatever your calling is. Ask for help in understanding, at each stage of your life, what God wants you to do and be. Ask for the grace to live out your calling.

The Year in Our Church

ADVENT

CHRISTMAS

ORDINARY TIME

LENT

HOLY WEEK

EASTER

Christmas

Epiphany

Ash Wednesday

Palm Sunday
Holy Thursday
Good Friday
Holy Saturday

Easter

First Sunday of Advent

All Souls Day

All Saints Day

Winter

Spring

Summer

Fall

Ascension
Pentecost

ORDINARY TIME

Liturgical Calendar

The liturgical calendar highlights the feast days and seasons of the Church year. Various colors symbolize the different seasons.

Liturgical Year

Advent marks the beginning of the Church year. It is a time of anticipation of Christmas and begins four Sundays before the feast.

The Christmas Season includes **Christmas,** the celebration of Jesus' birth, and Epiphany, the celebration of his manifestation to the world.

Lent is a season of conversion that begins on Ash Wednesday. It is a time of turning toward God in preparation for Easter.

During **Holy Week** we recall the events leading to the suffering and death of Jesus. Holy Week begins with Palm Sunday and ends on Holy Saturday.

Easter celebrates Jesus' being raised from the dead. The Resurrection is the central mystery of the Christian faith. The **Ascension** celebrates Jesus' return to the Father in heaven.

The coming of the Holy Spirit is celebrated on **Pentecost.** With this feast, the Easter Season ends.

All Saints Day celebrates the victory of all of the holy persons in heaven. On **All Souls Day,** we pray for those who have died but are still in purgatory.

The time set aside for celebrating our call to follow Jesus day by day as his disciples is Ordinary Time.

Advent

During Advent we remember how the People of God awaited the birth of the Messiah, and we prepare ourselves to celebrate the birth of Jesus.

Advent lasts four weeks. For many of us, four weeks can seem like a long time to wait. The People of God lived in hope of the coming of the Messiah for hundreds of years.

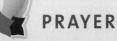

PRAYER

Loving God, help me to spend the season of Advent remembering your promise to send a Messiah. Help me to prepare to celebrate the birth of your only son, Jesus.

John the Baptist

This year we are studying the people and events in the Old Testament. The Old Testament tells the history of the People of God as God prepared them to receive the Messiah. The covenant with Abraham and Sarah, the Exodus event, the formation of Israel and the Temple, and the work of the prophets all anticipate the arrival of the Messiah.

John the Baptist was the last prophet to proclaim the arrival of Jesus. He told people that he himself was the messenger promised by the prophet Isaiah. With the help of the Holy Spirit, John prepared people to receive the Messiah.

John Prepares the Way

This is what the Bible says about John the Baptist:

> As it is written in Isaiah the prophet:
> > "Behold, I am sending my messenger ahead of you;
> > > he will prepare your way.
> > A voice of one crying out in the desert:
> > > 'Prepare the way of the Lord,
> > make straight his paths.'"
>
> John [the] Baptist appeared in the desert proclaiming a baptism of repentance for the forgiveness of sins. People of the whole Judean countryside and all the inhabitants of Jerusalem were going out to him and were being baptized by him in the Jordan River as they acknowledged their sins. John was clothed in camel's hair, with a leather belt around his waist. He fed on locusts and wild honey. And this is what he proclaimed: "One mightier than I is coming after me. I am not worthy to stoop and loosen the thongs of his sandals. I have baptized you with water; he will baptize you with the holy Spirit."

Mark 1:2-8

Saint John the Baptist,
Donatello, 1438

Jesse Tree

During Advent, many people make Jesse trees. A Jesse tree is a bare-branch tree that has ornaments on it representing prophecies, people, and events leading up to the birth of Jesus. The idea for a Jesse tree comes from a verse in Isaiah:

> But a shoot shall sprout
> from the stump of Jesse,
>   and from his
>   roots a bud
>   shall blossom.

Isaiah 11:1

To make a Jesse tree, your group will need a tree branch that is two or three feet tall. Decorate the tree with illustrated ornaments to stand for people such as Noah, Abraham, Isaiah, Mary, John the Baptist, David, and Ruth.

PRAYER SERVICE

Leader: Today we remember the people who came before Jesus to prepare his way.

Group A: We remember how God made a covenant with Sarah and Abraham and promised that they would be the founders of a great people.

All: We thank you for fulfilling all that you promised.

Group B: We remember Moses, who was chosen by God to lead the Chosen People out of slavery. ℟

Group A: We remember the Old Testament prophets who preached social justice and of the coming of the Messiah. ℟

Group B: We remember John the Baptist, who prepared the people to receive Jesus. ℟

Leader: God, our Father, we remember all of the people who waited for the coming of your son, Jesus. May this Jesse tree remind us of all those who patiently awaited the arrival of the Messiah.

All: Thanks be to God.

Christmas

Adoration of the Shepherds, Georges de la Tour, 17th century

The season of Christmas is the time when we remember the promises God fulfilled when he gave us his only Son, Jesus. It is also the season to share Jesus' message of love with the world.

 PRAYER

Gracious God, help me to spend the Christmas season remembering the gift that you gave to us when you sent us your only Son, Jesus.

The Presentation at the Temple

Jesus was born into a poor family. The customary way to celebrate the birth of an Israelite couple's son was to present him to God.

When Mary and Joseph entered the Temple, two people, Simeon and Anna, greeted them and rejoiced at the sight of the baby Jesus. They recognized Jesus as the Messiah who would fulfill not only their own hopes but the hopes of the entire world as well. This is what Simeon said after he saw Jesus:

> "Now, Master, you may let your servant go
>   in peace, according to your word,
> for my eyes have seen your salvation,
>   which you prepared in sight of all the peoples,
> a light for revelation to the Gentiles,
>   and glory for your people Israel."

The child's father and mother were amazed at what was said about him; and Simeon blessed them and said to Mary his mother, "Behold, this child is destined for the fall and rise of many in Israel, and to be a sign that will be contradicted (and you yourself a sword will pierce) so that the thoughts of many hearts may be revealed."

Luke 2:29-35

Presentation in the Temple, Giovanni Bellini, 15th century

Sharing Jesus' Presence

During the Christmas Season we celebrate God's love. We remember the Messiah, the Son of God who became man, God's gift to the world. We also celebrate our mission to bring love to others, especially those most in need of love. We are challenged during Christmas to share the presence of Jesus with all people, regardless of who they are.

Peace Chain

We celebrate the birth of Jesus on December 25. Seven days after his birth, his parents took him to the Temple. On this day, January 1, people all over the world celebrate World Peace Day, and the pope issues his yearly message for world peace.

In honor of Jesus' message of peace and the pope's message to all of us on World Peace Day, you will create a Peace Chain with your group. Each of you will make a paper chain link out of green or red construction paper. On your link write a verse from the Bible that is about peace. Several suggested passages have been listed below; however, feel free to use a Scripture passage of your own choosing. Decorate your link and then attach it to someone else's finished link. Hang up the entire chain when everyone is finished.

Passages of Peace: Psalm 29:11, Psalm 34:14, Isaiah 52:7, Matthew 5:9, 1 Corinthians 14:33, James 3:18.

"The pillars of true peace are justice and that form of love which is forgiveness."

PRAYER SERVICE

Leader: As Christmas approaches, let us reflect on the meaning of the birth of Jesus by remembering the joy that Simeon and Anna felt when they recognized Jesus as the Son of God.

Reader: A reading from the holy Gospel according to Luke
[Luke 2: 29–32]

The Gospel of the Lord.

All: Praise to you, Lord Jesus Christ.

Leader: We share the joy that Anna and Simeon felt when they saw the baby Jesus in the Temple. They had been waiting a long time for the Messiah, but they never gave up hope. They knew that God's promise to send his only Son would be fulfilled.

All: God, like Simeon and Anna, we remember your promise to send your only son, Jesus Christ, to the world. Help us to remember to welcome Jesus just as Simeon and Anna did, with gladness in our hearts.

Leader: Jesus Christ, you help us to accept God in our lives.

All: Thank you for showing us the way.

Leader: You help us to love others as God loves us. ℟

Leader: You help us to bring healing to those who are in need. ℟

Leader: You help us to bring peace to the world. ℟

Leader: Let's spend a few minutes telling God how happy we are that he sent his only Son, Jesus Christ.

Lent

Lent is the time we spend preparing ourselves for Easter. During this 40-day period we remember the 40 days Jesus spent in the wilderness, fasting and praying. Like Jesus, we are called to make sacrifices during Lent to help us grow closer to God. What will you do during Lent that brings you closer to God?

PRAYER

Loving God, help me to spend the season of Lent in prayer and sacrifice so that I may grow closer to you.

Jesus in the Desert

After John baptized Jesus in the Jordan River, the Holy Spirit led Jesus to the harsh desert wilderness, where he ate nothing for 40 days. On the final night, the devil came to test Jesus' faith and trust in God. Just as the Holy Spirit had sustained Jesus through hunger, the Holy Spirit would sustain him through temptation.

First, the devil tempted Jesus with food, knowing that Jesus was hungry. The devil showed Jesus some large stones, saying, "If you are the Son of God, command that these stones become loaves of bread." Jesus refused to be tempted and said, "It is written, 'One does not live by bread alone.'"

Christ Borne Up Unto a Pinnacle of the Temple, James Jacques-Joseph Tissot, 19th century

Then the devil took Jesus to the top of a high mountain. He showed Jesus all of the kingdoms of the world and told Jesus that he could be king of all those kingdoms if only he would worship the devil. Again, Jesus refused. Jesus said, "It is written: 'You shall worship the Lord, your God, and him alone shall you serve.'"

Finally, the devil took Jesus to the top of a high tower at the Temple in Jerusalem. The devil tried to trick him again by telling Jesus to jump from the tower if he was certain that God's angels could catch him. Jesus refused to do this as well. He said, "It also says, 'You shall not put the Lord, your God, to the test.'"

After that final test, the devil left him, and Jesus returned from the desert.

adapted from Luke 4:1-13

Growing Closer to God

We mark the beginning of Lent by receiving ashes on our foreheads at a special ceremony. During Lent we think about those 40 days and nights Jesus spent in the desert. We see his act of fasting as a sign of his willingness to identify with the poor and the weak. We hope that, by following his example, we too may identify with people in need so that we may free ourselves from personal wants in order to serve others with charitable acts.

Like Jesus we turn our attention to God during Lent by praying and making small personal sacrifices, such as giving up unhealthful foods. At the age of 14, we are required to give up eating meat on Fridays during Lent. Reading parts of the Bible, praying, and attending Mass as often as we can are also ways that we can celebrate Lent.

A third Lenten practice is giving alms or gifts to those in need. Like prayer and fasting, giving alms focuses our attention on God by emphasizing our dependence on his gifts, which are to be shared with all.

PRAYER SERVICE

Leader: Let us praise God. Blessed be God forever.

All: Blessed be God forever.

Leader: God, as we enter into the season of Lent, help us to resist the temptations of the world, just as your only Son, Jesus, resisted the devil in the desert.

All: God, let us spend Lent growing closer to you as we pray, reading your word in the Bible, and resisting temptation, just as your Son, Jesus, resisted the temptations of the devil when he was in the desert.

Reader: A reading from the holy Gospel according to Luke. [Luke 4:1–13]

The Gospel of the Lord.

All: Praise to you, Lord Jesus Christ.

Leader: Let us take time to remember the good things we have done to celebrate Lent. Spend a few minutes telling God things we have done to observe Lent and ways we will observe Lent in the week to come.

Thank you for sending your only Son, Jesus, to help us turn from sin.

All: Help us to use prayer and sacrifice to grow closer to you as we observe the season of Lent.

Holy Week

Christ Entering Jerusalem, Pieto Lorenzetti, 14th century

Holy Week is a time when we remember Jesus' passing from death to new life. It is also a time to reflect on how Jesus, through prayer, was able to make the difficult decision to follow God's will. During this Holy Week, how will you grow closer to God in prayer? What can you do to follow God's will better?

 PRAYER

Almighty God, give me the strength and courage to listen to you and obey your will, just as your Son did.

Jesus Prays in the Garden

After the Last Supper, Jesus knew that he had important tasks to finish. He went with Peter, James, and John to pray at a place called Gethsemane, a garden just outside Jerusalem. Jesus told the others to keep watch while he went away and prayed. He asked God whether it was possible for the hour of his death to pass him by. Jesus prayed, "Father, all things are possible to you. Take this cup away from me, but not what I will but what you will."

The Agony in the Garden, Simon Bening, illumination from prayer book, 16th century

When Jesus came back, he found the apostles sleeping. He asked them, "Are you asleep? Could you not keep watch for one hour? Watch and pray that you may not undergo the test. The spirit is willing but the flesh is weak." Jesus then returned to prayer.

Jesus went back to the apostles a second time and found them sleeping again. He returned to his prayers. When he finished praying, he returned a third time and said to them, "Are you still sleeping and taking your rest? It is enough. The hour has come. Behold, the Son of Man is to be handed over to sinners. Get up, let us go. See, my betrayer is at hand."

adapted from Mark 14:32-42

Jesus was ready to follow God's plan. Soon Judas would betray Jesus, Jesus would be brought to trial and crucified, and Jesus would rise from the dead to win new life for all.

Obeying God's Will

As we see in this Scripture passage, Jesus was totally focused on doing his Father's will. He is troubled and distressed, but he knows that all things are possible with God. In prayer to God he could say, "Not what I will but what you will." When he knew that the hour of his betrayal had come, he woke his disciples, who did not have the strength to watch and pray.

We often find ourselves struggling to make the right decisions in difficult situations. Although we are called to act in obedience to God when making these difficult choices, our obedience is not meant to be simply mechanical. Obedience to God is the result of listening to God and connecting our hearts with God's love. We can find the strength needed to make difficult choices by asking Jesus to help.

Gethsemane today

PRAYER SERVICE

Leader: *The grace of our Lord Jesus Christ be with us all, now and forever.*

All: *Amen.*

Leader: *As we prepare for Holy Week and Easter, let us remember the story of Jesus in Gethsemane.*

All: *God, help us to find the courage and the strength to follow your will, just as Jesus did when he found the courage and the strength to obey your will and die on the cross for our sins.*

Reader: *A reading from the holy Gospel according to Mark.* [Mark 14:32–42]

The Gospel of the Lord.

All: *Praise to you, Lord Jesus Christ.*

Leader: *Let us take a few minutes to talk to God about a dilemma we face and how we can find the strength and the courage to follow God's will.*

Leader: *Thank you for helping us to turn from sin and follow your will.*

All: *Amen.*

Easter and Ascension

The Holy Women at the Sepulchre, Annibale Carracci, late 16th century

After Jesus' Resurrection and Ascension, his followers were prepared to proclaim everything that they had witnessed and spread the good news from Jerusalem to the entire world.

 PRAYER

Risen Savior, as we celebrate Easter, help us to remember to live out our faith every day while we await your return.

The Disciples Bear Witness

Before Jesus left them, the disciples had questions about the future of Israel. The kingdom of Israel had been destroyed, and the country was controlled by Rome. Prophets had told the people that the Messiah would restore the kingdom, so Jesus' followers were curious about whether Jesus would restore the kingdom of Israel right away or sometime in the future.

Jesus answered that they should be patient and wait for God to reveal his plan: "It is not for you to know the times or seasons that the Father has established by his own authority. But you will receive the power when the Holy Spirit comes upon you, and you will be my witnesses in Jerusalem, throughout Judea and Samaria, and to the ends of the earth."

Then something truly incredible took place: Jesus rose up into the air, and a cloud took him out of their sight. Jesus' followers were amazed. They stood, staring into the sky where Jesus had disappeared. Then two angels appeared and reminded Jesus' followers that they had work to do: "Men of Galilee, why are you standing there looking at the sky? This Jesus who has been taken up from you into heaven will return in the same way as you have seen him going into heaven."

Jesus' followers listened and returned to Jerusalem.

adapted from the Acts of the Apostles 1:6-12

The Ascension of Christ, Hans Memling, panel from a tryptich, late 15th century

Living Out Our Faith

Jesus' words to his followers before he ascended into heaven convey an important message. They remind us that we should not spend our time thinking about when Jesus will return. Rather, we should live our faith by helping others and by discovering God's presence in every aspect of life.

Renewing Our Baptismal Promises

When a baby is baptized, his or her parents answer three questions for the child with "I do." The questions are these:

Do you believe in God, the Father almighty, Creator of heaven and earth?

Do you believe in Jesus Christ, his only Son, our Lord, who was born of the Virgin Mary, was crucified, died, and was buried, rose from the dead, and is now seated at the right hand of the Father?

Do you believe in the Holy Spirit, the holy catholic Church, the communion of saints, the forgiveness of sins, the resurrection of the body, and the life everlasting?

Renewing Baptismal vows at an Easter Vigil

As we grow, we reaffirm these promises at important times and on special days, such as our First Communion, Confirmation, and Easter Sunday. Today think about the meaning of these promises and write a short prayer that expresses how you will serve the world according to these promises. Think about how you can do God's work by helping others.

PRAYER SERVICE

Leader: *Let us praise our loving God. Blessed be God forever.*

All: *Blessed be God forever.*

Leader: *As we observe Easter, let us remember that God wants us to live our faith in everything we do.*

All: *God, help us to live our faith by reading the Bible, praying, helping others, and following your commandments.*

Reader: *A reading from the Acts of the Apostles.*
[Acts 1:6–12]

The Word of the Lord.

All: *Thanks be to God.*

Leader: *Let's spend a few minutes reflecting on how we will live out our baptismal promises and be Jesus' witnesses.*

All: *God, encourage us to live our faith this week by helping people who are in need.*

Pentecost

The Descent of the Holy Spirit, Titian, 16th century

The disciples felt as if they could do anything when the Holy Spirit came to them after Jesus ascended. The Holy Spirit entered their hearts and gave them the strength to carry out the mission Jesus had entrusted to them. We celebrate the gift of the Holy Spirit on the feast of Pentecost.

PRAYER

Father of Light, help me to find strength in the Holy Spirit as I live out my faith.

God's Spirit Encourages the Exiled Jews

During the Pentecost vigil we often read from the Old Testament Book of Ezekiel. Although this message was for the exiled Jews in Babylon, it continues to remind us of the presence of the Holy Spirit in our lives.

In 597 B.C. the Babylonians conquered Jerusalem, captured many of the Israelites, and deported them to Babylon. The people who were taken lost everything—their homes, the Temple, and their families.

Imagine how discouraged the people felt. During this time God called on Ezekiel to be a prophet who would give hope to the Israelites. The prophet told them that God had shown him a vision of a plain covered with dried bones. In the vision God had asked him, "How can these bones come back to life?"

Ezekiel had responded, "LORD God, you alone know that."

Then God had said, "Prophesy over these bones, and say to them: Dry bones, hear the word of the LORD! . . . I will bring spirit into you, that you may come to life."

When the Israelites heard Ezekiel, they realized that God had not abandoned them. They knew that God would send the spirit to end their discouragement and help them build a life in Babylon. Eventually, the Israelites were able to leave Babylon and return to Jerusalem. In the same way, the Holy Spirit gives us the strength and power to live out our faith, especially when we are discouraged.

adapted from Ezekiel 37:1-12

The Fruits of the Holy Spirit

The spirit that gave the exiled Jews strength is the same spirit that Jesus' followers received at Pentecost. The Holy Spirit gave the apostles the power and encouragement to begin preaching the good news.

When we are baptized, we receive the Holy Spirit permanently in our lives. With the presence of the Holy Spirit, we are empowered and encouraged to live out our faith. Specifically, the presence of the Holy Spirit in our lives helps us to express the "fruits" of the Holy Spirit.

In the Letter to the Galatians, 5:22–23, these fruits are named. They are

love: the charity we express to others

joy: the happiness we receive from our faith

peace: the tranquility of our souls

patience: the ability to endure difficulties

kindness: the goodness we show people

generosity: the ability to share with others

faithfulness: the commitment we make to God

gentleness: the ability to act without harshness or anger

self-control: the ability to avoid acting on temptation

Which of the fruits of the Holy Spirit are most important to you right now? Do you need to be generous to others? Do you need to be more patient with someone?

PRAYER SERVICE

Leader: Let us praise the God of wisdom and grace. Blessed be God forever.

All: Blessed be God forever.

Leader: As we observe Pentecost, let us think about the importance of the Holy Spirit in our lives.

All: God, may the Holy Spirit strengthen and guide us as we live out our faith.

Reader 1: A reading from the Book of Ezekiel.
[Ezekiel 37:1–6]

The Word of the Lord.

All: Thanks be to God.

Leader: Let us spend a moment asking the Holy Spirit to dwell in our hearts and grant us the spiritual gifts that we cherish.

Reader 2: Spirit of love, joy, and peace.

All: Enter our hearts.

Reader 3: Spirit of patience, kindness, and generosity. ℟

Reader 4: Spirit of faithfulness, gentleness, and self-control. ℟

Leader: God, grant us these fruits of the Holy Spirit so that others may recognize your presence.

All Saints Day and All Souls Day

Paradise, Giovanni di Paolo, 15th century

All Saints and All Souls Days are celebrated on November 1 and 2. On these days we remember those who have died and who are either in heaven or in purgatory.

 PRAYER

God our Father, thank you for the sacraments, which keep us in contact with you and with all other believers, living and dead.

Celebrating the Saints

The Catholic Church has recognized thousands of individuals as saints for their exceptional commitment to faith and charity.

We look to the saints as role models and leaders; we also ask for their help and guidance in our prayers.

Although the Church has named only specific people as saints, in a larger sense all of us who believe in Jesus and live virtuous lives are saints. Together we are united with God in the communion of saints, which we celebrate in the sacraments. The Eucharist especially brings all Christians into a special relationship with God and each other.

When we are united with Christ, we are able to live virtuous lives, just as the saints did. As a result Christians are set apart in three ways: First, Christians are to know that their first priority must be for things of God. Second, Christians are to live lives of holiness and good works. Third, Christians are to be confident that one day they will live with God forever.

Think of a saint whom you admire. Why do you admire that person so much? Did he or she start a religious order? How was that saint's life virtuous?

Saint Elizabeth of Hungary

Saint Dymphna

Saint John Baptist de LaSalle

The Communion of Saints

We celebrate the union of believers on All Saints Day. On this day we remember all of those who have gone before us and are now living in God's presence. On All Souls Day we remember those who have died but whose souls are being prepared in purgatory to live with God forever. They are on the final part of the journey. We remember these people because we are united to all believers through the sacraments.

Saint Cards

This is an example of a saint card that you will be making. Use the example to create a card for your favorite saint. On the front of the card, draw a picture of the saint and write a prayer. Then add something about the accomplishments of that saint on the back of the card.

Remember that we are all in communion with the saints, so make a second card for yourself. Draw your picture on the front of the card. On the back put your name, date of birth, and place of birth. Then write some of the good things you have done to show how you are also becoming a saint. Have you helped others? Have you done any service for your community? Do you pray regularly? Write all of those things and any others you can think of.

PRAYER SERVICE

Leader: Praise be to God, who fills our lives with joy.

All: Praise be to God.

Leader: As we observe All Saints Day and All Souls Day, let us remember that God unites all his followers, living and dead, in the communion of saints.

Reader 1: A reading from the First Letter of John. [1 John 3:1–3]

The Word of the Lord.

All: Thanks be to God.

Leader: Let's spend a few minutes talking to God. On All Saints Day we remember those who are living with God. On All Souls Day we pray for those who are in purgatory.

Reader 2: God, help us to live our faith in service to others so that we may grow closer to you.

Reader 3: God, help us to follow in the footsteps of the saints, who have shown us how to serve the Kingdom of God right here on earth.

Reader 4: God, help us to remember those who are already with you in heaven and help us to pray for those who are still waiting to be with you.

All: God, thank you for the sacraments, especially the sacrament of the Eucharist, which unites us, your followers, in the communion of saints.

Prayers and Practices of Our Faith

KNOWING AND PRAYING OUR FAITH

CELEBRATING OUR FAITH

LIVING OUR FAITH

SONGS OF OUR FAITH

UNDERSTANDING THE WORDS OF OUR FAITH

The Bible and You

God speaks to us in many ways. One way God speaks to us is through the Bible. The Bible is the most important book in Christian life because it is God's message, or revelation. The Bible is the story of God's promise to care for us, especially through his Son, Jesus. At Mass we hear stories from the Bible. We can also read the Bible on our own.

The Bible is not just one book; it is a collection of many books. The writings in the Bible were inspired by the Holy Spirit and written by many different authors using different styles.

The Bible is made up of two parts: The Old Testament and the New Testament. The Old Testament contains 46 books that tell stories about the Jewish people and their faith in God before Jesus was born.

The first five books of the Old Testament— Genesis, Exodus, Leviticus, Numbers, and Deuteronomy—are referred to as the Torah, meaning "instruction" or "law." The central story in the Torah is the Exodus, the liberation of the Hebrew slaves as Moses led them out of Egypt and to the Promised Land. During the journey God gave the Ten Commandments to Moses and the people.

Torah scroll

A beautiful part of the Old Testament is the Book of Psalms. A psalm is a prayer in the form of a poem. Each psalm expresses an aspect, or feature, of the depth of human emotion. Over several centuries 150 psalms were gathered to form the Book of Psalms. They were once sung at the Temple in Jerusalem, and they have been used in the public worship of the Church since its beginning. Catholics also pray the Psalms as part of their private prayer and reflection.

The prophets were called by God to speak for him and urge the Jewish people to be faithful to the Covenant. A large part—18 books—of the Old Testament presents the messages and actions of the prophets.

The New Testament contains 27 books that tell the story of Jesus' life, death, and resurrection and the experience of the early Christians. For Christians the most important books of the New Testament are the four Gospels—Matthew, Mark, Luke, and John. Many of the 27 books are letters written by leaders such as Saint Paul.

How can you find a passage in the Bible? Bible passages are identified by book, chapter, and verse, for example, Ex 3:1–4. The name of the book comes first. It is in abbreviated form. Your Bible's table of contents will help you determine what the abbreviation means. In our example, *Ex* stands for *Exodus*. After the name of the book, there are two numbers. The first one identifies the chapter, which in our example is chapter three; it is followed by a colon. The second number identifies the verse or verses, which in our example are verses one to four.

Locating a Scripture Passage

BOOK   VERSES

Ex 3:1–4

CHAPTER

Prayer and Forms of Prayer

God is always with us. He wants us to talk to him and to listen to him. In prayer we raise our hearts and minds to God. We are able to speak to and listen to God because, through the Holy Spirit, God teaches us how to pray.

We Pray in Many Ways

Because prayer is so important, the Church teaches us to pray often and in many ways. Sometimes we bless or adore God (prayer of blessing and adoration). Other times we ask God for something for ourselves (prayer of petition). Sometimes we pray for others (prayer of intercession). We also thank God in prayer (prayer of thanksgiving). Finally, we can also praise God (prayer of praise). We can pray silently or aloud. We can pray alone or with others. Praying with others is called communal prayer.

We Meditate and Contemplate

One way to pray is to meditate. To meditate is to think about God. We try to keep our attention and focus on God. In meditation we may use Scripture, prayer books, or icons, which are religious images, to help us concentrate and to spark our imagination.

Another way to pray is to contemplate. This means that we rest quietly in God's presence.

We Get Ready to Pray

We live in a very busy, noisy, and fast-paced world. Sometimes, because of this, we have difficulty concentrating. In order to meditate or reflect, we need to prepare ourselves.

We can get ready for meditation by resting our bodies in a comfortable position. Sitting with our backs straight and both feet on the floor is one comfortable position. We can close our eyes, fold our hands comfortably in front of us, and silently take a deep breath and then let it out slowly. We can establish a rhythm by slowly counting to three while breathing in and slowly counting to three while breathing out. Concentrating on our breathing helps us to quiet our thoughts.

We Avoid Distractions

If we become distracted by thinking about something, such as the day at school or a sports event, we can just go back to thinking about our breathing.

After a little practice we will be able to avoid distractions, pray with our imagination, and spend time with God or Jesus in our hearts.

Prayers to Take to Heart

We can pray with any words that come to mind. Sometimes, when we find that choosing our own words is difficult, we can use traditional prayers. Likewise, when we pray aloud with others, we rely on traditional prayers to unite our minds, hearts, and voices. Memorizing traditional prayers such as the following can be very helpful. When we memorize prayers, we take them to heart, meaning that we not only learn the words but also try to understand and live them.

Lord's Prayer

Our Father, who art in heaven,
hallowed be thy name;
thy kingdom come,
thy will be done
on earth as it is in heaven.
Give us this day our daily bread,
and forgive us our trespasses,
as we forgive those who trespass against us;
and lead us not into temptation,
but deliver us from evil.
Amen.

Hail Mary

Hail Mary, full of grace,
the Lord is with you.
Blessed are you among women,
and blessed is the fruit of your womb, Jesus.
Holy Mary, Mother of God,
pray for us sinners,
now and at the hour of our death.
Amen.

Morning Offering

My God, I offer you my prayers,
works, joys and sufferings of this day
in union with the holy sacrifice of the Mass throughout the world.
I offer them for all the intentions of your Son's Sacred Heart,
for the salvation of souls, reparation for sin,
and the reunion of Christians.
Amen.

Prayer Before Meals

Bless us, O Lord, and these your gifts
which we are about to receive from your goodness.
Through Christ our Lord.
Amen.

Prayer After Meals

We give you thanks
for all your gifts,
almighty God,
living and reigning
now and for ever.
Amen.

Act of Contrition

My God,
I am sorry for my sins with all my heart.
In choosing to do wrong
and failing to do good,
I have sinned against you
whom I should love above all things.
I firmly intend, with your help,
to do penance,
to sin no more,
and to avoid whatever leads me to sin.
Our Savior Jesus Christ
suffered and died for us.
In his name, my God, have mercy.

Apostles' Creed

I believe in God,
the Father almighty,
Creator of heaven and earth,
and in Jesus Christ, his only Son, our Lord,
who was conceived by the Holy Spirit,
born of the Virgin Mary,
suffered under Pontius Pilate,
was crucified, died and was buried;
he descended into hell;
on the third day he rose again from the dead;
he ascended into heaven,
and is seated at the right hand of God the Father almighty;
from there he will come to judge the living and the dead.

I believe in the Holy Spirit,
the holy catholic Church,
the communion of saints,
the forgiveness of sins,
the resurrection of the body,
and life everlasting. Amen.

Nicene Creed

I believe in one God,
the Father almighty,
maker of heaven and earth,
of all things visible and invisible.

I believe in one Lord Jesus Christ,
the Only Begotten Son of God,
born of the Father before all ages.
God from God, Light from Light,
true God from true God,
begotten, not made, consubstantial with the Father;
through him all things were made.
For us men and for our salvation
he came down from heaven,
and by the Holy Spirit was incarnate of the Virgin Mary,
and became man.

For our sake he was crucified under Pontius Pilate,
he suffered death and was buried,
and rose again on the third day
in accordance with the Scriptures.
He ascended into heaven
and is seated at the right hand of the Father.
He will come again in glory
to judge the living and the dead
and his kingdom will have no end.

I believe in the Holy Spirit, the Lord, the giver of life,
who proceeds from the Father and the Son,
who with the Father and the Son is adored and glorified,
who has spoken through the prophets.

I believe in one, holy, catholic and apostolic Church.
I confess one Baptism for the forgiveness of sins
and I look forward to the resurrection of the dead
and the life of the world to come. Amen.

Act of Faith

O my God, I firmly believe that you are one God in three divine Persons, Father, Son, and Holy Spirit. I believe that your divine Son became man and died for our sins, and that he will come to judge the living and the dead. I believe these and all the truths which the holy Catholic Church teaches, because you have revealed them, who can neither deceive nor be deceived.
Amen.

Act of Hope

O my God, relying on your infinite mercy and promises, I hope to obtain pardon of my sins, the help of your grace, and life everlasting, through the merits of Jesus Christ, my Lord and Redeemer.
Amen.

Act of Love

O my God, I love you above all things with my whole heart and soul, because you are all good and worthy of all my love. I love my neighbor as myself for the love of you. I forgive all who have injured me and I ask pardon of those whom I have injured.
Amen.

Hail, Holy Queen

Hail, holy Queen, Mother of mercy,
hail, our life, our sweetness, and our hope.
To you we cry, the children of Eve;
to you we send up our sighs,
mourning and weeping in this land of exile.
Turn, then, most gracious advocate,
your eyes of mercy toward us;
lead us home at last
and show us the blessed fruit of your womb, Jesus:
O clement, O loving, O sweet Virgin Mary.

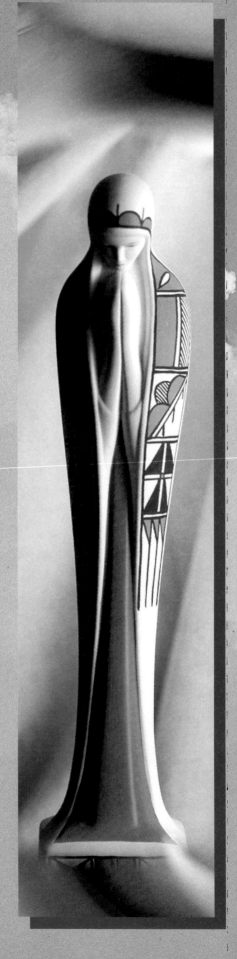

Prayer to the Holy Spirit

Come, Holy Spirit, fill the hearts of your faithful.
And kindle in them the fire of your love.
Send forth your Spirit and they shall be created.
And you will renew the face of the earth.

Lord,
by the light of the Holy Spirit
you have taught the hearts of your faithful.
In the same Spirit
help us to relish what is right
and always rejoice in your consolation.
We ask this through Christ our Lord.
Amen.

Prayer for Vocations

God, in Baptism you called me by name
and made me a member of your people,
    the Church.
Help all your people to know their vocation
    in life,
and to respond by living a life of holiness.
For your greater glory and for the service
    of your people,
raise up dedicated and generous leaders
who will serve as sisters, priests,
brothers, deacons, and lay ministers.

Send your Spirit to guide and strengthen me
that I may serve your people
following the example of your Son, Jesus Christ,
in whose name I offer this prayer.
Amen.

The Rosary

The Rosary helps us to pray to Jesus through Mary. When we pray the Rosary, we think about the special events, or mysteries, in the lives of Jesus and Mary.

The Rosary is made up of a string of beads and a crucifix. We hold the crucifix in our hands as we pray the Sign of the Cross. Then we pray the Apostles' Creed.

Next to the crucifix, there is a single bead, followed by a set of three beads and another single bead. We pray the Lord's Prayer as we hold the first single bead and a Hail Mary at each bead in the set of three that follows. Then we pray the Glory Be to the Father. On the next single bead we think about the first mystery and pray the Lord's Prayer.

There are five sets of ten beads; each set is called a decade. We pray a Hail Mary on each bead of a decade as we reflect on a particular mystery in the lives of Jesus and Mary. The Glory Be to the Father is prayed at the end of each set. Between sets is a single bead on which we think about one of the mysteries and pray the Lord's Prayer.

We end by holding the crucifix in our hands as we pray the Sign of the Cross.

Praying the Rosary

10. Think about the fourth mystery. Pray the Lord's Prayer.

9. Pray ten Hail Marys and one Glory Be to the Father.

11. Pray ten Hail Marys and one Glory Be to the Father.

8. Think about the third mystery. Pray the Lord's Prayer.

12. Think about the fifth mystery. Pray the Lord's Prayer.

7. Pray ten Hail Marys and one Glory Be to the Father.

6. Think about the second mystery. Pray the Lord's Prayer.

5. Pray ten Hail Marys and one Glory Be to the Father.

4. Think about the first mystery. Pray the Lord's Prayer.

13. Pray ten Hail Marys and one Glory Be to the Father.

3. Pray three Hail Marys and one Glory Be to the Father.

2. Pray the Lord's Prayer.

14. Pray the Sign of the Cross.

1. Pray the Sign of the Cross and the Apostles' Creed.

Mysteries of the Rosary

The Church has used three sets of mysteries for many centuries. In 2002 Pope John Paul II proposed a fourth set of mysteries—the Mysteries of Light, or Luminous Mysteries. According to his suggestion, the four sets of mysteries might be prayed on the following days: the Joyful Mysteries on Monday and Saturday, the Sorrowful Mysteries on Tuesday and Friday, the Glorious Mysteries on Wednesday and Sunday, and the Luminous Mysteries on Thursday.

The Joyful Mysteries

1. **The Annunciation**

   Mary learns that she has been chosen to be the mother of Jesus.

2. **The Visitation**

   Mary visits Elizabeth, who tells her that she will always be remembered.

3. **The Nativity**

   Jesus is born in a stable in Bethlehem.

4. **The Presentation**

   Mary and Joseph take the infant Jesus to the Temple to present him to God.

5. **The Finding of Jesus in the Temple**

   Jesus is found in the Temple discussing his faith with the teachers.

The Mysteries of Light

1. **The Baptism of Jesus in the River Jordan**

   God proclaims that Jesus is his beloved Son.

2. **The Wedding Feast at Cana**

   At Mary's request, Jesus performs his first miracle.

3. **The Proclamation of the Kingdom of God**

   Jesus calls all to conversion and service to the Kingdom.

4. **The Transfiguration of Jesus**

   Jesus is revealed in glory to Peter, James, and John.

5. **The Institution of the Eucharist**

   Jesus offers his Body and Blood at the Last Supper.

The Sorrowful Mysteries

1. The Agony in the Garden

Jesus prays in the Garden of Gethsemane on the night before he dies.

2. The Scourging at the Pillar

Jesus is lashed with whips.

3. The Crowning With Thorns

Jesus is mocked and crowned with thorns.

4. The Carrying of the Cross

Jesus carries the cross that will be used to crucify him.

5. The Crucifixion

Jesus is nailed to the cross and dies.

The Glorious Mysteries

1. The Resurrection

God the Father raises Jesus from the dead.

2. The Ascension

Jesus returns to his Father in heaven.

3. The Coming of the Holy Spirit

The Holy Spirit comes to bring new life to the disciples.

4. The Assumption of Mary

At the end of her life on earth, Mary is taken body and soul into heaven.

5. The Coronation of Mary

Mary is crowned as Queen of Heaven and Earth.

Stations of the Cross

The 14 Stations of the Cross represent events from Jesus' Passion and Death. At each station we use our senses and our imagination to reflect prayerfully upon Jesus' suffering, Death, and Resurrection.

1. **Jesus Is Condemned to Death.**
   Pontius Pilate condemns Jesus to death.

2. **Jesus Takes Up His Cross.**
   Jesus willingly accepts and patiently bears his cross.

3. **Jesus Falls the First Time.**
   Weakened by torments and by loss of blood, Jesus falls beneath his cross.

4. **Jesus Meets His Sorrowful Mother.**
   Jesus meets his mother, Mary, who is filled with grief.

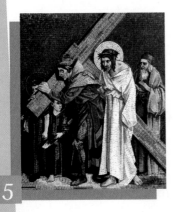

5. **Simon of Cyrene Helps Jesus Carry the Cross.**
   Soldiers force Simon of Cyrene to carry the cross.

6. **Veronica Wipes the Face of Jesus.**
   Veronica steps through the crowd to wipe the face of Jesus.

7. Jesus Falls a Second Time.
Jesus falls beneath the weight of the cross a second time.

8. Jesus Meets the Women of Jerusalem.
Jesus tells the women to weep not for him but for themselves and for their children.

9. Jesus Falls the Third Time.
Weakened almost to the point of death, Jesus falls a third time.

10. Jesus Is Stripped of His Garments.
The soldiers strip Jesus of his garments, treating him as a common criminal.

11. Jesus Is Nailed to the Cross.
Jesus' hands and feet are nailed to the cross.

12. Jesus Dies on the Cross.
After suffering greatly on the cross, Jesus bows his head and dies.

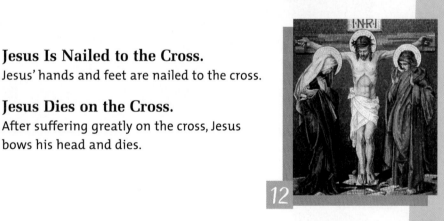

13. Jesus Is Taken Down From the Cross.
The lifeless body of Jesus is tenderly placed in the arms of Mary, his mother.

14. Jesus Is Laid in the Tomb.
Jesus' disciples place his body in the tomb.

The closing prayer—sometimes included as a 15th station—reflects on the Resurrection of Jesus.

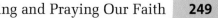

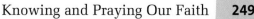

The Seven Sacraments

Jesus touches our lives through the sacraments. Our celebrations of the sacraments are signs of Jesus' presence in our lives and a means for receiving his grace. The Church celebrates seven sacraments, which are divided into three categories.

Sacraments of Initiation

These sacraments lay the foundation of every Christian life.

Baptism

In Baptism we receive new life in Christ. Baptism takes away original sin and gives us a new birth in the Holy Spirit. Its sign is the pouring of water.

Confirmation

Confirmation seals our life of faith in Jesus. Its signs are the laying on of hands on a person's head, most often by a bishop, and the anointing with oil. Like Baptism, Confirmation is received only once.

Eucharist

The Eucharist—the Body and Blood of Christ—nourishes our life of faith. Its signs are bread and wine.

Sacraments of Healing

These sacraments celebrate the healing power of Jesus.

Penance

Through Penance we receive God's forgiveness. Forgiveness requires being sorry for our sins. In Penance we receive Jesus' healing grace through absolution by the priest. The signs of this sacrament are our confession of sins and the words of absolution.

Anointing of the Sick

This sacrament unites a sick person's suffering with that of Jesus and brings forgiveness of sins. Oil, a symbol of strength, is the sign of this sacrament. A person is anointed with oil and receives the laying on of hands from a priest.

Sacraments at the Service of Communion

These sacraments help members serve the community.

Matrimony

In Matrimony a baptized man and woman are united with each other as a sign of the unity between Jesus and his Church. Matrimony requires the consent of the couple, as expressed in the marriage promises. The couple and their wedding rings are the signs of this sacrament.

Holy Orders

In Holy Orders men are ordained as priests, deacons, or bishops. Priests serve as spiritual leaders of their communities, and deacons serve to remind us of our baptismal call to help others. Bishops carry on the teachings of the apostles. The signs of this sacrament are the laying on of hands and the anointing with oil by the bishop.

Celebrating the Lord's Day

Sunday is the day on which we celebrate the Resurrection of Jesus. Sunday is the Lord's Day. We gather for Mass, rest from work, and perform works of mercy. People all over the world gather at God's eucharistic table as brothers and sisters.

The Order of Mass

The Mass is the high point of the Christian life, and it always follows a set order.

Introductory Rites—preparing to celebrate the Eucharist

Entrance Chant

We gather as a community and praise God in song.

Greeting

We pray the Sign of the Cross. The priest welcomes us.

Penitential Act

We remember our sins and ask God for mercy.

Gloria

We praise God in song.

Collect

We ask God to hear our prayers.

Liturgy of the Word—hearing God's plan of salvation

First Reading

We listen to God's Word, usually from the Old Testament.

Responsorial Psalm

We respond to God's Word
in song.

Second Reading

We listen to God's Word from
the New Testament.

Gospel Acclamation

We sing "Alleluia!" to praise
God for the Good News.
During Lent, we use a different
acclamation.

Gospel Reading

We stand and listen to the
Gospel of the Lord.

Homily

The priest or the deacon
explains God's Word.

Profession of Faith

We proclaim our faith through
the Nicene Creed.

Prayer of the Faithful

We pray for our needs and the needs of others.

Liturgy of the Eucharist—celebrating Christ's presence in the Eucharist

Presentation and Preparation of the Gifts

We bring gifts of bread and wine to the altar.

Prayer over the Offerings

The priest prays that God will accept our sacrifice.

Eucharistic Prayer

This prayer of thanksgiving is the center and high point of the entire celebration.

- **Preface**—We give thanks and praise to God.
- **Holy, Holy, Holy**—We sing an acclamation of praise.
- **Consecration**—The bread and wine become the Body and Blood of Jesus Christ.
- **The Mystery of Faith**—We proclaim the mystery of our faith.
- **Amen**—We affirm the words and actions of the Eucharistic Prayer.

Communion Rite—receiving the Body and Blood of Jesus Christ

The Lord's Prayer

We pray the Our Father.

Sign of Peace

We offer one another Christ's peace.

Lamb of God

We pray for forgiveness, mercy, and peace.

Communion

We receive the Body and Blood of Jesus Christ.

Prayer after Communion

We pray that the Eucharist will strengthen us to live as Jesus did.

Concluding Rites—going forth to glorify the Lord by our lives

Final Blessing

We receive God's blessing.

Dismissal

We go in peace, glorifying the Lord by our lives.

Holy Days of Obligation

The Holy Days of Obligation are the days other than Sundays on which we celebrate the great things God has done for us through Jesus and the saints. On Holy Days of Obligation, Catholics attend Mass.

Six Holy Days of Obligation are celebrated in the United States.

January 1—Mary, Mother of God
Fortieth day after Easter—Ascension
August 15—Assumption of the Blessed Virgin Mary
November 1—All Saints
December 8—Immaculate Conception
December 25—Nativity of Our Lord Jesus Christ

Assumption of the Virgin, Paolo Veronese

The Birth of Christ, detail, Emil Nolde

Precepts of the Church

The Precepts of the Church describe the minimum effort we must make in prayer and in living a moral life. All Catholics are called to move beyond the minimum by growing in love of God and love of neighbor. The Precepts are as follows:

1. attendance at Mass on Sundays and Holy Days of Obligation
2. confession of sin at least once a year
3. reception of Holy Communion at least once a year during the Easter season
4. observance of the days of fast and abstinence
5. providing for the needs of the Church

An Examination of Conscience

An examination of conscience is the act of looking prayerfully into our hearts to ask how we have hurt our relationships with God and other people through our thoughts, words, and actions. We reflect on the Ten Commandments and the teachings of the Church. The questions below help us in our examination of conscience.

My Relationship With God

What steps am I taking to help me grow closer to God and to others? Do I turn to God often during the day, especially when I am tempted?

Do I participate at Mass with attention and devotion on Sundays and holy days? Do I pray often and read the Bible?

Do I use God's name and the names of Jesus, Mary, and the saints with love and reverence?

My Relationships With Family, Friends, and Neighbors

Have I set a bad example through my words or actions? Do I treat others fairly? Do I spread stories that hurt other people?

Am I loving of those in my family? Am I respectful of my neighbors, my friends, and those in authority?

Do I show respect for my body and for the bodies of others? Do I keep away from forms of entertainment that do not respect God's gift of sexuality?

Have I taken or damaged anything that did not belong to me? Have I cheated, copied homework, or lied?

Do I quarrel with others just so I can get my own way? Do I insult others to try to make them think they are less than I am? Do I hold grudges and try to hurt people who I think have hurt me?

How to Make a Good Confession

An examination of conscience is an important part of preparing for the Sacrament of Penance. The Sacrament of Penance includes the following steps:

1. The priest greets us, and we pray the Sign of the Cross. He invites us to trust in God. He may read God's Word with us.

2. We confess our sins. The priest may help and counsel us.

3. The priest gives us a penance to perform. Penance is an act of kindness or prayers to pray, or both.

4. The priest asks us to express our sorrow, usually by reciting the Act of Contrition.

5. We receive absolution. The priest says, "I absolve you from your sins in the name of the Father, and of the Son, and of the Holy Spirit." We respond, "Amen."

6. The priest dismisses us by saying, "Go in peace." We go forth to perform the act of penance he has given us.

The Ten Commandments

As believers in Jesus Christ, we are called to a new life and are asked to make moral choices that keep us united with God. With the help and grace of the Holy Spirit, we can choose ways to act to keep us close to God, to help other people, and to be witnesses to Jesus.

The Ten Commandments guide us in making choices that help us to live as God wants us to live. The first three commandments tell us how to love God; the other seven tell us how to love our neighbor.

1. I am the Lord your God: you shall not have strange gods before me.
2. You shall not take the name of the Lord your God in vain.
3. Remember to keep holy the Lord's Day.
4. Honor your father and your mother.
5. You shall not kill.
6. You shall not commit adultery.
7. You shall not steal.
8. You shall not bear false witness against your neighbor.
9. You shall not covet your neighbor's wife.
10. You shall not covet your neighbor's goods.

The Great Commandment

The Ten Commandments are fulfilled in Jesus' Great Commandment: "You shall love God with all your heart, with all your soul, with all your mind, and with all your strength. You shall love your neighbor as yourself."

adapted from Mark 12:30–31

The New Commandment

Before his death on the cross, Jesus gave his disciples a new commandment: "Love one another. As I have loved you, so you also should love one another" (John 13:34).

The Beatitudes

The Beatitudes are the teachings of Jesus in the Sermon on the Mount (Matthew 5:1–10). Jesus teaches us that if we live according to the Beatitudes, we will live a happy Christian life. The Beatitudes fulfill God's promises made to Abraham and his descendants and describe the rewards that will be ours as loyal followers of Christ.

Blessed are the poor in spirit,
  for theirs is the kingdom of heaven.

Blessed are they who mourn,
  for they will be comforted.

Blessed are the meek,
  for they will inherit the land.

Blessed are they who hunger and
    thirst for righteousness,
  for they will be satisfied.

Blessed are the merciful,
  for they will be shown mercy.

Blessed are the clean in heart,
  for they will see God.

Blessed are the peacemakers,
  for they will be called children
    of God.

Blessed are they who are
    persecuted for the sake
    of righteousness,
  for theirs is the kingdom of heaven.

Making Good Choices

Our conscience is the inner voice that helps us to know the law God has placed in our hearts. Our conscience helps us to judge the moral qualities of our own actions. It guides us to do good and avoid evil.

The Holy Spirit can help us to form a good conscience. We form our conscience by studying the teachings of the Church and following the guidance of our parents and pastoral leaders.

God has given every human being freedom of choice. This does not mean that we have the right to do whatever we please. We can live in true freedom if we cooperate with the Holy Spirit, who gives us the virtue of prudence. This virtue helps us to recognize what is good in every situation and to make correct choices. The Holy Spirit gives us the gifts of wisdom and understanding to help us make the right choices in life in relationship to God and others. The gift of counsel helps us to reflect on making correct choices in life.

The Ten Commandments help us to make moral choices that are pleasing to God. We have the grace of the sacraments, the teachings of the Church, and the good example of saints and fellow Christians to help us make good choices.

Making moral choices involves the following steps:

1. Ask the Holy Spirit for help.

2. Think about God's law and the teachings of the Church.

3. Think about what will happen as a result of your choice. Ask yourself, will the consequences be pleasing to God? Will my choice hurt someone else?

4. Seek advice from someone you respect and remember that Jesus is with you.

5. Ask yourself how your choice will affect your relationships with God and others.

Making moral choices takes into consideration the object of the choice, our intention in making the choice, and the circumstances in which the choice is made. It is never right to make an evil choice in the hope of gaining something good.

Virtues

Virtues are gifts from God that lead us to live in a close relationship with him. Virtues are like habits. They need to be practiced; they can be lost if they are neglected. The three most important virtues are called *theological* virtues because they come from God and lead to God. The *cardinal* virtues are human virtues, acquired by education and good actions. *Cardinal* comes from *cardo,* the Latin word for *hinge,* meaning "that on which other things depend."

Theological Virtues

faith   hope   charity

Cardinal Virtues

prudence   justice   fortitude   temperance

Gifts of the Holy Spirit

The Holy Spirit makes it possible for us to do what God asks of us by giving us these many gifts.

wisdom	understanding	counsel
fortitude	knowledge	piety	fear of the Lord

Fruits of the Holy Spirit

The Fruits of the Holy Spirit are signs of the Holy Spirit's action in our lives.

love	joy	peace
patience	kindness	generosity
faithfulness	gentleness	self-control

Church tradition also includes **goodness, modesty,** and **chastity** as Fruits of the Holy Spirit.

Works of Mercy

The Corporal and Spiritual Works of Mercy are actions we can perform that extend God's compassion and mercy to those in need.

Corporal Works of Mercy

The Corporal Works of Mercy are these kind acts by which we help our neighbors with their material and physical needs.

feed the hungry	shelter the homeless
clothe the naked	visit the sick and imprisoned
bury the dead	give alms to the poor

Can Fire in the Park, Beauford Delaney

Spiritual Works of Mercy

The Spiritual Works of Mercy are acts of compassion, as listed below, by which we help our neighbors with their emotional and spiritual needs.

instruct	advise	console
comfort	forgive	bear wrongs patiently

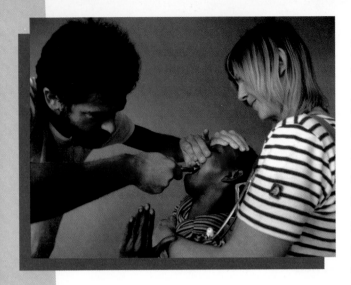

Showing Our Love for the World

In the story of the Good Samaritan (Luke 10:29–37), Jesus makes clear our responsibility to care for those in need. The Catholic Church teaches this responsibility in the following themes of Catholic Social Teaching.

Life and Dignity of the Human Person

All human life is sacred, and all people must be respected and valued over material goods. We are called to ask whether our actions as a society respect or threaten the life and dignity of the human person.

Call to Family, Community, and Participation

Participation in family and community is central to our faith and to a healthy society. Families must be supported so that people can participate in society, build a community spirit, and promote the well-being of all, especially the poor and vulnerable.

Rights and Responsibilities

Every person has a right to life as well as a right to those things required for human decency. As Catholics, we have a responsibility to protect these basic human rights in order to achieve a healthy society.

Option for the Poor and Vulnerable

In our world many people are very rich while at the same time many are extremely poor. As Catholics, we are called to pay special attention to the needs of the poor by defending and promoting their dignity and by meeting their immediate material needs.

The Dignity of Work and the Rights of Workers

The basic rights of workers must be respected: the right to productive work, fair wages, and private property; and the right to organize, join unions, and pursue economic opportunity. Catholics believe that the economy is meant to serve people and that work is not merely a way to make a living but an important way in which we participate in God's creation.

Solidarity

Because God is our Father, we are all brothers and sisters with the responsibility to care for one another. Solidarity is the attitude that leads Christians to share spiritual and material goods. Solidarity unites rich and poor, weak and strong, and helps to create a society that recognizes that we all depend upon one another.

Care for God's Creation

God is the creator of all people and all things, and he wants us to enjoy his creation. The responsibility to care for all God has made is a requirement of our faith.

Song of Love

Chorus

Thank you Je - sus for help - ing me to

see. Thank you God for the

heart you've giv - en me.

Thank you Spir - it for com - ing to me,

and for show - ing me how to sing

your song of love.

(to Verse 1)

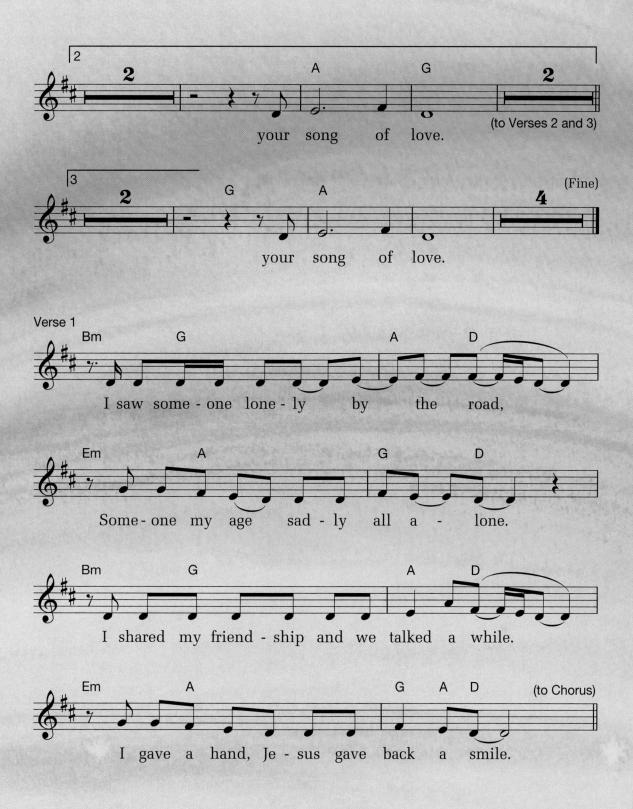

Song of Love *(continued)*

Verse 2

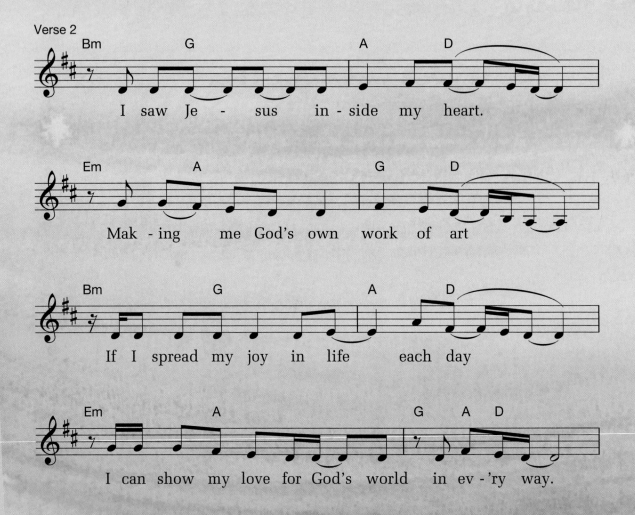

I saw Je - sus in - side my heart.

Mak - ing me God's own work of art

If I spread my joy in life each day

I can show my love for God's world in ev - 'ry way.

Verse 3

I saw Je - sus in friends and fam - i - ly

By my side, shar - ing and sup - port - ing me.

I found my heart had room for ev - 'ry - one.

Thank you Spir - it for what you have be - gun.

(to Chorus)

Lord, You Have the Words

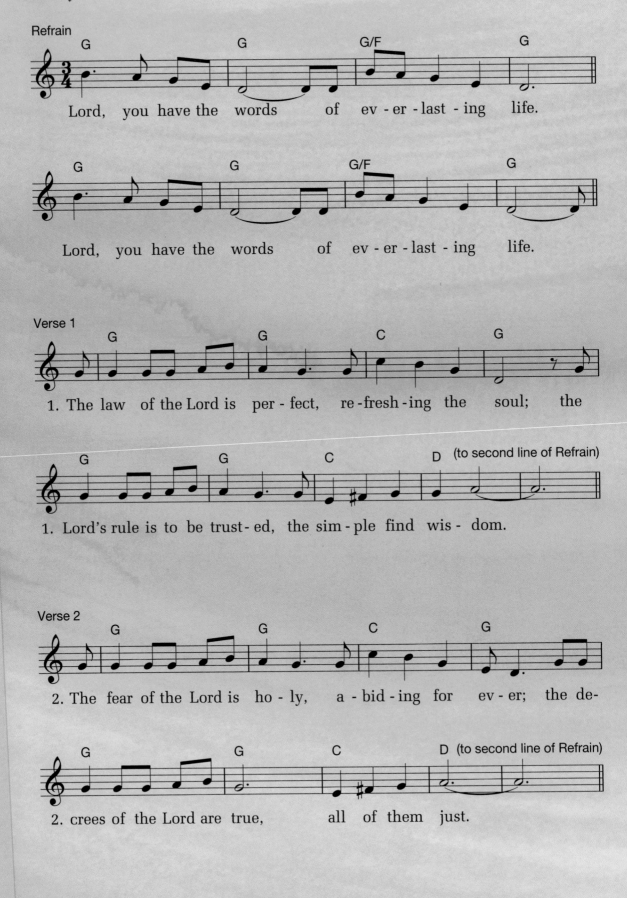

Refrain

Lord, you have the words of ev - er - last - ing life.

Lord, you have the words of ev - er - last - ing life.

Verse 1

1. The law of the Lord is per - fect, re - fresh - ing the soul; the

(to second line of Refrain)

1. Lord's rule is to be trust - ed, the sim - ple find wis - dom.

Verse 2

2. The fear of the Lord is ho - ly, a - bid - ing for ev - er; the de-

(to second line of Refrain)

2. crees of the Lord are true, all of them just.

Verse 3

3. The pre-cepts of the Lord are right, they glad-den the heart, the com-

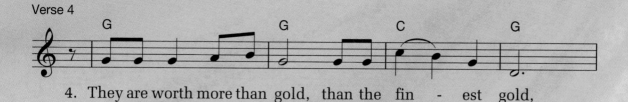

3. mand of the Lord is clear, giv-ing light to the eye.

Verse 4

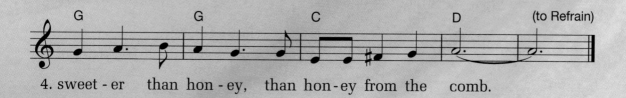

4. They are worth more than gold, than the fin - est gold,

4. sweet - er than hon - ey, than hon-ey from the comb.

If (Si)

English Refrain

If to-day you hear the voice of God, har-den not your heart.

(to Coda last time)

If to-day you hear the voice of God, har-den not your heart.

Verses

1. To the ti - ny wind and the voice of the hur-ri-cane, O-pen up my heart.
2. To the strang-er's need, to the need of my fam-i- ly, O-pen up my heart.

(to English Refrain)

1. To the child at play or the cry of a-noth-er's pain, O-pen up my heart.
2. To the law's firm rule, to the pro-phets who call to me, O-pen up my heart.

Coda (if singing English only; not on the CD)

heart. Har-den not your heart.

Spanish
Refrain

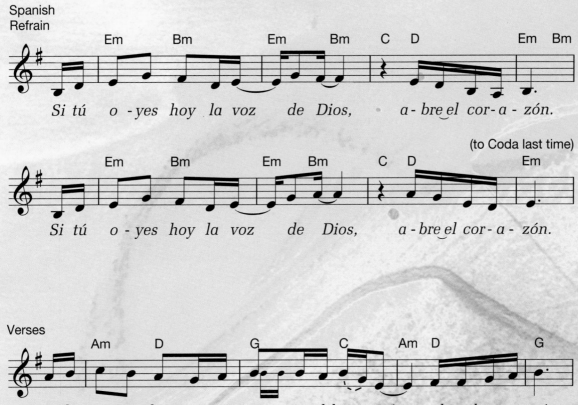

Si tú o-yes hoy la voz de Dios, a-bre el cor-a-zón.

(to Coda last time)

Si tú o-yes hoy la voz de Dios, a-bre el cor-a-zón.

Verses

3. A la tier-na bri-sa a-si co-mo al hu-ra-cán, a-bre el cor-a-zón.
4. Al des-co-no-ci-do y los llan-tos de mi ho-gar, a-bre el cor-a-zón.

(to Spanish Refrain)

3. A la dul-ce voz de a-quel ni-ño que jue-ga, a-bre el cor-a-zón.
4. A la du-ra ley, al pro-fe-ta que me in-vi-ta, a-bre el cor-a-zón.

Coda (if singing Spanish only)

zón. a-bre el cor-a-zón.

I Say "Yes," Lord/Digo "Sí," Señor

Verses

1.   To the God who can-not die: I say "Yes," my Lord.
2. Like that of Job un-ceas-ing-ly: *Di-go "Sí," Se-ñor.*

1. (Echo)   To the One who hears me cry: I say
2. (Echo) Like that of Ma - ri - a whole heart-ed - ly: *Di - go*

1. "Yes," my Lord. (Echo)   To the God of the op-pressed:
2. *"Sí," Se-ñor.* (Echo)   Like that of Da-vid in a song:

1. _____ I say "Yes," my Lord. (Echo)   To the
2. _____ *Di - go "Sí," Se - ñor.* (Echo)   Like Is - ra-

1. God of all jus - tice: I say "Yes," my Lord. (Echo)
2. el, for you I long: *Di - go "Sí," Se - ñor.* (Echo)

Refrain

G	D7	D7

1. I say "Yes," my Lord, in all the good times, through
2. *Di - go "Sí," Se - ñor, en tiem - pos mal - os, en*

G	G	D7

1. all the bad times, I say "Yes," my Lord, to
2. *tiem - pos bue - nos, Di - go "Sí," Se - ñor, a*

D7	G

1. ev - 'ry word you speak.
2. *to - do lo que ha - blas.*

Sí, Señor!
Yes, my Lord!

Shepherd Me, O God

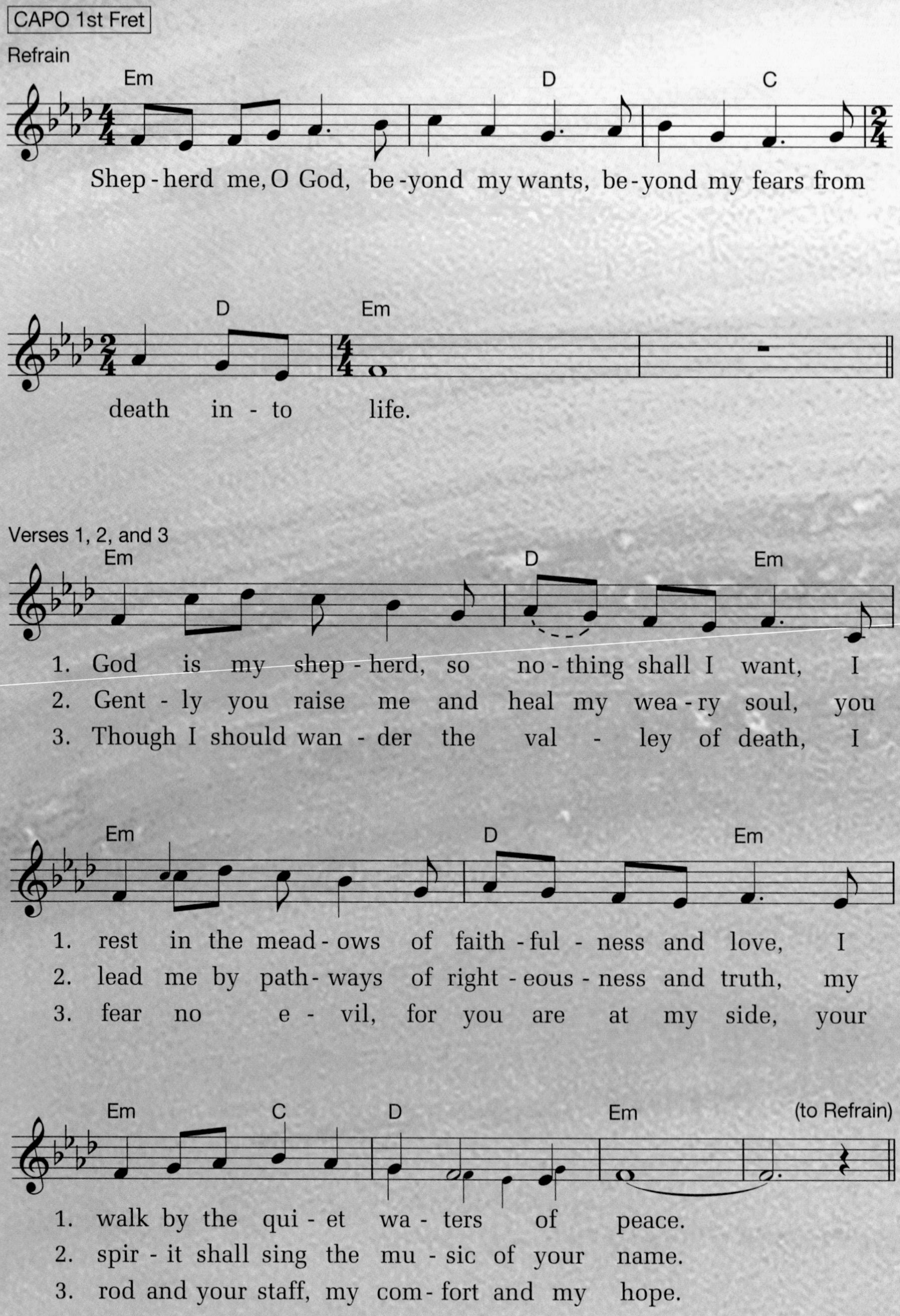

CAPO 1st Fret
Refrain
Em D C
Shep - herd me, O God, be - yond my wants, be - yond my fears from
D Em
death in - to life.
Verses 1, 2, and 3
Em D Em
1. God is my shep - herd, so no - thing shall I want, I
2. Gent - ly you raise me and heal my wea - ry soul, you
3. Though I should wan - der the val - ley of death, I
Em D Em
1. rest in the mead - ows of faith - ful - ness and love, I
2. lead me by path - ways of right - eous - ness and truth, my
3. fear no e - vil, for you are at my side, your
Em C D Em (to Refrain)
1. walk by the qui - et wa - ters of peace.
2. spir - it shall sing the mu - sic of your name.
3. rod and your staff, my com - fort and my hope.

We Are Marching

1. We are march - ing in the light of God, we are
2. We are sing - ing in the light of God, we are

1. march - ing in the light of God.   We are
2. sing - ing in the light of God.   We are

1. march - ing in the light of God, we are
2. sing - ing in the light of God, we are

1. march - ing in the light of God,   we are
2. sing - ing in the light of God,   we are

1. march - ing,   Oo   We   are
2. sing - ing,   Oo   We   are

1. march - ing in the light of God,   we are
2. sing - ing in the light of God,   we are

1. march - ing,   Oo   We   are
2. sing - ing,   Oo   We   are

1. march - ing in the light of God.
2. sing - ing in the light of God.

Give Your Gifts

CAPO 1st Fret

Verses

1. My friends, there are dif-fer-ent kinds of gifts from the
2. Like parts of one bod-y we are not the same, but to-

1. Spir - it. The Lord gives each one of us a call to share
2. geth - er, for we are the bod-y of Christ to-day

1. ———— if we hear it. We all serve the same
2. ———— and for - ev - er. Some can hear but not

1. Lord in our dif - fer - ent ways,
2. see. Some can see but not hear.

1. and the Fa-ther will help us ev-er-y day.
2. But when we work to - geth - er there's noth-ing to fear.

Lead Me, Guide Me

Verses

D   D   Em   Em

1. I am weak   and I need thy strength and power to
2. I am lost   if you take your hand from me,   I am

G   A7   D   D

1. help   me   o - ver   my   weak - est   hour.   Help me
2. blind   with - out   thy   Light   to   see,   Lord, just

D   Bm   Em   Em

1. through the dark - ness thy face   to   see,
2. al - ways let me thy ser - vant be.

D   A   D   (to Refrain)

1. Lead me, oh   Lord,   lead   me.
2. Lead me, oh   Lord,   lead   me.

Open Your Ears, O Faithful People

Verses

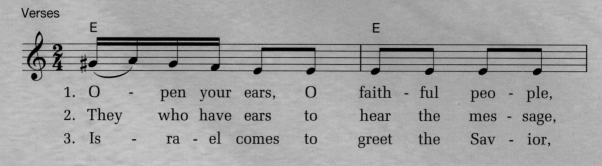

1. O - pen your ears, O faith - ful peo - ple,
2. They who have ears to hear the mes - sage,
3. Is - ra - el comes to greet the Sav - ior,

1. o - pen your ears and hear God's Word. O - pen your hearts, O
2. they who have ears, now let them hear; they who would learn the
3. Ju - dah is glad to see his day, from east and west the

1. roy - al priest - hood, God has come to you.
2. way of wis - dom, let them hear God's Word.
3. peo - ples trav - el, God will show the way.

Refrain

Am / Am / Am / E
God has spok-en to the peo-ple, hal-le-lu-jah!

E / E / E / Am
God has spok-en words of wis-dom, hal-le-lu-jah!

Am / Am / Am / E
To-rah o-ra, To-rah o-ra, hal-le-lu-jah!

E / E / E / Am
To-rah o-ra, To-rah o-ra, hal-le-lu-jah!

Blessing Prayer

Refrain

May the road rise up to meet you. May the

wind be al - ways with you. May the sun -shine warm you

al - ways. 'til we meet a - gain.

Verses

1. May the rain fall soft - ly on you.
2. Christ be - fore you, Christ be - hind you.
3. Christ to shield you, Christ be with you.

(to Refrain)

1. May the hand of God up - hold you.
2. Christ be - neath you, Christ a - bove you.
3. Christ be with you now and al - ways.

Glossary

A

Abba an informal word for *father* in Aramaic, the language Jesus spoke. It is like "dad" in English. When Jesus spoke to God the Father, he called him "Abba." [Abba]

absolution the forgiveness we receive from God through the priest in the Sacrament of Penance [absolución]

Advent the four weeks before Christmas. It is a time of joyful preparation for the celebration of the Incarnation, Jesus' birth as our savior, and a time for anticipating the coming of Jesus Christ at the end of time. [Adviento]

Advocate Jesus' name for the Holy Spirit. The Holy Spirit comforts us, speaks for us in difficult times, and makes Jesus present to us. [Abogado]

All Saints Day November 1, the day on which the Church honors all who have died and now live with God as saints in heaven. This group includes those who are officially recognized as saints as well as many unknown people who after a good life have died and now live in God's presence. The feast celebrates our union with those who have gone before us and points to our ultimate goal of union with God. [Día de Todos los Santos]

All Souls Day November 2, the day on which the Church prays that all friends of God who have died may rest in peace. Those who have died may need purification in purgatory before living fully in God's presence. Our prayers and good works can help them in this process. Along with All Saints Day, this feast reminds us that all who love God, living and dead, are united in living communion with Jesus Christ and with one another. [Día de los Fieles Difuntos]

altar the table in the church on which the priest celebrates Mass, where the sacrifice of Christ on the cross is made present in the Sacrament of the Eucharist. The altar represents two aspects of the mystery of the Eucharist. It is the place where Jesus Christ offers himself for our sins and where he gives us himself as our food for eternal life. [altar]

ambo a raised stand from which a person reads the Word of God during Mass [ambón]

ambo

Amen the Hebrew word used to conclude Jewish and Christian prayers. It means "This is true," "So be it," or "Let it be so." We end prayers with "Amen" to show that we mean what we have just said. [Amén]

angel a spiritual creature who worships God in heaven. Angels serve God as messengers. They tell us of his plans for our salvation. [ángel]

Annunciation the announcement to Mary by the angel Gabriel that God had chosen her to be the mother of Jesus. When Mary agreed, the Son of God became human in her. The feast of the Annunciation is celebrated on March 25, nine months before Christmas. [Anunciación]

Anointing of the Sick one of the seven sacraments. In this sacrament a sick person has holy oil applied and receives the strength, peace, and courage to overcome the difficulties associated with illness. Through this sacrament, Jesus brings the sick person spiritual healing and forgiveness of sins. If it is God's will, healing of the body is given as well. [Unción de los enfermos]

apostle one of twelve special men who accompanied Jesus in his ministry and were witnesses to the Resurrection. *Apostle* means "one sent." These were the people sent to preach the gospel to the whole world. [apóstol]

Apostles' Creed a statement of Christian belief that developed out of a creed used in Baptism in Rome. The Apostles' Creed lists simple statements of belief in God the Father, Jesus Christ the Son, and the Holy Spirit. The profession of faith used in Baptism today is based on it. [Credo de los Apóstoles]

apostolic one of the four Marks of the Church. The Church is apostolic because it continues to hand on the teaching of the apostles through their successors, the bishops, in union with the successor of Saint Peter, the pope. [apostólico]

Ark of the Covenant a portable box in which were placed the tablets of the Ten Commandments. The Ark was the most important item in the shrine that was carried through the desert and then placed in the holiest part of the Temple in Jerusalem. Two angels are depicted on the cover of the Ark of the Covenant. The wings of the angels curve upward, representing the place where God came close to Israel and revealed his will. [Arca de la Alianza]

Ark of the Covenant

Ascension the entry of Jesus into God's presence in heaven. In the Acts of the Apostles, it is written that Jesus, after his Resurrection, spent 40 days on earth, instructing his followers. He then returned to his Father in heaven. [Ascensión]

Ash Wednesday the first day of Lent, on which we receive ashes on our foreheads. The ashes remind us to prepare for Easter by repenting and showing sorrow for the choices we make that offend God and hurt our relationships with others. [Miércoles de Ceniza]

assembly the people of God when they are gathered together to worship him [asamblea]

Assumption Mary's being taken, body and soul, into heaven. Mary had a special relationship with her son, Jesus, from the very beginning, when she conceived him. Catholics believe that because of this relationship, she enjoys a special participation in Jesus' Resurrection and has been taken into heaven where she now lives with him. We celebrate this event in the Feast of the Assumption on August 15. [Asunción]

Assumption

B

Baptism the first of the seven sacraments. Baptism frees us from original sin and is necessary for salvation. Baptism gives us new life in Jesus Christ through the Holy Spirit. The celebration of Baptism consists of immersing a person in water while declaring that the person is baptized in the name of the Father, the Son, and the Holy Spirit. [Bautismo]

Beatitudes the teachings of Jesus in the Sermon on the Mount in Matthew's Gospel. The Beatitudes are eight ways of living the Christian life. They are the fulfillment of the commandments given to Moses. These teachings present the way to true happiness. [Bienaventuranzas]

Bible the collection of books containing the truths of God's revelation to us. These writings were inspired by the Holy Spirit and written by human beings. The Bible is made up of the 46 books in the Old Testament and 27 books in the New Testament. [Biblia]

bishop a man who has received the fullness of Holy Orders. As a successor to the original apostles, he takes care of the Church and is a principal teacher in it. [obispo]

Blessed Sacrament the bread that has been consecrated by the priest at Mass. It is kept in the tabernacle to adore and to be taken to the sick. [Santísimo Sacramento]

blessing a prayer that calls for God's power and care upon some person, place, thing, or special activity [bendición]

Body and Blood of Christ the bread and wine that has been consecrated by the priest at Mass. In the Sacrament of the Eucharist, all of the risen Lord Jesus Christ—body, blood, soul, and divinity—is present in the form of bread and wine. [Cuerpo y Sangre de Cristo]

C

canonize to declare that a Christian who has died is already in heaven and may be looked to as a model of Christian life who may intercede for us as a saint [canonizar]

capital sins those sins that can lead us to more serious sin. They are pride, covetousness, envy, anger, gluttony, lust, and sloth. [pecados capitales]

catechumen a person being formed in the Christian life through instruction and by the example of the parish community. Through conversion and maturity of faith, a catechumen is preparing to be welcomed into the Church at Easter through the Sacraments of Baptism, Confirmation, and Eucharist. [catecúmeno]

catholic one of the four Marks of the Church. The Church is catholic because Jesus is fully present in it and because Jesus has given the Church to the whole world. It is universal. [católico]

character a permanent spiritual mark. Character shows that a person has a new relationship with Jesus and a special standing in the Church. Baptism, Confirmation, and Holy Orders each have a specific permanent character and therefore may be received only once. [carácter]

charity a virtue given to us by God that helps us love God above all things and our neighbor as ourselves [caridad]

chastity the integration of our physical sexuality with our spiritual nature. Chastity helps us to be completely human, able to give to others our whole life and love. All people, married and single, are called to practice chastity. [castidad]

Chosen People the people set apart by God to have a special relationship with him. God first formed a Chosen People when he made a covenant, or solemn agreement, with Abraham. He reaffirmed the covenant through Moses at Mount Sinai. The covenant is fulfilled in Jesus and his Church. [pueblo elegido]

chrism a perfumed oil, consecrated by a bishop, that is used in the Sacraments of Baptism, Confirmation, and Holy Orders. Anointing with chrism signifies the call of the baptized to the threefold ministry of priest, prophet, and king. [crisma]

Christ a title that means "anointed with oil." It is from a Greek word that means the same thing as the Hebrew word *Messiah*, or "anointed." It is the name given to Jesus after the Resurrection when he completed his mission as priest, prophet, and king. [Cristo]

Christian the name given to all those who have been anointed through the gift of the Holy Spirit in Baptism and have become followers of Jesus Christ [cristiano]

Christmas the feast of the birth of Jesus (December 25) [Navidad]

Church the people of God throughout the whole world, or diocese (the local Church), or the assembly of those called together to worship God. The Church is one, holy, catholic, and apostolic. [Iglesia]

clergy those men who are set apart as sacred ministers to serve the Church through Holy Orders [clero]

commandment a standard, or rule, for living as God wants us to live. Jesus summarized all of the commandments into two: love God and love your neighbor. [mandamiento]

communal prayer the worship of God together with others. The Liturgy of the Hours and the Mass are the main forms of communal prayer. [oración común]

Communion of Saints the unity of all, dead or living, who have been saved in Jesus Christ. The Communion of Saints is based on our one faith, and it is nourished by our participation in the Eucharist. [Comunión de los Santos]

confession the act of telling our sins to a priest in the Sacrament of Penance. The sacrament itself is sometimes referred to as "Confession." [confesión]

Confirmation the sacrament that completes the grace we receive in Baptism. It seals, or confirms, this grace through the seven gifts of the Holy Spirit that we receive as part of Confirmation. This sacrament also makes us better able to participate in the worship and apostolic life of the Church. [Confirmación]

conscience the inner voice that helps each of us to judge the morality of our own actions. It guides us to follow God's law by doing good and avoiding evil. [consciencia]

consecration the making of a thing or a person to be special to God through a prayer or blessing. At Mass, the words of the priest are a consecration of the bread and wine that become the Body and Blood of Christ. People or objects set apart for God in a special way are also consecrated. For example, churches and altars are consecrated for use in liturgy, and bishops are consecrated as they receive the fullness of the Sacrament of Holy Orders. [consagración]

contrition the sorrow we feel when we know that we have sinned, followed by the decision not to sin again. Perfect contrition arises from a love that loves God above all else. Imperfect contrition arises on other motives. Contrition is the most important act of the penitent preparing to celebrate the Sacrament of Penance. [contrición]

conversion a radical or serious change of the whole life, away from sin and toward God. The call to change of heart is a key part of the preaching of Jesus. Throughout our entire lives, Jesus calls us to change in this way. [conversión]

Corporal Works of Mercy kind acts by which we help our neighbors with their everyday, material needs. Corporal Works of Mercy include feeding the hungry, finding a home for the homeless, clothing the naked, visiting the sick and those in prison, giving alms to the poor, and burying the dead. [obras corporales de misericordia]

counsel one of the seven Gifts of the Holy Spirit. Counsel helps us to make correct choices in life through reflection, discernment, consulting, and the advising of others. [consejo]

covenant a solemn agreement between people or between people and God. God made covenants with humanity through agreements with Noah, Abraham, and Moses. These covenants offered salvation. God's new and final covenant was established through Jesus' life, death, and resurrection. *Testament* is another word for *covenant*. [alianza]

creation God's act of making everything that exists outside himself. Creation is everything that exists. God said that all of creation is good. [creación]

Creator God, who made everything that is and whom we can come to know through everything he created [Creador]

creed a brief summary of what people believe. The word *creed* comes from the Latin *credo*, "I believe." The Nicene Creed is the most important summary of Christian beliefs. [credo]

crozier the staff carried by a bishop that shows he cares for us in the same way that a shepherd cares for his sheep. It also reminds us that he represents Jesus, the Good Shepherd. [báculo]

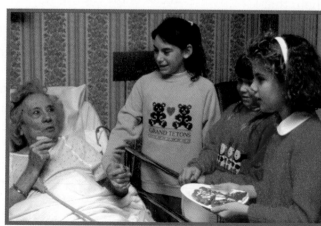

Corporal Works of Mercy

Understanding the Words of Our Faith   **293**

culture the collection of knowledge, belief, and behavior of a particular group of people. Culture expresses the shared attitudes, values, goals, and social practices of the group. In order to take root in a culture, the gospel must be adapted to live in that culture as well as transform it. [cultura]

D

deacon a man ordained through the Sacrament of Holy Orders to the ministry of service in the Church. Deacons help the bishop and priests by serving in the various charitable practices of the Church. They also help by proclaiming the gospel and preaching and by assisting at the Liturgy of the Eucharist. Deacons also celebrate Baptism, bless marriages, and preside at funerals. [diácono]

detraction the act of talking about the faults and sins of another person to someone who has no reason to hear this and cannot help the person. Detraction damages the reputation of another person without any intent to help that person. [detracción]

diocese the members of the Church in a particular area, united in faith and the sacraments, and gathered under the leadership of a bishop [diócesis]

disciple a person who has accepted Jesus' message and tries to live as he did, sharing his mission, his suffering, and his joys [discípulo]

discrimination the act of mistreating other people because of how they look or act, or just because they are different [discriminación]

Divine Providence the guidance of God over all he has created. Divine Providence exercises care for all creation and guides it toward its final perfection. [Divina Providencia]

Doctor of the Church, Teresa of Ávila

Doctor of the Church a man or a woman recognized as a model teacher of the Christian faith [Doctor de la Iglesia]

domestic church the Christian home, which is a community of grace and prayer and a school of human virtues and Christian charity [Iglesia doméstica]

E

Easter the celebration of the bodily raising of Jesus Christ from the dead. Easter is the festival of our redemption and the central Christian feast, the one from which other feasts arise. [Pascua]

Easter Vigil the celebration of the first and greatest Christian feast, the Resurrection of Jesus. It occurs on the first Saturday evening after the first full moon of spring. During this night watch before Easter morning, catechumens are baptized, confirmed, and receive Eucharist for the first time. [Vigilia Pascual]

Eastern Catholic Churches a group of churches that developed in the East (in countries such as Lebanon) that are in union with the Roman Catholic Church but have their own liturgical, theological, and administrative traditions. They show the truly catholic nature of the Church, which takes root in many cultures. [Iglesias Católicas Orientales]

Emmanuel a Hebrew name from the Old Testament that means "God with us." In Matthew's Gospel, Jesus is called Emmanuel. [Emanuel]

encyclical a letter written by the pope and sent to the whole Church and sometimes to the whole world. It expresses Church teaching on some specific and important issue. [encíclica]

envy a feeling of resentment or sadness because someone has a quality, a talent, or a possession that we want. Envy is one of the seven capital sins, and it is contrary to the tenth commandment. [envidia]

Epiphany the day on which we celebrate the visit of the Magi to Jesus after his birth. This is the day that Jesus was revealed as the savior of the whole world. [Epifanía]

Epiphany

epistle a letter written by Saint Paul or another leader to a group of Christians in the early Church. Twenty-one of the twenty-seven books of the New Testament are epistles. The second reading at Mass on Sundays and holy days is always from one of these books. [epístola]

eternal life the never-ending life after death with God, granted to those who die as God's friends, with the grace of God alive in them [vida eterna]

Eucharist the sacrament in which we give thanks to God for giving us the consecrated bread and wine that become the Body and Blood of Jesus Christ. This sacrament brings us into union with Jesus Christ and his saving Death and Resurrection. [Eucaristía]

Eucharistic liturgy the public worship, held by the Church, in which the consecrated bread and wine become the Body and Blood of Jesus Christ. The Sunday celebration of the Eucharistic liturgy is at the heart of Church life. [liturgia eucarística]

evangelization the proclamation, or declaring by word and by example, of the good news about the salvation we have received in Jesus Christ. Evangelization is a sharing of our faith with others, both those who do not know Jesus and those who are called to follow Jesus more closely. [evangelización]

examination of conscience the act of prayerfully thinking about what we have said or done in light of what the gospel asks of us. We also think about how our actions may have hurt our relationship with God or others. An examination of conscience is an important part of our preparing to celebrate the Sacrament of Penance. [examen de conciencia]

Understanding the Words of Our Faith   **295**

Exile ordered by King Nebuchadnezzar

Exile the period in the history of Israel between the destruction of Jerusalem in 587 B.C. and the return to Jerusalem in 537 B.C. During this time, many of the Jewish people were forced to live in Babylon, far from home. [exilio]

Exodus God's liberation of the Hebrew people from slavery in Egypt and his leading them to the Promised Land [Éxodo]

F

faith a gift of God that helps us to believe in him. We profess our faith in the creed, celebrate it in the sacraments, live by it through our good conduct of loving God and our neighbor, and express it in prayer. [fe]

fasting limiting the amount we eat for a period of time to express sorrow for sin and to make ourselves more aware of God's action in our lives. Adults 18 years old and older fast on Ash Wednesday and Good Friday. The practice is also encouraged as a private devotion at other times of penitence. [ayuno]

fear of the Lord one of the seven Gifts of the Holy Spirit. This gift leads us to a sense of wonder and awe in the presence of God because we recognize his greatness. [temor de Dios]

forgiveness the willingness to be kind to those who have hurt us but have then shown that they are sorry. In the Lord's Prayer, we pray that since God will forgive us for our sins, we are able to forgive those who have hurt us. [perdón]

fortitude the strength to choose to do the right thing even when that is difficult. Fortitude is one of the four central human virtues, called the Cardinal Virtues, by which we guide our conduct through faith and the use of reason. It is also one of the Gifts of the Holy Spirit. [fortaleza]

free will the ability to choose to do good because God has made us like him. Our free will is what makes us truly human. Our exercise of free will to do good increases our freedom. Using free will to choose sin makes us slaves to sin. [libre albedrío]

Fruits of the Holy Spirit the demonstration through our actions that God is alive in us. Saint Paul lists the Fruits of the Holy Spirit in Galatians 5:22–23: love, joy, peace, patience, kindness, generosity, faithfulness, gentleness, and self-control. Church tradition has added goodness, modesty, and chastity to make a total of twelve. [frutos del Espíritu Santo]

G

genuflect to show respect in church by touching a knee to the ground, especially before the Blessed Sacrament in the tabernacle [genuflexión, hacer la]

Gifts of the Holy Spirit the permanent willingness, given to us by the Holy Spirit, that makes it possible for us to do what God asks of us. The Gifts of the Holy Spirit are drawn from Isaiah 11:1–3. They include wisdom, understanding, counsel, fortitude, knowledge, and fear of the Lord. Church tradition has added piety to make a total of seven. [dones del Espíritu Santo]

God the Father, Son, and Holy Spirit, one God in three distinct persons. God created all that exists. He is the source of salvation, and he is truth and love. [Dios]

godparent a witness to Baptism who assumes the responsibility for helping the baptized person along the road of Christian life [padrino/madrina de Bautismo]

Gospel the good news of God's mercy and love that we experience by hearing the story of Jesus' life, Death, and Resurrection. The story is passed on in the teaching ministry of the Church as the source of all truth and right living. It is presented to us in four books in the New Testament, the Gospels of Matthew, Mark, Luke, and John. [Evangelio]

grace the gift of God, given to us without our meriting it. Sanctifying grace fills us with his life and makes it possible for us always to be his friends. Grace is the Holy Spirit alive in us, helping us to live our Christian vocation. Grace helps us to live as God wants us to. [gracia]

Great Commandment Jesus' commandment that we are to love both God and our neighbor as we love ourselves. Jesus tells us that this commandment sums up everything taught in the Old Testament. [El Mandamiento Mayor]

H

heaven union with God the Father, Son, and Holy Spirit in life and love that never ends. Heaven is a state of complete happiness and the goal of the deepest wishes of the human heart. [cielo]

Hebrews the descendants of Abraham, Isaac, and Jacob, who were enslaved in Egypt. God helped Moses lead these people out of slavery. [hebreos]

hell a life of total separation from God forever. In his infinite love for us, God can only desire our salvation. Hell is the result of the free choice of a person to reject God's love and forgiveness once and for all. [infierno]

holiness the fullness of Christian life and love. All people are called to holiness, which is made possible by cooperating with God's grace to do his will. As we do God's will, we are transformed more and more into the image of the Son, Jesus Christ. [santidad]

holy one of the four Marks of the Church. It is the kind of life we live when we share in the life of God, who is all holiness. The Church is holy because it is united with Jesus Christ. [santa]

Holy Communion the consecrated bread and wine that we receive at Mass, which is the Body and Blood of Jesus Christ. It brings us into union with Jesus and his saving Death and Resurrection. [Sagrada Comunión]

Holy Days of Obligation the principal feast days, other than Sundays, of the Church. On Holy Days of Obligation, we celebrate the great things that God has done for us through Jesus and the Saints. Catholics are obliged to participate in the Eucharist on these days, just as we are on Sundays. [días de precepto]

Holy Family the family of Jesus as he grew up in Nazareth. It included Jesus; his mother, Mary; and his foster father, Joseph. [Sagrada Familia]

Holy of Holies the holiest part of the Temple in Jerusalem. The high priest entered this part of the Temple once a year to address God and ask God's forgiveness for the sins of the people. [Sanctasanctórum]

Holy Orders the sacrament through which the mission given by Jesus to his apostles continues in the Church. The sacrament has three degrees: deacon, priest, and bishop. Through the laying on of hands in the Sacrament of Holy Orders, men receive a permanent sacramental mark that calls them to minister to the Church. [sacramento del Orden]

Holy Spirit the third person of the Trinity, who is sent to us as our helper and, through Baptism and Confirmation, fills us with God's life. Together with the Father and the Son, the Holy Spirit brings the divine plan of salvation to completion. [Espíritu Santo]

holy water water that has been blessed and is used as a sacramental to remind us of our Baptism [agua bendita]

Holy Week the celebration of the events surrounding Jesus' suffering, Death, Resurrection, and establishment of the Eucharist. Holy Week commemorates Jesus' triumphal entry into Jerusalem on Palm Sunday, the gift of himself in the Eucharist on Holy Thursday, his Death on Good Friday, and his Resurrection at the Easter Vigil on Holy Saturday. [Semana Santa]

Holy Week celebration

Homily the explanation by a bishop, a priest, or a deacon of the Word of God in the liturgy. The Homily relates the Word of God to our life as Christians today. [homilía]

hope the confidence that God will always be with us, make us happy now and forever, and help us to live so that we will be with him forever [esperanza]

I

Incarnation the Son of God, Jesus, being born as a full human being in order to save us. The Son of God, the second person of the Trinity, is both true God and true man. [Encarnación]

indulgence a lessening of the punishment due for sins that have been forgiven. Indulgences move us toward our final purification, when we will live with God forever. [indulgencia]

inspired influenced by the Holy Spirit. The human authors of Scripture were influenced by the Holy Spirit. The creative inspiration of the Holy Spirit makes sure that the Scripture is taught according to the truth God wants us to know for our salvation. [inspirado]

interpretation explanation of the words of Scripture, combining human knowledge and the teaching office of the Church under the guidance of the Holy Spirit [interpretación]

Islam the third great religion, along with Judaism and Christianity, professing belief in one God. *Islam* means "submission" to that one God. [islamismo]

Israelites the descendants of Abraham, Isaac, and Jacob. God changed Jacob's name to "Israel," and Jacob's twelve sons and their children became the leaders of the twelve tribes of Israel. (*See* Hebrews.) [israelitas]

J

Jesus the Son of God, who was born of the Virgin Mary and who died and was raised from the dead for our salvation. He returned to God and will come again to judge the living and the dead. His name means "God saves." [Jesús]

Jews the name given to the Hebrew people, from the time of the exile to the present. The name means "the people who live in the territory of Judah," the area of Palestine surrounding Jerusalem. [judíos]

Joseph the foster father of Jesus, who was engaged to Mary when the angel announced that Mary would have a child through the power of the Holy Spirit. In the Old Testament, Joseph was the son of Jacob who was sold into slavery in Egypt by his brothers and then saved them from starvation when famine came. [José]

Judaism the name of the religion of Jesus and all of the people of Israel after they returned from exile in Babylon and built the second Temple [judaísmo]

justice the virtue that guides us to give to God and others what is due them. Justice is one of the four central human virtues, called the Cardinal Virtues, by which we guide our Christian life. [justicia]

K

Kingdom of God God's rule over us, announced in the gospel and present in the Eucharist. The beginning of the Kingdom here on earth is mysteriously present in the Church, and it will come in completeness at the end of time. [reino de Dios]

knowledge one of the seven Gifts of the Holy Spirit. This gift helps us to know what God asks of us and how we should respond. [conocimiento]

L

laity those who have been made members of Christ in Baptism and who participate in the priestly, prophetic, and kingly functions of Christ in his mission to the whole world. The laity is distinct from the clergy, whose members are set apart as ministers to serve the Church. [laicado]

Joseph

Last Supper the last meal Jesus ate with his disciples on the night before he died. At the Last Supper, Jesus took bread and wine, blessed it, and said that it was his Body and Blood. Jesus' Death and Resurrection, which we celebrate in the Eucharist, was anticipated in this meal. [Última Cena]

Last Supper

Lectionary for Mass the official book that contains all of the Scripture readings used in the Liturgy of the Word [Leccionario]

Lent the 40 days before Easter (not counting Sundays) during which we prepare, through prayer, fasting, and giving aid to the poor, to change our lives and live the gospel more completely [Cuaresma]

liturgical year the celebrations throughout the year of all of the mysteries of Jesus' birth, life, Death, and Resurrection. The celebration of Easter is at the heart of the liturgical year. The other feasts celebrated throughout the year make up the basic rhythm of the Christian's life of prayer. [Año Litúrgico]

liturgy the public prayer of the Church that celebrates the wonderful things God has done for us in Jesus Christ, our high priest, and the way in which he continues the work of our salvation. The original meaning of *liturgy* was "a public work or service done for the people." [liturgia]

Liturgy of the Eucharist the part of the Mass in which the bread and wine are consecrated and become the Body and Blood of Jesus Christ, which we then receive in Holy Communion [Liturgia de la Eucaristía]

Liturgy of the Hours the public prayer of the Church to praise God and sanctify the day. It includes an office of readings before sunrise, morning prayer at dawn, evening prayer at sunset, and prayer before going to bed. The chanting of psalms makes up a major portion of each of these services. [Liturgia de las Horas]

Liturgy of the Word the part of the Mass in which we listen to God's Word from the Bible and consider what it means for us today. The Liturgy of the Word can also be a public prayer and proclamation of God's Word that is not followed by the Liturgy of the Eucharist. [Liturgia de la Palabra]

M

Magisterium the living, teaching office of the Church. This office, through the bishops and with the pope, provides an authentic interpretation of the Word of God. It ensures faithfulness to the teaching of the Apostles in matters of faith and morals. [Magisterio]

Magnificat Mary's song of praise to God for the great things he has done for her and planned for us through Jesus [Magníficat]

Marks of the Church the four most important aspects of the Church found in the Nicene Creed. According to the Nicene Creed, the Church is one, holy, catholic, and apostolic. [atributos de la Iglesia]

Mary the mother of Jesus. She is called blessed and "full of grace" because God chose her to be the mother of the Son of God, the second person of the Trinity. [María]

Mary, Queen of Heaven

Mass the most important sacramental celebration of the Church, established by Jesus at the Last Supper as a remembrance of his Death and Resurrection. At Mass we listen to God's Word from the Bible and receive Jesus Christ in the consecrated bread and wine that is his Body and Blood. [misa]

Matrimony a solemn agreement between a woman and a man to be partners for life, both for their own good and for bringing up children. Marriage is a sacrament when the agreement is properly made between baptized Christians. [Matrimonio]

memorial a remembrance of events that have taken place in the past. We recall these events because they continue to affect us because they are part of God's saving plan for us. Every time we remember these events, we make God's saving action present. [conmemoración]

Messiah a title that means "anointed with oil." It is from a Hebrew word that means the same thing as the Greek word *Christ*. "Messiah" is the title that was given to Jesus after the Resurrection, when he had completed his mission as priest, prophet, and king. [Mesías]

ministry service or work done for others. Ministry is done by bishops, priests, and deacons, who are all ordained to ministry in the celebration of the sacraments. All those baptized are called to a variety of ministries in the liturgy and in service to the needs of others. [ministerio]

miracle signs or acts of wonder that cannot be explained by natural causes but are works of God. In the Gospels, Jesus works miracles as a sign that the Kingdom of God is present in his ministry. [milagro]

mission the work of Jesus Christ that is continued in the Church through the Holy Spirit. The mission of the Church is to proclaim salvation in Jesus' life, Death, and Resurrection. [misión]

Understanding the Words of Our Faith   **301**

monastery a place where men or women live out their solemn vows of poverty, chastity, and obedience in a stable community life. They spend their days in public prayer, work, and meditation. [monasterio]

moral choice a choice to do what is right or not do what is wrong. We make moral choices because they are what we believe God wants and because we have the freedom to choose what is right and avoid what is wrong. [opción moral]

moral law a rule for living that has been established by God and people in authority who are concerned about the good of all. Moral laws are based on God's direction to us to do what is right and avoid what is wrong. Some moral laws are "written" in the human heart and can be known through our own reasoning. Other moral laws have been revealed to us by God in the Old Testament and in the new law given by Jesus. [ley moral]

mortal sin a serious decision to turn away from God by doing something that we know is wrong. For a sin to be mortal it must be a very serious offense, the person must know how serious the sin is, and freely chose to do it anyway. [pecado mortal]

Muslim a follower of the religion of Islam. *Muslim* means "one who submits to God." [musulmán]

mystery a religious truth that we can know only through God's revelation and that we cannot fully understand. Our faith is a mystery that we profess in the creed and celebrate in the liturgy and sacraments. [misterio]

Mystical Body of Christ the members of the Church formed into a spiritual body and bound together by the life communicated by Jesus Christ through the sacraments. Christ is the center and source of the life of this body. In it, we are all are united. Each member of the body receives from Christ gifts fitting for him or her. [Cuerpo Místico de Cristo]

N

natural law the moral law that is "written" in the human heart. We can know natural law through our own reason because the Creator has placed the knowledge of it in our hearts. It can provide the solid foundation on which we can make rules to guide our choices in life. Natural law forms the basis of our fundamental rights and duties and is the foundation for the work of the Holy Spirit in guiding our moral choices. [ley natural]

New Testament the 27 books of the second part of the Bible which tell of the teaching, ministry, and saving events of the life of Jesus. The four Gospels present Jesus' life, Death, and Resurrection. The Acts of the Apostles tells the story of the message of salvation as it spread through the growth of the Church. Various letters instruct us in how to live as followers of Jesus Christ. The Book of Revelation offers encouragement to Christians living through persecution. [Nuevo Testamento]

New Testament

Nicene Creed the summary of Christian beliefs developed by the bishops at the first two councils of the Church, held in A.D. 325 and 381. It is the creed shared by most Christians, in the East and in the West. [Credo Niceno]

O

obedience the act of willingly following what God asks us to do for our salvation. The fourth commandment requires children to obey their parents, and all people are required to obey civil authority when it acts for the good of all. To imitate the obedience of Jesus, members of religious communities make a special vow of obedience. [obediencia]

oil of catechumens the oil blessed by the bishop during Holy Week and used to anoint catechumens. This anointing strengthens them on their path to initiation into the Church. Infants are anointed with this oil right before they are baptized. [óleo de los catecúmenos]

oil of the sick the oil blessed by the bishop during Holy Week and used in the Sacrament of Anointing of the Sick, which brings spiritual and, if it is God's will, physical healing as well [óleo de los enfermos]

Old Testament the first 46 books of the Bible, which tell of God's covenant with the people of Israel and his plan for the salvation of all people. The first five books are known as the Torah. The Old Testament is fulfilled in the New Testament, but God's covenant presented in the Old Testament has permanent value and has never been revoked. [Antiguo Testamento]

one one of the four Marks of the Church. The Church is one because of its source in the one God and because of its founder, Jesus Christ. Jesus, through his Death on the cross, united all to God in one body. Within the unity of the Church, there is great diversity because of the variety of the gifts given to its members. [una]

ordination the rite of the Sacrament of Holy Orders, by which a bishop gives to men, through the laying on of hands, the ability to minister to the Church as bishops, priests, and deacons [ordenación]

original sin the consequence of the disobedience of the first human beings. They disobeyed God and chose to follow their own will rather than God's will. As a result, human beings lost the original blessing God had intended and became subject to sin and death. In Baptism we are restored to life with God through Jesus Christ although we still experience the effects of original sin. [pecado original]

P

Palm Sunday the celebration of Jesus' triumphant entry into Jerusalem on the Sunday before Easter. It begins a week-long commemoration of the saving events of Holy Week. [Domingo de Ramos]

Palm Sunday

parable one of the simple stories that Jesus told to show us what the Kingdom of God is like. Parables present images drawn from everyday life. These images show us the radical choice we make when we respond to the invitation to enter the Kingdom of God. [parábola]

parish a stable community of believers in Jesus Christ who meet regularly in a specific area to worship God under the leadership of a pastor [parroquia]

Paschal Mystery the work of salvation accomplished by Jesus Christ through his Passion, Death, and Resurrection. The Paschal Mystery is celebrated in the liturgy of the Church, and its saving effects are experienced by us in the sacraments. [Misterio Pascual]

Passover the Jewish festival that commemorates the delivery of the Hebrew people from slavery in Egypt. In the Eucharist we celebrate our passover from death to life through Jesus' Death and Resurrection. [Pascua Judía]

Passover plate

pastor a priest who is responsible for the spiritual care of the members of a parish community. It is the job of the pastor to see that the Word of God is preached, the faith is taught, and sacraments are celebrated. [pastor]

penance the turning away from sin with a desire to change our life and more closely live the way God wants us to live.

We express our penance externally by praying, fasting, and helping the poor. This is also the name of the action that the priest asks us take or the prayers that he asks us to pray after he absolves us in the Sacrament of Penance. (*See* Sacrament of Penance.) [penitencia]

Pentecost

Pentecost the 50th day after Jesus was raised from the dead. On this day the Holy Spirit was sent from heaven, and the Church was born. It is also the Jewish feast that celebrated the giving of the Ten Commandments on Mount Sinai 50 days after the Exodus. [Pentecostés]

People of God another name for the Church. In the same way that the people of Israel were God's people through the Covenant he made with them, the Church is a priestly, prophetic, and royal people through the new and eternal Covenant with Jesus Christ. [pueblo de Dios]

personal prayer the kind of prayer that rises up in us in everyday life. We pray with others in the liturgy, but in addition we can listen and respond to God through personal prayer every moment of our lives. [oración personal]

personal sin a sin we choose to commit, whether serious (mortal) or less serious (venial). Although the consequences of original sin leave us with a tendency to sin, God's grace, especially through the sacraments, helps us to choose good over sin. [pecado personal]

petition a request to God asking him to fulfill a need. When we share in God's saving love, we understand that every need is one that we can ask God to help us with through petition. [petición]

piety one of the seven Gifts of the Holy Spirit. It calls us to be faithful in our relationships both with God and with others. Piety helps us to love God and to behave responsibly and with generosity and affection toward others. [piedad]

pope the bishop of Rome, successor of Saint Peter, and leader of the Roman Catholic Church. Because he has the authority to act in the name of Christ, the pope is called the Vicar of Christ. The pope and all of the bishops together make up the living, teaching office of the Church, the Magisterium. [Papa]

praise the expression of our response to God, not only for what he does, but simply because he is. In the Eucharist the whole Church joins with Jesus Christ in expressing praise and thanksgiving to the Father. [alabanza]

prayer the raising of our hearts and minds to God. We are able to speak to and listen to God in prayer because he teaches us how to pray. [oración]

Precepts of the Church those positive requirements that the pastoral authority of the Church has determined are necessary to provide a minimum effort in prayer and the moral life. The Precepts of the Church ensure that all Catholics move beyond the minimum by growing in love of God and love of neighbor. [preceptos de la Iglesia]

presbyter a word that originally meant "an elder or trusted advisor to the bishop." From this word comes the English word *priest*, one of the three degrees of the Sacrament of Holy Orders. All the priests of a diocese under the bishop form the presbyterate. [presbítero]

pride a false image of ourselves that goes beyond what we deserve as God's creation. Pride puts us in competition with God. It is one of the seven capital sins. [soberbia]

priest a man who has accepted God's special call to serve the Church by guiding it and building it up through the ministry of the Word and the celebration of the sacraments [sacerdote]

priesthood all the people of God who have been given a share of the one mission of Christ through the Sacraments of Baptism and Confirmation. The ministerial priesthood, which is made up of those men who have been ordained bishops and priests in Holy Orders, is essentially different from the priesthood of all the faithful because its work is to build up and guide the Church in the name of Christ. [sacerdocio]

Promised Land the land first promised by God to Abraham. It was to this land that God told Moses to lead the Chosen People after they were freed from slavery in Egypt and received the Ten Commandments at Mount Sinai. [Tierra prometida]

prophet one called to speak for God and call the people to be faithful to the covenant. A major section of the Old Testament presents, in eighteen books, the messages and actions of the prophets. [profeta]

the prophet Isaiah

prudence the virtue that directs us toward the good and helps us to choose the correct means to achieve that good. When we act with prudence, we carefully and thoughtfully consider our actions. Prudence is one of the cardinal moral virtues that guide our conscience and influence us to live according to the law of Christ. [prudencia]

psalm a prayer in the form of a poem, written to be sung in public worship. Each psalm expresses an aspect of the depth of human prayer. Over several centuries 150 psalms were assembled into the Book of Psalms in the Old Testament. Psalms were used in worship in the Temple in Jerusalem, and they have been used in the public worship of the Church since its beginning. [salmo]

purgatory a state of final cleansing after death of all of our human imperfections to prepare us to enter into the joy of God's presence in heaven [purgatorio]

R

racism the opinion that race determines human traits and capacities and that a particular race has an inherent, or inborn, superiority. Discrimination based on a person's race is a violation of human dignity and a sin against justice. [racismo]

Real Presence the way in which the risen Jesus Christ is present in the Eucharist under the form of bread and wine. Jesus Christ's presence is called real because in the Eucharist his body and blood, soul and divinity, are wholly and entirely present. [Presencia Real]

reconciliation the renewal of friendship after that friendship has been broken by some action or lack of action. In the Sacrament of Penance, through God's mercy and forgiveness, we are reconciled with God, the Church, and others. [reconciliación]

Redeemer Jesus Christ, whose life, sacrificial Death on the cross, and Resurrection from the dead set us free from the slavery of sin and bring us redemption [Redentor]

redemption our being set free from the slavery of sin through the life, sacrificial Death on the cross, and Resurrection from the dead of Jesus Christ [redención]

reform to put an end to a wrong by introducing a better or changed course of action. The prophets called people to reform their lives by returning to being faithful to their covenant with God. [reformarse]

religious life a state of life recognized by the Church. In the religious life, men and women freely respond to a call to follow Jesus by living the vows of poverty, chastity, and obedience in community with others. [vida religiosa]

repentance our turning away from sin, with a desire to change our lives and live more closely as God wants us to live. We express our penance externally by prayer, fasting, and helping the poor. [arrepentimiento]

Resurrection the bodily raising of Jesus Christ from the dead on the third day after his Death on the cross. The Resurrection is the crowning truth of our faith. [Resurrección]

Revelation God's communication of himself to us through the words and deeds he has used throughout history to show us the mystery of his plan for our salvation. This Revelation reaches its completion in his sending of his Son, Jesus Christ. [revelación]

rite one of the many forms followed in celebrating liturgy in the Church. A rite may differ according to the culture or country where it is celebrated. *Rite* also means the special form for celebrating each sacrament. [rito]

Rosary a prayer in honor of the Blessed Virgin Mary. When we pray the Rosary, we meditate on the mysteries of Jesus Christ's life while praying the Hail Mary on five sets of ten beads and the Lord's Prayer on the beads in between. In the Latin Church, praying the Rosary became a way for ordinary people to reflect on the mysteries of Christ's life. [Rosario]

S

Sabbath the seventh day, when God rested after finishing the work of creation. The third commandment requires us to keep the Sabbath holy. For Christians the Sabbath became Sunday because it was the day Jesus rose from the dead and the new creation in Jesus Christ began. [Sabat]

sacrament one of seven ways through which God's life enters our lives through the work of the Holy Spirit.

oils used in sacraments

Jesus gave us three sacraments that bring us into the Church: Baptism, Confirmation, and the Eucharist. He gave us two sacraments that bring us healing: Penance and Anointing of the Sick. He also gave us two sacraments that help members serve the community: Matrimony and Holy Orders. [sacramento]

Sacrament of Penance the sacrament in which we celebrate God's forgiveness of sin and our reconciliation with God and the Church. Penance includes sorrow for the sins we have committed, confession of sins, absolution by the priest, and doing the penance that shows our willingness to amend our ways. [sacramento de la Penitencia]

sacramental an object, a prayer, or a blessing given by the Church to help us grow in our spiritual life [sacramental]

Sacraments at the Service of Communion the Sacraments of Holy Orders and Matrimony. These two sacraments contribute to the personal salvation of individuals by giving them a way to serve others. [sacramentos al servicio de la comunidad]

Sacraments of Healing the Sacraments of Penance and Anointing of the Sick, by which the Church continues the healing ministry of Jesus for soul and body [sacramentos de curación]

Sacraments of Initiation the sacraments that are the foundation of our Christian life. We are born anew in Baptism, strengthened by Confirmation, and receive in the Eucharist the food of eternal life. By means of these sacraments, we receive an increasing measure of divine life and advance toward the perfection of charity. [sacramentos de iniciación]

sacrifice a ritual offering of animals or produce made to God by the priest in the Temple in Jerusalem. Sacrifice was a sign of the people's adoration of God, giving thanks to God, or asking for his forgiveness. Sacrifice also showed union with God. The great high priest, Christ, accomplished our redemption through the perfect sacrifice of his Death on the cross. [sacrificio]

Sacrifice of the Mass the sacrifice of Jesus on the cross, which is remembered and mysteriously made present in the Eucharist. It is offered in reparation for the sins of the living and the dead and to obtain spiritual or temporal blessings from God. [Sacrificio de la misa]

saint a holy person who has died united with God. The Church has said that this person is now with God forever in heaven. [santo]

salvation the gift, which God alone can give, of forgiveness of sin and the restoration of friendship with him [salvación]

sanctifying grace the gift of God, given to us without our earning it, that unites us with the life of the Trinity and heals our human nature, wounded by sin. Sanctifying grace continues the work of making us holy that began at our Baptism. [gracia santificante]

Savior Jesus, the Son of God, who became human to forgive our sins and restore our friendship with God. *Jesus* means "God saves." [Salvador]

scriptorium the room in a monastery in which books were copied by hand. Often, beautiful art was created on the page to illustrate the story. [scriptorium]

Scriptures the holy writings of Jews and Christians collected in the Old and New Testaments of the Bible [Sagrada Escritura]

seraphim the heavenly beings who worship before the throne of God. One of them purified the lips of Isaiah with a burning coal so that he could speak for God. [serafines]

Sermon on the Mount the words of Jesus, written in Chapters 5 through 7 of the Gospel of Matthew, in which Jesus reveals how he has fulfilled God's law given to Moses. The Sermon on the Mount begins with the eight Beatitudes and includes the Lord's Prayer. [Sermón de la montaña]

Sermon on the Mount

sexism a prejudice or discrimination based on sex, especially discrimination against women. Sexism leads to behaviors and attitudes that foster a view of social roles based only on sex. [sexismo]

sin a deliberate thought, word, deed, or failure to act that offends God and hurts our relationships with other people. Some sin is mortal and needs to be confessed in the Sacrament of Penance. Other sin is venial, or less serious. [pecado]

slander a false statement that harms the reputation of someone and makes other people think bad of that person. Slander is an offense against the eighth commandment. [calumnia]

sloth a carelessness of heart that leads a person to ignore his or her development as a person, especially spiritual development and a relationship with God. Sloth is one of the seven capital sins, and it is contrary to the first commandment. [pereza]

solidarity the attitude of strength and unity that leads to the sharing of spiritual and material goods. Solidarity unites rich and poor, weak and strong, to create a society in which all give what they can and receive what they need. The idea of solidarity is based on the common origin of all humanity. [solidaridad]

Son of God the title revealed by Jesus that indicates his unique relationship to God the Father. The revelation of Jesus' divine sonship is the main dramatic development of the story of Jesus of Nazareth as it unfolds in the Gospels. [Hijo de Dios]

soul the part of us that makes us human and an image of God. Body and soul together form one unique human nature. The soul is responsible for our consciousness and for our freedom. The soul does not die and is reunited with the body in the final resurrection. [alma]

Spiritual Works of Mercy the kind acts through which we help our neighbors meet the needs that are more than material. The Spiritual Works of Mercy include instructing, advising, consoling, comforting, forgiving, and bearing wrongs with patience. [obras espirituales de misericordia]

Stations of the Cross a tool for meditating on the final hours of Jesus' life, from his condemnation by Pilate to his Death and burial. We do this by moving to representations of 14 incidents, each one based on the traditional sites in Jerusalem where these incidents took place. [Estaciones del Vía Crucis]

stewardship the careful and responsible management of something entrusted

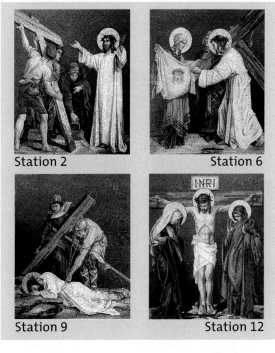

Station 2

Station 6

Station 9

Station 12

to one's care, especially the goods of creation, which are intended for the whole human race. The sixth precept of the Church makes clear our part in this stewardship by requiring us to provide for the material needs of the Church according to our abilities. [administración]

T

tabernacle the container in which the Blessed Sacrament is kept so that Holy Communion can be taken to the sick and the dying. *Tabernacle* is also the name of the tent sanctuary in which the Israelites kept the Ark of the Covenant from the time of the Exodus to the construction of Solomon's temple. [sagrario]

model of tabernacle tent sanctuary, Israel

temperance the cardinal virtue that helps us to control our attraction to pleasure so that our natural desires are kept within proper limits. This moral virtue helps us choose to use created goods in moderation. [templanza]

Temple the house of worship of God, first built by Solomon. The Temple provided a place for the priests to offer sacrifice, to adore and give thanks to God, and to ask for forgiveness. It was destroyed and rebuilt. The second Temple was also destroyed, this time by the Romans in A.D. 70, and was never rebuilt. Part of the outer wall of the Temple mount remains to this day in Jerusalem. [Templo]

temptation an attraction, from outside us or inside us, that can lead us to disobey God's commands. Everyone is tempted, but the Holy Spirit helps us to resist temptation and choose to do good. [tentación]

Ten Commandments the ten rules given by God to Moses on Mount Sinai that sum up God's law and show us what is required to love God and our neighbor. By following the Ten Commandments, the Hebrews accepted their covenant with God. [Diez Mandamientos]

Theological Virtues those virtues given us by God and not by human effort. They are faith, hope, and charity. [virtudes teologales]

Torah the Hebrew word for "instruction" or "law." It is also the name of the first five books of the Old Testament: Genesis, Exodus, Leviticus, Numbers, and Deuteronomy. [Torá]

Torah

transubstantiation the unique change of the bread and wine in the Eucharist into the Body and Blood of the risen Jesus Christ, while retaining its physical form as bread and wine [transubstanciación]

trespasses unlawful acts committed against the property or rights of another person or acts that physically harm a person [ofensas]

Trinity the mystery of the existence of God in three persons, the Father, the Son, and the Holy Spirit. Each person is God, whole and entire. Each is distinct only in the relationship of each to the others. [Trinidad]

U

understanding one of the seven Gifts of the Holy Spirit. This gift helps us make the right choices in life and in our relationships with God and others. [entendimiento]

universal Church the entire Church as it exists throughout the world. The people of every diocese, along with their bishops and the pope, make up the universal Church. [Iglesia universal]

V

venial sin a choice we make that weakens our relationship with God or other people. Venial sin wounds and lessens the divine life in us. If we make no effort to do better, venial sin can lead to more serious sin. Through our participation in the Eucharist, venial sin is forgiven, strengthening our relationship with God and others. [pecado venial]

Trinity

viaticum the Eucharist that a dying person receives. It is spiritual food for the last journey we make as Christians, the journey through death to eternal life. [viático]

Vicar of Christ the title given to the pope who, as the successor of Saint Peter, has the authority to act in Christ's place. A vicar is someone who stands in for and acts for another. [Vicario de Cristo]

virtue an attitude or way of acting that enables us do good [virtud]

Visitation Mary's visit to Elizabeth to share the good news that Mary is to be the mother of Jesus. Elizabeth's greeting of Mary forms part of the Hail Mary. During this visit, Mary sings the Magnificat, her praise of God. [Visitación]

vocation the call each of us has in life to be the person God wants each to be and the way we each serve the Church and the Kingdom of God. Each of us can live out his or her vocation as a layperson, as a member of a religious community, or as a member of the clergy. [vocación]

vow a deliberate and free promise made to God by people who want especially to dedicate their lives to God. The vows give witness now to the kingdom that is to come. [voto]

Vulgate the Latin translation of the Bible by Saint Jerome from the Hebrew and Greek it was originally written in. Most Christians of Saint Jerome's day no longer spoke Hebrew or Greek. The common language, or vulgate, was Latin. [Vulgata]

illumination from a 7th century calfskin Vulgate

W

wisdom one of the seven Gifts of the Holy Spirit. Wisdom helps us to understand the purpose and plan of God and to live in a way that helps to bring about this plan. It begins in wonder and awe at God's greatness. [sabiduría]

Wisdom Literature the Old Testament books of Job, Proverbs, Ecclesiastes, the Song of Songs, Wisdom, and Sirach. The purpose of these books is to give instruction on ways to live and how to understand and cope with the problems of life. [Libros Sapienciales]

witness the passing on to others, by our words and by our actions, the faith that we have been given. Every Christian has the duty to give witness to the good news about Jesus Christ that he or she has come to know. [testimonio]

worship the adoration and honor given to God in public prayer [culto]

Y

Yahweh the name of God in Hebrew, which God told Moses from the burning bush. *Yahweh* means "I am who am" or "I cause to be all that is." [Yavé]

worship

Glosario

A

Abba vocablo familiar que significa "padre" en arameo, idioma que hablaba Jesús. Viene a ser como "papá" en español. Al hablar con Dios Padre, Jesús le decía *Abba*. [Abba]

Abogado nombre dado por Jesús al Espíritu Santo. El Espíritu Santo nos conforta, nos habla en tiempos difíciles y nos manifiesta la presencia de Jesús. [Advocate]

absolución perdón que recibimos de Dios a través del sacerdote en el sacramento de la Penitencia. [absolution]

administración supervisión cuidadosa y responsable de algo que ha sido confiado a nuestro cuidado, en particular los bienes de la creación, que han sido destinados a toda la raza humana. El sexto precepto de la Iglesia deja clara nuestra participación en la administración al exigirnos que suplamos las necesidades materiales de la Iglesia según nuestra capacidad. [stewardship]

Adviento las cuatro semanas antes de la Navidad. Es una época de jubilosa preparación para la celebración de la Encarnación, el nacimiento de Jesús como nuestro salvador, y la espera de la venida de Jesucristo en el fin de los tiempos. [Advent]

agua bendita agua que ha sido bendecida y que se usa como sacramental para recordarnos nuestro Bautismo. [holy water]

alabanza la expresión de nuestra respuesta a Dios no sólo por lo que hace sino por quien es. En la Eucaristía la Iglesia entera se une a Jesucristo para alabar y dar gracias al Padre. [praise]

alianza pacto solemne que hacen las personas entre sí o que hacen las personas con Dios. Dios hizo alianzas con la humanidad mediante los pactos hechos con Noé, Abraham y Moisés. Estas alianzas ofrecían la salvación. La nueva y final alianza de Dios fue pactada mediante la vida, muerte y Resurrección de Jesús. *Testamento* es sinónimo de *alianza*. [covenant]

alma parte de la persona que la hace a la vez humana e imagen de Dios. Juntos, el cuerpo y el alma forman una naturaleza humana única. El alma es responsable de nuestra conciencia y de nuestra libertad. El alma no muere y se reune con el cuerpo en la resurrección final. [soul]

altar mesa que tienen las iglesias en la que el sacerdote celebra la misa. En la misa el sacrificio de Cristo en la cruz se hace presente en el sacramento de la Eucaristía. El altar representa dos aspectos del misterio de la Eucaristía: en primer lugar es el sitio donde Jesucristo se ofrece a sí mismo por nuestros pecados; y, en segundo lugar, es el sitio donde él se nos ofrece como alimento de vida eterna. [altar]

ambón plataforma elevada desde donde una persona lee la Palabra de Dios durante la misa. [ambo]

Amén vocablo hebreo usado al final de las oraciones judías y cristianas que quiere decir "es verdad", "así es", o "así sea". Al terminar nuestras oraciones decimos *Amén* para dar a entender que lo que acabamos de decir es lo que realmente creemos. [Amen]

ángel criatura espiritual que adora a Dios en el cielo. Los ángeles sirven a Dios como mensajeros y nos cuentan los planes que él tiene para nuestra salvación. [angel]

Año Litúrgico las celebraciones en el transcurso del año de todos los misterios del nacimiento, vida, muerte y Resurrección de Jesús. La Pascua es la celebración central del Año Litúrgico. Las otras fiestas celebradas a lo largo del año constituyen el ritmo básico de la vida de oración del cristiano. [liturgical year]

Antiguo Testamento los 46 primeros libros de la Biblia que hablan de la alianza de Dios con el pueblo de Israel y su plan de salvación para todas la humanidad. Los cinco primeros libros se conocen como el Torá. El Antiguo Testamento se cumple en el Nuevo Testamento, pero la alianza de Dios presentada en la escritura del Antiguo Testamento sigue teniendo un valor permanente y nunca ha sido revocada. [Old Testament]

Anunciación anuncio traído a María por el ángel Gabriel de que Dios la había elegido para ser madre de Jesús. Al aceptar María, el Hijo de Dios se hizo hombre dentro de ella. La fiesta de la Anunciación se celebra el 25 de marzo, nueve meses antes de la Navidad. [Annunciation]

apóstol uno de los doce hombres específicos que acompañaron a Jesús en su ministerio y fueron testigos de su Resurrección. *Apóstol* quiere decir "enviado". Los apóstoles fueron los enviados a predicar el Evangelio al mundo entero. [apostle]

apostólica uno de los cuatro atributos de la Iglesia. La Iglesia es apostólica porque sigue transmitiendo las enseñanzas de los apóstoles a través de sus sucesores, los obispos, en unión con el sucesor de San Pedro, el Papa. [apostolic]

Arca de la Alianza caja portátil donde se guardaban las tablas de los Diez Mandamientos. El Arca, el objeto más importante del santuario, fue transportada por todo el desierto y luego colocada en la parte más sagrada del Templo de Jerusalén. Sobre la tapa del Arca de la Alianza se encontraban dos ángeles cuyas alas se curvaban hacia arriba, representando el sitio donde Dios se acercó a Israel y le reveló su voluntad. [Ark of the Covenant]

arrepentimiento el apartarnos del pecado con el deseo de cambiar nuestra vida y acercarnos más a la forma de vida que Dios quiere que vivamos. Expresamos externamente nuestra penitencia mediante la oración, el ayuno y ayudando a los pobres. [repentance]

asamblea pueblo de Dios congregado para rendirle culto. [assembly]

Ascensión entrada de Jesús a la gloria divina junto al Padre. En los Hechos de los Apóstoles se escribe que, después de la Resurrección, Jesús estuvo 40 días en la tierra instruyendo a sus seguidores y luego volvió al cielo junto a su Padre. [Ascension]

Asunción el ascenso de María al cielo en cuerpo y alma. Desde el momento mismo en que María concibió a su Hijo Jesús fue muy especial la relación que hubo entre ellos. Los católicos creen que a raíz de esta relación ella goza de una participación especial en la Resurrección de Jesús y ha sido llevada al cielo, donde ahora vive con él. Este acontecimiento se celebra el 15 de agosto, Día de la Asunción. [Assumption]

atributos de la Iglesia las cuatro características más importantes de la Iglesia que se hallan en el Credo de Nicea. Según este credo la Iglesia es una, santa, católica y apostólica. [Marks of the Church]

ayuno limitar la cantidad de alimento que comemos durante un tiempo determinado, para expresar arrepentimiento por nuestros pecados y hacernos más conscientes de la acción de Dios en nuestra vida. Los adultos, de dieciocho años o más, ayunan el Miércoles de Ceniza y el Viernes Santo. Se fomenta también esta práctica como devoción privada en otras ocasiones de penitencia. [fasting]

B

báculo cayado o vara que lleva el obispo. Al llevar este cayado el obispo muestra que vela por nosotros de la misma forma en que el pastor cuida sus ovejas. También nos recuerda que él representa a Jesús, el Buen Pastor. [crozier]

Bautismo el primero de los siete sacramentos. El Bautismo nos libera del pecado original y es necesario para la salvación. El Bautismo nos da una vida nueva en Jesucristo por medio del Espíritu Santo. La celebración del Bautismo consiste en sumergir en agua a la persona diciendo que es bautizado ". . . en el nombre del Padre, del Hijo y del Espíritu Santo". [Baptism]

bendición oración que invoca el poder y amparo de Dios por una persona, lugar, cosa, o una actividad específica. [blessing]

Biblia la colección de libros que contienen las verdades de la revelación hecha a nosotros por Dios. Estos libros fueron inspirados por el Espíritu Santo y escritos por seres humanos. La Biblia se compone de 46 libros del Antiguo Testamento y 27 del Nuevo Testamento. [Bible]

Bienaventuranzas enseñanzas de Jesús en el Sermón de la montaña del Evangelio de San Mateo. Las Bienaventuranzas son ocho formas de llevar una vida cristiana y son la culminación de los mandamientos dados a través de Moisés. Estas enseñanzas nos presentan el camino a la verdadera felicidad. [Beatitudes]

C

calumnia afirmación falsa que daña la reputación de una persona y hace que otros piensen mal de esa persona. La calumnia va en contra del octavo mandamiento. [slander]

canonizar declaración hecha por la Iglesia de que un cristiano difunto está ya en el cielo y puede servir de ejemplo de vida cristiana e interceder por nosotros como santo. [canonize]

carácter señal espiritual permanente. El carácter muestra que la persona ha entablado una nueva relación con Jesús y ha llegado a un nivel especial en la Iglesia. El Bautismo, la Confirmación y el sacramento del Orden imprimen un carácter permanente; y, por eso, sólo pueden ser recibidos una sola vez. [character]

caridad virtud que nos ha dado Dios. La caridad nos permite amar a Dios sobre todas las cosas y al prójimo como a nosotros mismos. [charity]

castidad la integración de nuestra sexualidad física con nuestra naturaleza espiritual. La castidad permite que seamos completamente humanos, capaces de dar a otros por entero nuestra vida y amor. Todos, ya seamos casados o solteros, somos llamados a observar la castidad. [chastity]

catecúmeno persona que está recibiendo formación cristiana mediante instrucción y mediante el ejemplo de la comunidad. Por medio de la conversión y madurez de fe, el catecúmeno se prepara para ser recibido en el seno de la Iglesia en la Pascua a través de los sacramentos del Bautismo, Confirmación y Eucaristía. [catechumen]

católica uno de los atributos de la Iglesia. La Iglesia es católica porque Jesús está totalmente presente en ella y porque la ha dado al mundo entero. Es universal. [catholic]

cielo unión con Dios Padre, Hijo y Espíritu Santo en vida y amor que nunca acaba. El cielo es el estado de felicidad completa y es la meta de los deseos más profundos del corazón humano. [heaven]

clero varones elegidos ministros sagrados para servir a la Iglesia a través del sacramento del Orden. [clergy]

Comunión de los Santos unidad de todos los que se han salvado en Jesucristo, vivos o muertos. La Comunión de los Santos se basa en nuestra fe única y se nutre de nuestra participación en la Eucaristía. [Communion of Saints]

conciencia voz interior que nos ayuda a cada uno a conocer la ley de Dios para que cada persona pueda juzgar las cualidades morales de sus acciones. La conciencia nos guía para hacer el bien y evitar el mal. [conscience]

confesión acto de contar nuestros pecados al sacerdote en el sacramento de la Penitencia. Al sacramento mismo se le suele llamar "confesión". [confession]

Confirmación sacramento que da plenitud a la gracia que recibimos en el Bautismo. La Confirmación sella, o confirma, esta gracia a través de los siete dones del Espíritu Santo que recibimos como parte de la Confirmación. Este sacramento también nos hace más capaces de participar en el culto y en la vida apostólica de la Iglesia. [Confirmation]

conmemoración recuerdo de sucesos ocurridos en el pasado. Recordamos estos sucesos porque nos siguen afectando en el presente ya que son parte del plan de salvación que Dios tiene para nosotros. Cada vez que recordamos estos acontecimientos, hacemos presente la acción redentora de Dios. [memorial]

conocimiento uno de los siete dones del Espíritu Santo. Este don nos permite saber lo que Dios nos pide y cómo debemos responder. [knowledge]

consagración el hacer a una cosa o persona especial ante los ojos de Dios por medio de una oración o bendición. En la misa, las palabras del sacerdote son una consagración del pan y el vino que se convierten en el Cuerpo y Sangre de Cristo. Las personas y objetos dedicados a Dios de forma especial también son consagrados. Por ejemplo, las iglesias y altares son consagrados para su uso en la liturgia. Del mismo modo los obispos son consagrados al recibir la integridad del sacramento del Orden. [consecration]

consejo uno de los siete dones del Espíritu Santo. El consejo nos ayuda a reflexionar sobre cómo tomar decisiones apropiadas en la vida a través de la reflexión, el discernimiento, la consulta y el consejo de otros. [counsel]

contrición pesar que sentimos cuando sabemos que hemos pecado, seguido por la decisión de no volver a pecar. Contrición perfecta brota de un amor que ama a Dios sobre todas las cosas. Contrición imperfecta está basada en otros motivos. La contrición es el acto más importante del penitente que se prepara para celebrar el sacramento de la penitencia. [contrition]

conversión cambio radical, serio y extremo de nuestra vida total, que nos aparta del pecado y nos dirige a Dios. Este llamado a cambiar de vida es parte fundamental de las enseñanzas de Jesús. A lo largo de nuestra vida Jesús nos llama a cambiar de esta forma. [conversion]

creación El acto en que Dios hace todo lo que existe fuera de él. La creación es todo lo que existe. Dios dijo que todo lo creado es bueno. [creation]

Creador Dios, quien hizo todo lo que es y a quien podemos llegar a conocer a través de todo lo que él creó. [Creator]

credo breve resumen de lo que la gente creen las personas. *Credo* proviene del verbo latino *credo,* que significa "creo". El Credo de Nicea es el resumen más importante de lo que creemos como cristianos. [creed]

Credo de los Apóstoles declaración de la creencia cristiana, originada de un credo usado en los bautizos en Roma. El Credo de los Apóstoles enumera sencillas declaraciones de la creencia en Dios Padre, su Hijo Jesucristo y el Espíritu Santo. La profesión de fe usada actualmente en el bautizo se basa en este credo. [Apostles' Creed]

Credo de Nicea resumen de las creencias cristianas desarrolladas por los obispos en los dos primeros concilios de la Iglesia, llevados a cabo en 325 y 381 d. de C. Éste es el credo que comparten todos los cristianos, de oriente y occidente. [Nicene Creed]

crisma óleo perfumado que se utiliza en los sacramentos del Bautismo, la Confirmación y el Orden. La unción con el crisma significa el llamado a los bautizados al triple ministerio de sacerdote, profeta y rey. [chrism]

cristiano nombre dado a aquellos que han sido ungidos por medio del don del Espíritu Santo en el Bautismo y se han convertido en seguidores de Jesucristo. [Christian]

Cristo título que quiere decir "ungido". Proviene de una palabra griega que quiere decir lo mismo que el vocablo hebreo *Mesías* o "ungido". Cristo es el nombre que se le da a Jesús después de su Resurrección tras haber cumplido su misión como sacerdote, profeta y rey. [Christ]

Cuaresma los cuarenta días antes de la Pascua (sin contar domingos), durante los cuales nos preparamos, por medio de la oración, el ayuno y ayudando a los pobres, a cambiar nuestra vida y a vivir el Evangelio más plenamente. [Lent]

Cuerpo Místico de Cristo miembros de la Iglesia que forman un cuerpo espiritual y están unidos por la vida comunicada por Jesucristo a través de los sacramentos. Cristo es el centro y la fuente de la vida de este cuerpo en el cual todos estamos unidos. Cada miembro de este cuerpo recibe de Cristo los dones que más necesita esa persona. [Mystical Body of Christ]

Cuerpo y Sangre de Cristo pan y vino que han sido consagrados por el sacerdote en la misa. En el sacramento de la Eucaristía, Nuestro Señor Jesucristo—todo cuerpo, sangre, alma y divinidad—está presente en forma de pan y vino. [Body and Blood of Christ]

culto adoración y honor que se le rinde a Dios en oración pública. [worship]

cultura conjunto de conocimientos, creencias y conductas de un determinado grupo de personas. La cultura expresa las actitudes, valores, objetivos y prácticas sociales que tiene el grupo en común. Para que el Evangelio se arraigue en una cultura debe ser adaptado para vivir en esa cultura y transformarla. [culture]

D

detracción el hablar de las faltas y pecados de alguien a otro que no tiene por qué enterarse de ello y que no puede ayudar a esa persona. La detracción daña la reputación de una persona sin que se tenga intención alguna de ayudarla. [detraction]

Día de los Fieles Difuntos el 2 de noviembre, día en que la Iglesia ora por el eterno descanso de todos los que han muerto estando en amistad con Dios. Algunos de estos necesitan purificación en el purgatorio antes de pasar a vivir en presencia total de Dios; y con nuestras plegarias y buenas obras les ayudamos en este proceso. Junto al Día de Todos los Santos, esta fiesta nos recuerda que todos los que aman a Dios, vivos o muertos, están unidos en comunión viva con Jesucristo y entre sí. [All Souls Day]

Día de Todos los Santos el 1° de noviembre, día en que la Iglesia conmemora a todos los muertos que pasaron a ser santos y ahora viven con Dios en el cielo. Entre estos figuran aquéllos que han sido declarados santos de forma oficial por la Iglesia así como muchos otros desconocidos que han muerto tras haber llevado una vida recta y ahora viven en presencia de Dios. Esta fiesta celebra nuestra unión con aquéllos que se han ido antes que nosotros y nos señala nuestra meta final de unión con Dios. [All Saints Day]

diácono varón ordenado mediante el sacramento del Orden al ministerio de servicio en la Iglesia. Los diáconos asisten al obispo y a los sacerdotes sirviendo en las distintas prácticas caritativas de la Iglesia. También dan su asistencia proclamando el Evangelio y predicando y ayudando en la liturgia de la Eucaristía. Los diáconos, además, celebran bautizos, bendicen matrimonios y presiden funerales. [deacon]

días de precepto principales días de fiesta de la Iglesia, a parte de los domingos. En los días de precepto celebramos las grandes cosas que Dios ha hecho por nosotros a través de Jesucristo y los Santos. Es obligación de los católicos participar de la Eucaristía en estos días, al igual que lo es los domingos. [Holy Days of Obligation]

Diez Mandamientos diez reglas que Dios dio a Moisés en el Monte Sinaí que resumen la ley de Dios y nos muestran lo que hay que hacer para amar a Dios y al prójimo. Al seguir los Diez Mandamientos los hebreos aceptaron su alianza con Dios. [Ten Commandments]

diócesis miembros de la Iglesia de una zona determinada, unidos en la fe y los sacramentos y congregados bajo la guía de un obispo. [diocese]

Dios Padre, Hijo y Espíritu Santo: un solo Dios en tres personas distintas. Dios creó todo lo que es; él es la fuente de la salvación y es verdad y amor. [God]

discípulo persona que ha aceptado el mensaje de Jesús y trata de vivir de la misma forma en que él vivió, compartiendo su misión, su sufrimiento, y sus alegrías. [disciple]

discriminación acto de tratar mal a otros a causa de su apariencia o comportamiento, o sencillamente porque son distintos a nosotros. [discrimination]

Divina Providencia guía que da Dios a todo lo creado por él. La Divina Providencia vela por toda la creación y la guía hacia su perfección final. [Divine Providence]

Doctor de la Iglesia persona declarada como maestro ejemplar de la fe cristiana. [Doctor of the Church]

Domingo de Ramos celebración de la entrada triunfal de Jesús en Jerusalén que tiene lugar el domingo antes de la Pascua. Esta celebración inicia una semana de conmemoración de los eventos de salvación de la Semana Santa. [Palm Sunday]

dones del Espíritu Santo voluntad permanente que nos ha sido dada por el Espíritu Santo que nos permite hacer lo que Dios nos pide. Los dones del Espíritu Santo se encuentran en el libro del profeta Isaías 11:1–3 y son: sabiduría, entendimiento, consejo, fortaleza, conocimiento y temor de Dios. La tradición de la Iglesia ha agregado piedad, lo cual hace un total de siete. [Gifts of the Holy Spirit]

E

Emanuel nombre hebreo del Antiguo Testamento que significa "Dios con nosotros". En el Evangelio de San Mateo, se le llama Emanuel a Jesús. [Emmanuel]

Encarnación acto por el que el Hijo de Dios, Jesús, se hace plenamente hombre para salvarnos. El Hijo de Dios, segunda persona de la Trinidad, es tanto Dios verdadero, como verdadero hombre. [Incarnation]

encíclica carta escrita por el Papa y enviada a toda la Iglesia y a veces a todo el mundo. Expresa la doctrina de la Iglesia sobre un determinado e importante asunto. [encyclical]

entendimiento uno de los siete dones del Espíritu Santo. Este don nos ayuda a tomar decisiones apropiadas en la vida y en nuestra relación con Dios y los demás. [understanding]

envidia sentimiento de resentimiento o tristeza que sentimos cuando alguien tiene una cualidad, talento o pertenencia que queremos. La envidia es uno de los siete pecados capitales y va en contra del décimo mandamiento. [envy]

Epifanía día en que se celebra la visita de los Reyes Magos a Jesús recién nacido. Éste es el día en que se reveló a Jesús como salvador del mundo entero. [Epiphany]

epístola carta escrita por San Pablo u otro líder espiritual a un grupo de cristianos en los primeros tiempos de la Iglesia. Veintiuno de los veintisiete libros del Nuevo Testamento son Epístolas. En la misa de los domingos y días santos la segunda lectura se hace siempre de uno de estos libros. [epistle]

esperanza confianza en que Dios estará siempre con nosotros, nos dará felicidad ahora y siempre y nos ayudará a vivir de forma que vivamos con él para siempre. [hope]

Espíritu Santo tercera Persona de la Trinidad que es enviada a nosotros para asistirnos y, mediante el Bautismo y la Confirmación, nos llena de la vida de Dios. Junto con el Padre y el Hijo, el Espíritu Santo da plenitud al plan divino de salvación. [Holy Spirit]

Estaciones del Vía Crucis forma de meditar las horas finales de la vida de Jesús, desde su condena a muerte por Pilatos hasta su muerte y sepultura. Consiste en recorrer representaciones de catorce incidentes distintos, cada uno de ellos basado en los sitios tradicionales de Jerusalén donde tuvieron lugar estos incidentes. [Stations of the Cross]

Eucaristía sacramento en el cual damos gracias a Dios por habernos dado a Jesucristo en el pan y el vino consagrados que se convierten en el Cuerpo y Sangre de Jesús. Este sacramento nos hace entrar en unión con Jesús y su muerte y Resurrección redentoras. [Eucharist]

Evangelio buena nueva de la misericordia y amor de Dios que experimentamos al oír la historia de la vida, muerte y Resurrección de Jesús. Esta historia es transmitida en el ministerio de enseñanza de la Iglesia como fuente de toda verdad y de vida recta. Se nos presenta en el Nuevo Testamento en cuatro libros: los Evangelios de San Mateo, San Marcos, San Lucas y San Juan. [Gospel]

evangelización proclamación, o declaración por medio de la palabra y el ejemplo, de la buena nueva de salvación que hemos recibido en Jesucristo. Evangelizar es compartir nuestra fe con los demás, tanto con aquellos que no conocen a Jesús como aquellos que son llamados a seguir a Jesús más de cerca. [evangelization]

examen de conciencia acto de reflexionar en oración sobre aquello que hemos dicho o hecho considerando lo que el Evangelio pide de nosotros. Es también pensar acerca de cómo nuestras acciones pudieron haber dañado nuestra amistad con Dios y con otras personas. El examen de conciencia es una parte importante de la preparación para la celebración del sacramento de la Penitencia. [examination of conscience]

exilio período de la historia de Israel comprendido entre la destrucción de Jerusalén en 587 a. de C. y el regreso a Jerusalén en 537 a. de C. Durante este tiempo muchos de los judíos fueron obligados a vivir en Babilonia, lejos de su tierra. [Exile]

Éxodo obra de Dios que consistió en la liberación del pueblo hebreo de la esclavitud en Egipto y su peregrinaje a la Tierra prometida guiados por él. [Exodus]

F

fe don de Dios que nos llama a creer en él. Profesamos nuestra fe en el credo; la celebramos en los sacramentos; vivimos según ella mediante nuestra buena conducta de amar a Dios y al prójimo; y la expresamos en la oración. [faith]

fortaleza fuerza que nos ayuda a obrar bien aun cuando sea difícil hacerlo. La fortaleza es una de las cuatro virtudes humanas centrales, llamadas virtudes cardinales, por las cuales guiamos nuestra conducta mediante el uso de la razón y la fe. Es también uno de los dones del Espíritu Santo. [fortitude]

frutos del Espíritu Santo forma en que actuamos porque Dios está vivo en nosotros. San Pablo enumera los frutos del Espíritu Santo en Gálatas 5:22–23: amor, gozo, paz, paciencia, benignidad, generosidad, fe, mansedumbre y continencia. La tradición eclesial ha agregado bondad, modestia y castidad, lo que hace un total de doce. [Fruits of the Holy Spirit]

G

genuflexión, hacer la forma de mostrar respeto en la iglesia doblando una rodilla y haciéndola tocar el suelo, sobre todo cuando estamos ante el Santísimo Sacramento que está en el sagrario. [genuflect]

gracia don de Dios que se nos da gratuitamente. La gracia santificante nos llena de su vida y permite que seamos siempre amigos suyos. La gracia es el Espíritu Santo que habita en nosotros, ayudándonos a vivir nuestra vocación cristiana. La gracia también nos ayuda a vivir de la forma en que Dios quiere que vivamos. [grace]

gracia santificante don de Dios, dado a nosotros gratuitamente, que nos une con la vida de la Trinidad y sana nuestra naturaleza humana que ha sido herida por el pecado. La gracia santificante continúa la obra de nuestra santificación que se inició con nuestro bautismo. [sanctifying grace]

H

hebreos descendientes de Abraham, Isaac y Jacob que fueron esclavizados en Egipto. Dios ayudó a Moisés a liberar a este pueblo de la esclavitud. [Hebrews]

Hijo de Dios título revelado por Jesús que indica su relación única con Dios Padre. La revelación de Jesús como Hijo de Dios es el principal suceso de la historia de Jesús de Nazaret según la relatan los Evangelios. [Son of God]

homilía explicación de la Palabra de Dios en la liturgia hecha por el obispo, sacerdote o diácono. La homilía explica de qué forma se relaciona hoy la Palabra de Dios con nuestra vida cristiana. [Homily]

I

Iglesia pueblo de Dios congregado en todo el mundo, o la diócesis, la Iglesia local o la asamblea de los convocados a rendirle culto a Dios. La Iglesia es una, santa, católica, y apostólica. [Church]

iglesia doméstica el hogar cristiano, el cual es una comunidad de gracia y oración y una escuela de virtudes humanas y caridad cristiana. [domestic church]

Iglesia universal toda la Iglesia tal como existe en el mundo entero. La gente de todas las diócesis, junto con sus obispos y el Papa, forman la Iglesia universal. [universal Church]

Iglesias Católicas Orientales grupo de Iglesias que se desarrollaron en el oriente (en países como el Líbano) que están en unión con la Iglesia Católica Romana pero tienen tradiciones litúrgicas, teológicas y administrativas propias. Éstas muestran la verdadera naturaleza católica de la Iglesia, que se arraiga en numerosas culturas distintas. [Eastern Catholic Churches]

indulgencia reducción del castigo debido a pecados que han sido perdonados. Nos conduce hacia nuestra purificación final, cuando habremos de vivir con Dios para siempre. [indulgence]

infierno vida total y eternamente apartada de Dios. En su infinito amor hacia nosotros, Dios sólo puede desear nuestra salvación. El infierno es el resultado de la libre elección de la persona de rechazar el amor y perdón de Dios de forma definitiva. [hell]

inspirado asistencia del Espíritu Santo a los autores humanos de la Sagrada Escritura. La inspiración del Espíritu Santo asegura que la Sagrada Escritura enseñe la verdad que Dios quiere que conozcamos para nuestra salvación. [inspired]

interpretación explicación de las palabras de la Sagrada Escritura que combina el conocimiento humano con el oficio de enseñanza de la Iglesia bajo la guía del Espíritu Santo. [interpretation]

islamismo La tercera gran religión, con el judaísmo y el cristianismo, que profesa creencia en un solo Dios. *Islam* quiere decir "sumisión" a ese Dios único. [Islam]

israelitas descendientes de Abraham, Isaac y Jacob. Dios cambió el nombre de Jacob a "Israel"; los doce hijos de Jacob junto con los hijos de estos hijos se convirtieron en jefes de las doce tribus de Israel. (*Véase* hebreos.) [Israelites]

J

Jesús hijo de Dios, que nació de la Virgen María y murió y fue resucitado de entre los muertos para nuestra salvación. Jesús volvió a Dios y vendrá de nuevo a juzgar a vivos y a muertos. Su nombre significa "Dios salva". [Jesus]

José padre adoptivo de Jesús, que estaba desposado con María cuando el ángel anunció que ella tendría un hijo por obra del poder del Espíritu Santo. En el Antiguo Testamento José era el hijo de Jacob que fue vendido como esclavo en Egipto por sus hermanos y que luego los salvó de morir de hambre cuando hubo escasez de comida en la región. [Joseph]

judaísmo nombre de la religión de Jesús y de todo el pueblo de Israel después de su regreso del exilio en Babilonia y la construcción del segundo Templo. [Judaism]

judíos nombre dado al pueblo hebreo, desde el tiempo del exilio al presente. Este nombre quiere decir "pueblo del territorio de Judea", zona de Palestina en torno a Jerusalén. [Jews]

justicia deseo firme y poderoso de dar a Dios y a los demás lo que les corresponde. Es una de las cuatro virtudes humanas centrales, llamadas virtudes cardinales, por las cuales guiamos nuestra vida cristiana. [justice]

L

laicado los que se han convertido en miembros de Cristo en el bautismo y que participan en las funciones sacerdotales, proféticas y regias de Cristo en su misión destinada al mundo entero. El laicado es distinto al clero, cuyos miembros están dedicados a servir a la Iglesia como ministros suyos. [laity]

Leccionario libro oficial que contiene todas las lecturas de la Sagrada Escritura utilizadas en la Liturgia de la Palabra. [*Lectionary for Mass*]

ley moral regla de vida establecida por Dios y por personas de autoridad que se preocupan por el bien de todos. Las leyes morales se basan en la directiva que nos dio Dios de hacer lo que está bien y evitar lo que está mal. Algunas leyes morales están escritas en el corazón de la persona y se pueden conocer por medio de la razón. Otras nos han sido reveladas por Dios en el Antiguo Testamento y en la nueva ley dada por Jesús. [moral law]

ley natural ley moral que está escrita en el corazón de la persona. Podemos conocer la ley natural mediante la razón porque el Creador ha puesto en nuestros corazones su conocimiento. Esta ley puede brindarnos una base sólida sobre la cual podemos crear las reglas para guiar nuestras decisiones en la vida. La ley natural representa la base de nuestros derechos y deberes fundamentales y es el cimiento de la obra del Espíritu Santo al guiar nuestras opciones morales. [natural law]

libre albedrío capacidad de optar por hacer el bien porque Dios nos ha hecho semejantes a él. Nuestro libre albedrío es lo que nos hace verdaderamente humanos. Al ejercer nuestro libre albedrío para hacer el bien, nuestra libertad aumenta; pero si lo usamos para elegir el pecado, nos hace esclavos de ese pecado. [free will]

Libros Sapienciales libros siguientes del Antiguo Testamento: Job, Proverbios, Eclesiastés, Cantar de los Cantares, Sabiduría y Eclesiástico. Su objetivo es instruir acerca de cómo vivir y cómo entender y sobrellevar los problemas de la vida. [Wisdom Literature]

liturgia oración pública de la Iglesia que celebra las maravillas que Dios ha hecho por nosotros en Jesucristo, nuestro Sumo Sacerdote, y cómo él continúa la obra de nuestra salvación. El sentido original de *liturgia* era "obra pública o servicio prestado al pueblo". [liturgy]

Liturgia de la Eucaristía parte de la misa durante la que se consagran el pan y el vino, convirtiéndose así en el Cuerpo y la Sangre de Jesucristo, que luego recibimos en la Sagrada Comunión. [Liturgy of the Eucharist]

Liturgia de la Palabra parte de la misa durante la que escuchamos la Palabra de Dios en la Biblia y reflexionamos sobre lo que significa hoy para nosotros. La Liturgia de la Palabra también puede ser una oración pública y proclamación de la Palabra de Dios que no va seguida de la Liturgia de la Eucaristía. [Liturgy of the Word]

Liturgia de las Horas oración pública de la Iglesia para alabar a Dios y santificar el día. Consiste en: un Oficio de Lecturas antes del alba, los Laudes al amanecer, las Vísperas al anochecer, y una oración antes de acostarse. Recitar los salmos conforma la mayor parte de cada uno de estos oficios. [Liturgy of the Hours]

liturgia eucarística culto público rendido por la Iglesia en el cual se consagran el pan y el vino para que se conviertan en Cuerpo y Sangre de Jesucristo. La celebración dominical de la liturgia eucarística es el eje central de la vida eclesial. [Eucharistic liturgy]

M

Magisterio oficio de enseñanza viviente de la Iglesia. Este oficio, a través de los obispos y junto con el Papa, ofrece una interpretación auténtica de la Palabra de Dios. Su objetivo es mantenerse fiel a las enseñanzas de los apóstoles en cuestiones de fe y moral. [Magisterium]

Magníficat canto de María de alabanza a Dios. Ella lo alaba por las grandes cosas que ha hecho por ella y los grandes planes que ha hecho para nosotros a través de Jesús. [Magnificat]

mandamiento norma, o regla, para vivir de la forma en que Dios quiere que vivamos. Jesús resumió todos los mandamientos en dos: amar a Dios y amar al prójimo. [commandment]

Mandamiento Mayor, El enseñanza esencial de Jesús de amar a Dios y al prójimo como a nosotros mismos. Jesús nos dice que su mandamiento resume todo lo enseñado en el Antiguo Testamento. [Great Commandment]

María Madre de Jesús. Se le dice bendita y "llena de gracia" porque Dios la eligió para ser madre de su Hijo, segunda persona de la Trinidad. [Mary]

Matrimonio contrato solemne entre un varón y una mujer para ser compañeros para toda la vida, tanto para su bien propio como para procrear hijos. El Matrimonio es un sacramento cuando el contrato se hace de forma apropiada entre cristianos bautizados. [Matrimony]

Mesías título que quiere decir "ungido". Proviene de un vocablo hebreo que significa lo mismo que la palabra griega *Cristo*, que es el título dado a Jesús después de su resurrección, cuando ya había terminado su misión como sacerdote, profeta y rey. [Messiah]

Miércoles de Ceniza primer día de Cuaresma, en el que se nos coloca ceniza en la frente para que nos acordemos de que, para prepararnos para la Pascua, debemos mostrar arrepentimiento por decisiones que hemos tomado que ofenden a Dios y dañan nuestra relación con los demás. [Ash Wednesday]

milagro señales o actos maravillosos que no pueden ser explicados por causas naturales pero que son obras de Dios. En los Evangelios Jesús obra milagros como señal de que el Reino de Dios está presente en su ministerio. [miracle]

ministerio servicio u obra que se hace a otros. Lo hacen los obispos, sacerdotes y diáconos ordenados al ministerio en la celebración de los sacramentos. Todos los bautizados son llamados a una variedad de ministerios en la liturgia y en el servicio a las necesidades de los demás. [ministry]

misa la celebración sacramental más importante de la Iglesia. La celebración de la misa fue instituida por Jesús en la Última Cena para que fuera un recordatorio de su muerte y Resurrección. En la misa oímos la Palabra de Dios en la Biblia y recibimos a Jesucristo en el pan y el vino que han sido consagrados y convertidos en su Cuerpo y Sangre. [Mass]

misión obra de Jesucristo que continúa en la Iglesia a través del Espíritu Santo. La misión de la Iglesia es proclamar la salvación en la vida, muerte y Resurrección de Jesús. [mission]

misterio verdad religiosa que sólo podemos conocer por revelación de Dios y que no podemos comprender totalmente. Nuestra fe es un misterio que profesamos en el credo y que celebramos en la liturgia y los sacramentos. [mystery]

Misterio Pascual obra de salvación realizada por Jesucristo mediante su pasión, muerte y Resurrección. El Misterio Pascual se celebra en la liturgia de la Iglesia. En los sacramentos experimentamos sus efectos redentores. [Paschal Mystery]

monasterio lugar donde residen varones o mujeres cumpliendo sus votos de pobreza, castidad y obediencia en una vida de comunidad estable. Éstos pasan sus días en oración pública, trabajo y meditación. [monastery]

musulmán seguidor de la religión islámica. *Musulmán* quiere decir "que se somete a Dios". [Muslim]

N

Navidad fiesta del nacimiento de Jesús (el 25 de diciembre). [Christmas]

Nuevo Testamento los 27 libros de la segunda parte de la Biblia que relatan las enseñanzas, ministerio y acontecimientos de salvación de la vida de Jesús. El Nuevo Testamento se compone de: cuatro Evangelios, que presentan la vida, muerte y Resurrección de Jesús; los Hechos de los Apóstoles, que narran la historia del mensaje de salvación al irse extendiendo con el crecimiento de la Iglesia; varias cartas que nos instruyen sobre cómo vivir como seguidores de Jesucristo; y el Libro del Apocalipsis, que da ánimo a los cristianos que sufren persecución. [New Testament]

O

obediencia acto de seguir por voluntad propia lo que Dios nos pide que hagamos para nuestra salvación. Según el cuarto mandamiento, los niños deben obedecer a sus padres y todas las personas deben obedecer a la autoridad civil cuando obra en beneficio de todos. Imitando la obediencia de Jesús, los miembros de las comunidades religiosas hacen un voto especial de obediencia. [obedience]

obispo varón que ha recibido el sacramento del Orden en su totalidad. Como sucesor de los primeros apóstoles, el obispo vela por la Iglesia y es un educador importante dentro de la misma. [bishop]

obras corporales de misericordia buenas acciones con las que ayudamos a nuestro prójimo a cubrir sus necesidades materiales cotidianas. Las obras corporales de misericordia son: dar de comer al hambriento, dar techo al que no lo tiene, vestir al desnudo, visitar a los enfermos y a los presos, dar limosna a los pobres y enterrar a los muertos. [Corporal Works of Mercy]

obras espirituales de misericordia acciones caritativas mediante las cuales socorremos al prójimo en sus necesidades que van más allá de lo material. Las obras espirituales de misericordia son: instruir, aconsejar, consolar, confortar, perdonar y sufrir con paciencia las flaquezas ajenas. [Spiritual Works of Mercy]

ofensas actos contrarios a la ley cometidos contra la propiedad o los derechos de otra persona, o actos que físicamente lastiman a esa persona. [trespasses]

óleo de los catecúmenos óleo bendecido por el obispo durante la Semana Santa y usado para ungir a los catecúmenos. Esta unción los afianza en su camino de iniciación en la Iglesia. Los bebés son ungidos con este óleo momentos antes de ser bautizados. [oil of catechumens]

óleo de los enfermos óleo bendecido por el obispo durante la Semana Santa y usado en el sacramento de la unción de los enfermos, la cual brinda sanación espiritual y, si Dios quiere, sanación física también. [oil of the sick]

opción moral elegir hacer lo que está bien o no hacer lo que está mal. Elegimos opciones morales porque son lo que creemos que Dios quiere y porque tenemos la libertad de escoger lo que está bien y evitar lo que está mal. [moral choice]

oración el levantar el corazón y la mente a Dios. Podemos hablar y escuchar a Dios porque él nos enseña a orar. [prayer]

oración común culto a Dios que se rinde junto con otras personas. La Liturgia de las Horas y la misa son las principales formas de oración común. [communal prayer]

oración personal tipo de oración que surge en nuestra vida cotidiana. Oramos junto con otras personas en la liturgia; pero, además, cada momento de nuestra vida es una ocasión de escuchar y responder a Dios a través de la oración personal. [personal prayer]

ordenación rito del sacramento del Orden, mediante el cual el obispo da a los varones a través de la imposición de manos la capacidad de servir en el ministerio a la Iglesia como obispos, sacerdotes y diáconos. [ordination]

P

padrino/madrina de Bautismo testigo del Bautismo que asume la responsabilidad de ayudar al bautizado a seguir el camino de la vida cristiana. [godparent]

Papa el obispo de Roma, sucesor de San Pedro y cabeza de la Iglesia Católica Romana. Como tiene autoridad de actuar en nombre de Cristo, al Papa se le llama Vicario de Cristo. El Papa junto a todos los obispos conforma el oficio de enseñanza viviente de la Iglesia: el Magisterio. [pope]

parábola una de las sencillas narraciones que Jesús contaba que nos muestran cómo es el Reino de Dios. Las parábolas nos presentan imágenes, o escenas, tomadas de la vida cotidiana. Estas imágenes nos muestran la decisión radical, o seria, que tomamos cuando respondemos a la invitación de entrar en el reino de Dios. [parable]

parroquia comunidad de creyentes en Jesucristo que se reúne regularmente en un lugar determinado para rendirle culto a Dios bajo la guía de un pastor. [parish]

Pascua celebración de la Resurrección de Jesucristo de entre los muertos. La Pascua festeja nuestra redención y es la fiesta cristiana central de las que se originan otras fiestas. [Easter]

Pascua judía festival judío que conmemora la liberación del pueblo hebreo de la esclavitud de Egipto. *Pascua* viene de una palabra hebrea que significa "tránsito" o "pasaje". En la Eucaristía celebramos nuestro "tránsito" de la muerte a la vida a través de la muerte y Resurrección de Jesús. [Passover]

pastor sacerdote responsable del cuidado espiritual de los miembros de una comunidad parroquial. El deber del sacerdote es velar por que se predique la Palabra de Dios, se enseñe la fe y se celebren los sacramentos. [pastor]

pecado pensamiento, palabra, acción, o falta de acción deliberados que ofenden a Dios y dañan nuestra relación con otras personas. Algunos pecados son mortales y deben ser confesados en el sacramento de la penitencia. Otros son veniales, o menos graves. [sin]

pecado mortal decisión grave de apartarnos de Dios haciendo algo que sabemos que está mal. Para que un pecado sea mortal, debe ser una falta muy grave, la persona debe saber lo grave que es el pecado y, a pesar de ello, decidir libremente cometerlo. [mortal sin]

pecado original consecuencia de la desobediencia de los primeros seres humanos, que desobedecieron a Dios y decidieron seguir su propia voluntad y no la de Dios. A raíz de esto los seres humanos perdieron la bendición original que Dios les había destinado y se sometieron al pecado y la muerte. En el Bautismo se nos restaura la vida con Dios a través de Jesucristo, aunque aún seguimos sufriendo los efectos del pecado original. [original sin]

pecado personal pecado que decidimos cometer. Puede ser grave (mortal) o menos grave (venial). Aunque las consecuencias del pecado original nos dejan con una tendencia al pecado, la gracia de Dios, sobre todo a través de los sacramentos, nos ayuda a elegir el bien sobre el mal. [personal sin]

pecado venial decisión que tomamos que debilita nuestra relación con Dios y los demás. El pecado venial hiere y reduce la vida divina que hay en nosotros. Si no nos esforzamos por superarnos, el pecado venial puede llevarnos a pecados más graves. Nuestra participación en la Eucaristía perdona los pecados veniales y fortalece nuestra relación con Dios y los demás. [venial sin]

pecados capitales aquellos pecados que pueden llevarnos a cometer pecados más graves. Los pecados capitales son: soberbia, avaricia, envidia, ira, gula, lujuria y pereza. [capital sins]

penitencia apartarnos del pecado con el deseo de cambiar nuestras vidas y acercarnos más a la forma de vida que Dios quiere que vivamos. Expresamos externamente nuestra penitencia mediante la oración, el ayuno y ayudando a los pobres. También se le llama penitencia a la acción que el sacerdote nos pide hacer o a las oraciones que nos pide rezar después de que él nos absuelve en el sacramento de la Penitencia. (*Véase* sacramento de la Penitencia). [penance]

Pentecostés el 50° día después de la Resurrección de Jesús. En este día, el Espíritu Santo fue enviado del cielo y nació la Iglesia. También es el día de la fiesta judía que celebra el recibimiento de los Diez Mandamientos en el Monte Sinaí 50 días después del Éxodo. [Pentecost]

perdón voluntad de ser bondadosos con una persona que nos ha hecho daño pero que después dice haberse arrepentido. En la oración del Padrenuestro rogamos que, al igual que Dios siempre nos ha de perdonar nuestros pecados, nosotros también sepamos perdonar a los que nos han hecho daño. [forgiveness]

pereza dejadez que lleva a una persona a no hacer caso de su desarrollo como persona, en particular de su desarrollo espiritual y de su relación con Dios. La pereza es uno de los siete pecados capitales y va en contra del primer mandamiento. [sloth]

petición el pedir a Dios algo que necesitamos. Cuando participamos del amor redentor de Dios entendemos que para cada una de nuestras necesidades podemos pedirle a Dios que nos ayude mediante una petición. [petition]

piedad uno de los siete dones del Espíritu Santo. Nos llama a ser fieles en nuestras relaciones con Dios y los demás. Nos ayuda a amar a Dios y a comportarnos de una manera responsable y con generosidad y afecto en nuestra relación con los demás. [piety]

preceptos de la Iglesia aquellos requisitos positivos que la autoridad pastoral de la Iglesia ha determinado ser necesarios. Estos requisitos representan el esfuerzo mínimo que debemos hacer en la oración y en la vida moral. Los preceptos de la Iglesia se aseguran de que todos los católicos progresemos más allá del mínimo, creciendo en amor a Dios y en amor al prójimo. [Precepts of the Church]

presbítero palabra que originalmente quería decir "anciano" o "consejero de confianza del obispo". De esta palabra deriva el vocablo inglés *priest,* o "sacerdote" en español, uno de los tres grados del sacramento del Orden. Todos los sacerdotes de una diócesis que están bajo la guía de un obispo forman el presbiterio. [presbyter]

Presencia Real modo en que Cristo resucitado está presente en la Eucaristía en forma de pan y vino. Se le llama "real" a la presencia de Jesucristo porque en la Eucaristía su cuerpo y sangre, alma y divinidad, están total y enteramente presentes. [Real Presence]

profeta persona llamada a hablar por Dios y a llamar a la gente a ser fiel a la alianza. Una sección importante del Antiguo Testamento presenta en dieciocho libros los mensajes y acciones de los profetas. [prophet]

prudencia virtud que nos orienta hacia el bien. También nos ayuda a escoger los medios apropiados para alcanzar ese bien. Cuando actuamos con prudencia consideramos nuestros acciones con cuidado. La prudencia es una de las virtudes cardinales morales que guía nuestra conciencia e influye en nosotros para que vivamos según la ley de Cristo. [prudence]

pueblo de Dios otro de los nombres de la Iglesia. Al igual que el pueblo de Israel era el pueblo de Dios debido a la alianza que él hizo con ellos, la Iglesia es un pueblo sacerdotal, profético y regio gracias a la nueva y eterna alianza en Jesucristo. [people of God]

pueblo elegido pueblo escogido por Dios para que mantuviera con él una relación especial. La primera vez que Dios formó un pueblo elegido fue cuando hizo una alianza, o pacto solemne, con Abraham. Más tarde, él reafirmó esa alianza a través de Moisés en el Monte Sinaí. Esta alianza ha alcanzado su plenitud en Jesús y su Iglesia. [Chosen People]

purgatorio estado de purificación final de todas las imperfecciones humanas que viene después de la muerte y antes de entrar a gozar la presencia de Dios en el cielo. [purgatory]

R

racismo creencia de que la raza determina rasgos y capacidades humanas y que existe una superioridad inherente, o innata, de una raza determinada. La discriminación por razón de la raza de una persona es una violación de la dignidad humana y un pecado contra la justicia. [racism]

reconciliación reanudar la amistad que se había roto por alguna acción o falta de acción. En el sacramento de la Penitencia, mediante la misericordia y el perdón de Dios, nos reconciliamos con él, con la Iglesia y con los demás. [reconciliation]

redención liberación de la esclavitud del pecado mediante la vida, el sacrificio de la muerte en la cruz y la Resurrección de Jesucristo de entre los muertos. [redemption]

Redentor Jesucristo, cuya vida, sacrificio de su muerte en la cruz y Resurrección de entre los muertos, nos libró de la esclavitud del pecado y nos trajo la redención. [Redeemer]

reformarse poner fin a un error tomando un curso de acción mejor o distinto. Los profetas llamaban a la gente a reformar sus vidas volviendo a ser fieles a la alianza con Dios. [reform]

reino de Dios el dominio de Dios sobre nosotros anunciado en el Evangelio y presente en la Eucaristía. El principio del reino aquí en la Tierra está presente en forma misteriosa en la Iglesia y vendrá en su plenitud al final de los tiempos. [Kingdom of God]

Resurrección el volver a la vida el cuerpo de Jesucristo el tercer día después de haber muerto en la cruz. La Resurrección es la verdad culminante de nuestra fe. [Resurrection]

revelación comunicación que nos hace Dios de sí mismo por medio de las palabras y hechos que ha usado a lo largo de la historia, para mostrarnos el misterio del plan de salvación que tiene para nosotros. Esta revelación llega a su plenitud con el envío de su Hijo, Jesucristo. [Revelation]

rito una de las diversas formas de celebrar la liturgia en la Iglesia. Los ritos pueden ser distintos según la cultura o el país donde se celebren. *Rito* también quiere decir el modo especial en que celebramos cada sacramento. [rite]

Rosario oración en honor a la Virgen María. Durante el rezo del rosario meditamos los misterios de la vida de Jesucristo mientras rezamos el Avemaría en los cinco grupos de diez cuentas y el Padrenuestro en las cuentas que van en medio. En la Iglesia de rito latino rezar el rosario se convirtió en una manera en que la gente común podía reflexionar sobre los misterios de la vida de Jesús. [Rosary]

S

Sabat séptimo día, en el que Dios, habiendo terminado su obra de creación, descansó. El tercer mandamiento nos exige que consideremos santo el sabat. Para los cristianos el sabat se convirtió en domingo porque era el día en que resucitó Jesús y se inició la nueva creación en Jesucristo. [Sabbath]

sabiduría uno de los siete dones del Espíritu Santo. Nos ayuda a entender el propósito y el plan de Dios y a vivir de una forma que ayude a realizar este plan. La sabiduría se inicia con la admiración y portento ante la grandeza de Dios. [wisdom]

sacerdocio todo el pueblo de Dios que ha sido hecho partícipe de la misión de Cristo a través de los sacramentos del Bautismo y la Confirmación. El sacerdocio ministerial, compuesto de aquellos varones que han sido ordenados obispos y sacerdotes a través del orden sagrado, es en esencia distinto del sacerdocio de todos los fieles porque su labor es la de edificar y guiar a la Iglesia en nombre de Cristo. [priesthood]

sacerdote varón que ha aceptado el llamado especial de Dios para servir a la Iglesia, guiándola y edificándola mediante el ministerio de la Palabra y la celebración de los sacramentos. [priest]

sacramental objeto, oración o bendición dados por la Iglesia que nos ayudan a crecer en nuestra vida espiritual. [sacramental]

sacramento una de las siete formas en que la vida de Dios entra en nuestra vida a través de la obra del Espíritu Santo. Jesús nos dio tres sacramentos por medio de los cuales pasamos a ser miembros de la Iglesia (Bautismo, Confirmación y Eucaristía); dos sacramentos que nos traen sanación (Penitencia y Unción de los enfermos); y dos sacramentos que ayudan a los miembros a servir a la comunidad (Matrimonio y sacramento del Orden). [sacrament]

sacramento de la Penitencia sacramento en el cual celebramos el perdón de Dios de nuestros pecados y nuestra reconciliación con él y la Iglesia. La penitencia consiste en el arrepentimiento de los pecados cometidos, la confesión de los pecados, la absolución por el sacerdote y el cumplimiento de la penitencia para mostrar que estamos dispuestos a enderezar nuestra vida. [Sacrament of Penance]

sacramento del Orden sacramento mediante el cual la misión, o deber, dado por Jesús a sus apóstoles continúa en la Iglesia. Tiene tres grados: diaconado, presbiterado y episcopado. Mediante la imposición de manos en el sacramento del Orden, los varones reciben una marca o carácter sacramental permanente que los llama a servir a la Iglesia como ministros suyos. [Holy Orders]

sacramentos al servicio de la comunidad sacramentos que contribuyen a la salvación personal de los individuos dándoles un modo de servir a los demás. Son dos: sacramento del Orden y Matrimonio. [Sacraments at the Service of Communion]

sacramentos de curación sacramentos mediante los cuales la Iglesia continúa el ministerio de Jesús de sanación del alma y del cuerpo. Son dos: Penitencia y Unción de los enfermos. [Sacraments of Healing]

sacramentos de iniciación sacramentos que son los cimientos de nuestra vida cristiana. Volvemos a nacer en el Bautismo, nos fortalecemos en la Confirmación y recibimos en la Eucaristía el alimento de la vida eterna. Por medio de estos sacramentos, recibimos una creciente medida de vida divina y avanzamos hacia la perfección de la caridad. [Sacraments of Initiation]

sacrificio ritual en que el sacerdote en el Templo de Jerusalén ofrecía animales u hortalizas a Dios para dar muestra de la adoración del pueblo a Dios, para dar gracias a Dios o para pedir su perdón. El sacrificio también mostraba la unión con Dios. Cristo, el gran Sumo Sacerdote, alcanzó nuestra redención a través del sacrificio perfecto de su muerte en la cruz. [sacrifice]

Sacrificio de la misa sacrificio de Jesús en la cruz, el cual se recuerda y se hace presente de forma misteriosa en la Eucaristía. Es ofrecida en reparación de los pecados de los vivos y los difuntos y para obtener de Dios beneficios espirituales o temporales. [Sacrifice of the Mass]

Sagrada Comunión el pan y el vino consagrados que recibimos en la misa los cuales son el Cuerpo y Sangre de Jesucristo. La Sagrada Comunión nos hace entrar en unión con Jesucristo y su muerte y Resurrección redentoras. [Holy Communion]

Sagrada Escritura escritos sagrados de los judíos y cristianos recopilados en el Antiguo y Nuevo Testamento de la Biblia. [Scriptures]

Sagrada Familia familia de Jesús en la que creció Jesús en Nazaret. Estaba formada por Jesús, su madre María y su padre adoptivo José. [Holy Family]

sagrario lugar donde se guarda el Santísimo Sacramento para que la Sagrada Comunión pueda ser llevada a los enfermos y moribundos. Se le llama también tabernáculo. Para los israelitas el tabernáculo es el nombre de la tienda de campaña usada como santuario para guardar el Arca de la Alianza desde la época del éxodo hasta la construcción del templo de Salomón. [tabernacle]

salmo oración en forma de poema. Los salmos estaban destinados para ser cantados en cultos públicos. Cada salmo expresa un aspecto o característica de la profundidad de la oración humana. A lo largo de varios siglos se han recolectado 150 salmos que forman el Libro de los Salmos en el Antiguo Testamento. Estos salmos se usaban en el culto a Dios en el Templo de Jerusalén y han sido usados en el culto público de la Iglesia desde sus orígenes. [psalm]

salvación don que sólo Dios puede darnos del perdón del pecado; y la reanudación de nuestra amistad con Dios. [salvation]

Salvador Jesús, el Hijo de Dios, que se hizo hombre para perdonar nuestros pecados y reanudar nuestra amistad con Dios. *Jesús* quiere decir "Dios salva". [Savior]

Sanctasanctórum parte más sagrada del Templo de Jerusalén. El sumo sacerdote entraba a este recinto una vez al año para dirigirse a Dios y pedirle su perdón por los pecados del pueblo. [Holy of Holies]

santa uno de los cuatro atributos de la Iglesia. Es el tipo de vida que vivimos cuando participamos de la vida de Dios, que es todo santidad. La Iglesia es santa por su unión con Jesucristo. [holy]

santidad plenitud de la vida y el amor cristianos. Todos somos llamados a la santidad, la cual, al cooperar con la gracia de Dios, hace posible que se haga la voluntad de Dios en todas las cosas. Al hacer la voluntad de Dios, nos transformamos cada vez más en la imagen de su Hijo, Jesucristo. [holiness]

Santísimo Sacramento pan que ha sido consagrado por el sacerdote en la misa. Se guarda en el sagrario para su adoración y para ser llevado a los enfermos. [Blessed Sacrament]

santo persona virtuosa y ejemplar que ha muerto en unión con Dios. Además, la Iglesia ha declarado que esta persona está con Dios en el cielo ahora y para siempre. [saint]

scriptórium habitación que hay en los monasterios donde se hacían libros copiados a mano. Con frecuencia se creaban bellas obras de arte en la página para ilustrar el texto. [scriptorium]

Semana Santa celebración de los sucesos relacionados con la pasión, muerte y Resurrección de Jesús, y el don de la Eucaristía. Se inicia con la conmemoración de la entrada triunfal de Jesús a Jerusalén el Domingo de Ramos; sigue con la conmemoración del regalo que hace de sí mismo en la Eucaristía el Jueves Santo, su muerte el Viernes Santo, y su Resurrección durante la Vigilia Pascual el Sábado de Gloria. [Holy Week]

serafines seres celestiales que adoran a Dios ante su trono. Uno de ellos purificó los labios de Isaías con carbón ardiente para que pudiese hablar por Dios. [seraphim]

Sermón de la montaña palabras de Jesús que figuran en los capítulos 5 a 7 del Evangelio de San Mateo, en las que Jesús revela cómo él ha dado plenitud a la ley de Dios entregada a Moisés. El Sermón de la montaña comienza con las ocho Bienaventuranzas e incluye la oración del Padrenuestro. [Sermon on the Mount]

sexismo prejuicios o discriminación en razón del sexo de una persona, especialmente discriminación contra la mujer. El sexismo crea conductas y actitudes que fomentan una visión de los roles sociales basada sólo en el sexo de la persona. [sexism]

soberbia imagen falsa de lo que somos que exagera lo que nos corresponde como seres creados por Dios. La soberbia nos pone en competencia con Dios y es uno de los siete pecados capitales. [pride]

solidaridad actitud de fuerza y unidad que conduce a compartir los bienes espirituales y materiales. La solidaridad une a ricos y pobres, débiles y poderosos y crea una sociedad donde todos dan lo que pueden y reciben lo que necesitan. La idea de solidaridad se basa en el origen común de la humanidad. [solidarity]

T

temor de Dios uno de los siete dones del Espíritu Santo. Este don nos conduce a un sentimiento de admiración y portento ante la presencia de Dios debido a su grandeza. [fear of the Lord]

templanza virtud cardinal que nos ayuda a controlar nuestra atracción al placer de manera que nuestros deseos naturales se mantengan dentro de sus límites apropiados. Esta virtud moral nos ayuda a optar por usar con moderación los bienes creados. [temperance]

Templo casa donde se rinde culto a Dios, construida originalmente por Salomón. El Templo proporcionaba un lugar donde los sacerdotes podían ofrecer sacrificios, adorar y dar gracias a Dios y pedir su perdón. Fue destruido y reconstruido. El segundo templo fue destruido por los romanos en 70 d. de C. y nunca fue reconstruido. Parte del muro exterior del monte del Templo se conserva aún hoy en Jerusalén. [Temple]

tentación atracción, que viene de fuera o de dentro de nosotros mismos, que puede llevarnos a no seguir los mandamientos de Dios. Todos somos tentados, pero el Espíritu Santo nos ayuda a resistir la tentación y a optar por hacer el bien. [temptation]

testimonio el transmitir a los demás, mediante nuestras palabras y acciones, la fe que se nos ha dado. Cada cristiano tiene el deber de dar testimonio de la buena nueva de Jesucristo que ha llegado a conocer. [witness]

Tierra prometida tierra prometida originalmente por Dios a Abraham. Fue a esta tierra que Dios dijo a Moisés que llevara al pueblo elegido tras ser liberados de la esclavitud de Egipto y donde recibieron los Diez Mandamientos en el Monte Sinaí. [Promised Land]

Torá palabra hebrea que significa "instrucción" o "ley". Es también el nombre de los cinco primeros libros del Antiguo Testamento: Génesis, Éxodo, Levítico, Números y Deuteronomio. [Torah]

transubstanciación la transformación única del pan y el vino durante la Eucaristía en el Cuerpo y Sangre de Cristo resucitado, manteniendo las misma forma fisica del pan y el vino. [transubstantiation]

Trinidad misterio de la existencia de un Dios en tres Personas: Padre, Hijo y Espíritu Santo, donde cada una es Dios, todo y entero. Cada persona es distinta sólo en su relación a las otras. [Trinity]

U

Última Cena última comida que compartieron Jesús y sus discípulos la noche antes de que Jesús muriera. En la Última Cena Jesús tomó el pan y el vino, los bendijo y dijo que eran su Cuerpo y su Sangre. La muerte y Resurrección de Jesús, que celebramos en la Eucaristía, fue anticipada en esta cena. [Last Supper]

una uno de los cuatro atributos de la Iglesia. La Iglesia es una debido a su origen en un Dios único y a su fundador Jesucristo. Jesús, mediante su muerte en la cruz, unió todo a Dios en un cuerpo. Dentro de la unidad de la Iglesia hay una gran diversidad debido a la riqueza de los dones dados a sus miembros. [one]

Unción de los Enfermos uno de los siete sacramentos, en el cual la persona enferma es ungida con óleo santo y recibe fuerza, paz y coraje para superar las dificultades que conlleva la enfermedad. A través del sacramento Jesús brinda al enfermo sanación espiritual y perdón de sus pecados y, si Dios quiere, también sanación al cuerpo. [Anointing of the Sick]

V

viático Eucaristía que recibe el moribundo. Es el alimento espiritual para el viaje final que hacemos como cristianos: el viaje a través de la muerte hacia la vida eterna. [viaticum]

Vicario de Cristo título dado al Papa, quien como sucesor de San Pedro, tiene la autoridad de actuar en representación de Cristo. Un vicario es alguien que está, o actúa en representación de otra persona. [Vicar of Christ]

vida eterna vida con Dios después de la muerte y que nunca acaba. Es concedida a aquellos que mueren estando en amistad con Dios, con su gracia viva en ellos. [eternal life]

vida religiosa estado de vida reconocido por la Iglesia. Dentro de la vida religiosa varones y mujeres pueden responder libremente al llamado de seguir a Jesús viviendo sus votos de pobreza, castidad, y obediencia en comunidad con otros. [religious life]

Vigilia Pascual celebración de la primera y más grande de las fiestas cristianas: la Resurrección de Jesús. Tiene lugar la tarde del primer sábado que sigue a la luna llena que se observa después del primer día de primavera. Es en esta noche de vigilia antes de la mañana de Pascua que los catecúmenos son bautizados, confirmados y reciben por primera vez la Eucaristía. [Easter Vigil]

virtud actitud o forma de actuar que nos ayuda a hacer el bien. [virtue]

virtudes teologales aquellas virtudes que nos fueron dadas por Dios y no alcanzadas por esfuerzo humano. Son: la fe, la esperanza, y la caridad. [Theological Virtues]

Visitación visita de María a Isabel para contarle la buena nueva de que habrá de ser la madre de Jesús. El saludo de Isabel forma parte del Avemaría. Durante esta visita María hace su oración de alabanza a Dios: el Magníficat. [Visitation]

vocación llamado que se nos hace en la vida para que lleguemos a ser las personas que Dios quiere que seamos. También es la forma en que servimos a la Iglesia y al reino de Dios. Podemos ejercer nuestra vocación como laicos, como miembros de una comunidad religiosa o como miembros del clero. [vocation]

voto promesa deliberada y libre hecha a Dios por aquellas personas que desean dedicar de forma especial sus vidas a Dios. Los votos dan ahora testimonio del reino que ha de venir. [vow]

Vulgata traducción de la Biblia al latín que hizo San Jerónimo del original hebreo y griego. En la época de San Jerónimo la mayoría de los cristianos ya no hablaban hebreo o griego. La lengua común, o vulgata, era el latín. [Vulgate]

Y

Yavé nombre de Dios en hebreo dado por Dios a Moisés desde la zarza ardiente. *Yavé* quiere decir "Yo soy el que soy" o "Yo hago existir". [Yahweh]

Acknowledgments

Excerpts from the English translation of Rite of Marriage © 1969, International Committee on English in the Liturgy, Inc. (ICEL); excerpts from the English translation of Rite of Baptism for Children © 1969, ICEL; excerpts from the English translation of *The Roman Missal* © 2010, ICEL; excerpts from the English translation of Rite of Penance © 1974, ICEL; excerpts from the English translation of Rite of Confirmation, 2nd Edition © 1975, ICEL; excerpts from the English translation of Order of Deacons, Priests, and Bishops © 1975, ICEL; excerpts from the English translation of A Book of Prayers © 1982, ICEL; excerpts from the English translation of Book of Blessings © 1988, ICEL. All rights reserved. Used with permission.

For more information related to the English translation of the *Roman Missal, Third Edition*, see www.loyolapress.com/romanmissal.

Excerpts from The New American Bible with Revised New Testament and Psalms Copyright © 1991, 1986, 1970 Confraternity of Christian Doctrine, Inc., Washington, DC. Used with permission. All rights reserved. No portion of the New American Bible may be reprinted without permission in writing from the copyright holder.

209 Excerpts from Vatican conciliar, postconciliar, and papal documents are from the official translations, Libreria Editrice Vaticana, 00120 Citta del Vaticano.

Illustration

Kathleen Burke: 231, 232–233, 268–269, 270–271, 272–273, 278–279, 280–281, 284–285, 286–287, 288
Gino D'Achille: 3, 14, 28, 35, 37, 44–45, 47, 62, 67, 69, 70, 75, 76, 77, 84–85, 100–101, 117, 132, 158, 188, 224–225, 228, 260, 290
David Diaz: 4, 8, 12, 20, 23, 53, 86–87, 88, 95, 102, 109, 110–111, 126, 143, 166–167, 174, 184, 196–197, 201, 226, 250, 251, 264
Julie Downing: 273
Peter Siu: 2, 54, 59, 124, 183
John Stevens: 9, 134–135, 189, 198, 209, 274–275, 276–277, 282–283

Photography

Unless otherwise acknowledged, photos are the property of Loyola Press. When there is more than one picture on a page, credits are supplied in sequence, left to right, top to bottom. Page positions are abbreviated as follows: (t) top, (m) middle, (b) bottom, (l) left, (r) right, (bkgr) background, (ins) inset, (cl) clockwise from top, right.

UNIT 1: 1, 2 Art Resource, NY. 5 (t,r) Koninklijke Bibliotheek; (b,r) Biblioteca Medicea Laurenziana, Florence. 6 L'Osservatore Romano—The Vatican. 7 Christ in the Desert. 10 (t,l) Courtesy of Rev. George J. Dyer, S.T.D., St. Patrick Church, Wadsworth, IL; (m,l) © Bettmann/CORBIS. 11 (t) © Mary Kate Denny/Getty Images; (m,r) © David Young-Wolff/PhotoEdit; (b) © Stephen Frisch/Stock Boston. 13 (t,r) The British Museum; (b) Used with permission of Missionary Sisters of the Sacred Heart of Jesus. 15 (l) © Sheldan Collins/CORBIS. 16 (bkgr) © AFP/CORBIS. 17 Courtesy Jewish National Fund, NY. 18 (t,r) photodisc/Getty Images; (m,r) © Varie/Alt/CORBIS; (b,l) © Jim Cummins/Getty Images; (b,r) © Myrleen F. Cate/PhotoEdit. 19 (l) © Cheryl Maeder/Getty Images; (r) © Richard Hutchings/PhotoEdit. 21 © Archivo Iconografico, S.A./CORBIS. 22 Courtesy of Leonidas Orellano Castro, Peru. 24 © Yasuo Ueno, Japan/Asian Christian Art Association. 25 Cooperativa La Semilla De Dios de R.L. 26 (t,l) © Philadelphia Museum of Art/CORBIS; (m) © The Crosiers/Gene Plaisted OSC; (b,l) Courtesy John Brandi Company, White Plains, NY; (b,r) © Tony Freeman/PhotoEdit. 29 Art Resource, NY. 30 (t) © Jonathan Nourok/PhotoEdit. 31 photodisc. 32 © Ann Purcell, Carl Purcell/Words & Pictures/PictureQuest. 34 (t) © Stephen McBrady/PhotoEdit; (b,l) © David Young-Wolff/PhotoEdit; (b,r) © Gunter Marx Photography/CORBIS. 36 © Exploris, Diana Altman Collection/Photo courtesy North Carolina Museum of Art. 39 George A. Lane, S.J. 40 © The Crosiers/Gene Plaisted OSC.

UNIT 2: 41 Photo by Paul Pierlott. 42 (all) Through the kind permission of St. Peter the Apostle Catholic Church, Philadelphia, PA. 43 (t,l) © Christian Lantry/Getty Images; (t,r) © Phil Martin Photography; (b) photodisc/Getty Images. 46 © Phil Martin Photography. 48 © Holzenbecher/Premium Stock/PictureQuest. 49 George A. Lane, S.J. 50 (t,r) © Tony Freeman/PhotoEdit; (m,l) Courtesy St. Peter's Church, Philadelphia, PA; (b,r) © Myrleen F. Cate/PhotoEdit. 51 (l) © Bob Daemmrich Photography; (r) Courtesy of Villa Scalabrini Nursing and Rehabilitation Center. 52 © Scala/Art Resource, NY. 55 (t,r) © Mitch Hrdlicka/photodisc/PictureQuest; (bkgr) © Phil Martin Photography. 56 (bkgr) © Phil Martin Photography. 57 Karen Morris/Garden of Learning, a project of The Franciscan Friars' Justice, Peace, Integrity of Creation Office. 58 (t,l) Holy Cards courtesy of the Burke Family; (m,l) © Myrleen F. Cate/PhotoEdit; (m,r) © Rachel Epstein/PhotoEdit. 59 © David Young-Wolff/PhotoEdit. 60 Art Resource, NY. 61 © Gianni Dagli Orti/CORBIS. 65 © Phil Martin Photography. 66 (t) © The Crosiers/Gene Plaisted OSC; (m,l) © Photodisc/Getty; (b,l) © Robert Brenner/PhotoEdit; (b,r) © Rob Lewine/CORBIS. 68 Pierpont Morgan Library/Art Resource, NY. 72 (bkgr) © Phil Martin Photography. 73 © Lawrence Migdale/Stock, Boston. 74 (t) (b) © Spencer Grant/PhotoEdit. 79 (b) © Sonia Halliday Photographs; (bkgr) © Gary Braasch/CORBIS. 80 Private Collection.

UNIT 3: 81 St. Helena, c. 1495, Samuel H. Kress Collection, Image © 2003 Board of Trustees, National Gallery of Art, Washington, DC. (detail). 82 See Page 81 acknowledgment. 83 (m) photodisc/Getty Images. 87 (b,r) Courtesy of Brother Alfonso Wobeto. 89 © Nicholas de Vore III/Photographers Aspen/PictureQuest. 90 (t,l) © Jeff Greenberg/PhotoEdit; (m,l) © Stephen McBrady/PhotoEdit; (m,r) © Cleo Photography/PhotoEdit; (b,l) © Sculpture by Hamilton Reed Armstrong. 91 (t,l) © Nancy Richmond/The Image Works; (b,l) © Rudi Von Briel/PhotoEdit. 92 (t) Herzog August Bibliothek; (bkgr) © The Crosiers/Gene Plaisted OSC. 93 Lateran Christian Museum, The Vatican/Art Resource, NY. 94 © Christies Images, Inc./Christies Images, All Rights Reserved. 96 (bkgr) photodisc; (ins) © A. Ramey/Stock, Boston. 97 © Phil Martin Photography. 98 (t,r) © Myrleen F. Cate/PhotoEdit; (m,r) © National Gallery Collection; By kind permission of the trustees of the National Gallery, London/CORBIS; (b,l) © Myrleen F. Cate/PhotoEdit; (b,r) © Mary Kate Denny/PhotoEdit. 99 (l) © Journal-Courier/Steve Warmowski; (m) © Phil Martin Photography. 103 (all) © Phil Martin Photography. 104 (bkgr) © Phil Martin Photography. 106 (t,l) © Nik Wheeler/CORBIS; (b,l) Courtesy of St. Vladimir and Olga Ukrainian Catholic Church; (m,r) © Bill Aron/PhotoEdit; (b,r) photodisc/Getty Images. 107 (l) Courtesy of David Stillman; (m) © Maureen Collins Photography; (r) Courtesy of the Burke Family. 108 Victoria and Albert Museum/Bridgeman Art Library. 112 © CORBIS. 113 © Elizabeth Crews/The Image Works. 114 (t,l) © David Young-Wolf/PhotoEdit; (m,r) © James Noel Smith/Illustration Works./Getty Images; (b,l) © Bob Krist/CORBIS; (b,r) © Michael Newman/PhotoEdit. 115 (t,l) © Bob Daemmrich/Stock, Boston; (t,r) © Sean Sprague/Stock Boston; (b) © Tony Freeman/PhotoEdit. 119 (ins) Museo Nacional de Art de Catalunya, Barcelona. 120 (t)Courtesy of John Bretzlauf; (b) Private Collection.

UNIT 4: 121 © Erich Lessing/Art Resource, NY. 122 (bkgr) ARS Jesuitica; (ins) see pg. 121. 123 (t,l) © Myrleen F. Cate/PhotoEdit; (t,r) © Tony Freeman/PhotoEdit; (b,l) © Bob Daemmrich/Stock Boston. 125 © Archivo Iconografico S.A./CORBIS. 127 (t) © Bettmann/CORBIS; (b) CORBIS. 128 © Phil Martin Photography. 129 © Stewart Cohen/Index Stock Imagery/PictureQuest. 130 (t,l) © Myrleen F. Cate/PhotoEdit; (m,l and m,r) © Tony Freeman/PhotoEdit. 131 © David Young-Wolff/PhotoEdit. 133 Berlin Art Museum. 136 © Colin Mead/Image State-Pictor/PictureQuest. 138 (t,l) David Young-Wolff/PhotoEdit; (m,l) Courtesy of Stillwater Community Chapel; (m,r and b,l) Skjold Photographs. 139 (l) © Michael Newman; (m) © Richard Hutchings; (r) David Young-Wolff/all, PhotoEdit. 140 Private Collection. 141 © The Crosiers/Gene Plaisted OSC. 142 Private Collection. 144 Richard of Chichester by Rena Gardiner. 145 © Bob Daemmrich/Stock, Boston, Inc. 146 (t,l) © Myrleen F. Cate; (t,r) © David Young-Wolff/both, PhotoEdit; (b,l) © Cameramann, Int'l.,Milton and Joan Mann; (b,r) © The Crosiers/Gene Plaisted OSC. 147 (l) © Bob Daemmrich/Stock, Boston. Inc.; (r) © Michael Newman/PhotoEdit. 148 Art Resource, NY. 151 (bkgr) © Phil Martin Photography. 152 © Ken Hawkins/Focus Group/PictureQuest. 153 © Phil Martin Photography. 154 (t,l) © Bettmann/CORBIS; (m,r) © David Young-Wolff/PhotoEdit; (b,l) © Michael Newman and (b,r)